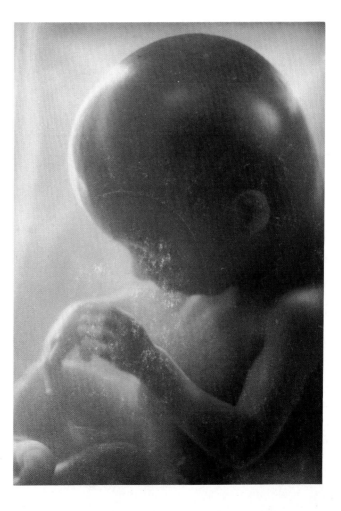

THE ZERO PEOPLE

The Zero People

Essays on Life

Edited by
Jeff Lane Hensley

SERVANT BOOKS
Ann Arbor, Michigan

Contents

Preface / vii

I. Responding in Love
1. The Silent Holocaust, *John Powell* / 3

II. Roe v. Wade, and Some Implications
2. Raw Judicial Power, *John T. Noonan, Jr.* / 15
3. A New Medical Ethic / 27

III. The Population Bomb Fizzles
4. The Population Bomb Threat:
A Look at the Facts, *Jacqueline R. Kasun* / 33

IV. A Doctor Who Saves Babies
5. The Right to Live, *Dr. C. Everett Koop* / 45

V. Abortion and Women
6. Abortion as a Feminist Concern, *Janet Smith* / 77
7. Complications of Legal Abortion:
A Perspective from Private Practice,
Matthew J. Bulfin, M.D. / 97

VI. Public Policy: Rape, Incest, and Children
8. The Hard Cases: Rape, Incest and Public Policy,
Basile Uddo / 109
9. A Consideration of Abortion Survivors,
Philip G. Ney, M.D. / 123

VII. The Experience of Pain by the Unborn
10. The Experience of Pain by the Unborn,
John T. Noonan, Jr. / 141

VIII. Abortion, Infanticide and Euthanasia: The Deadly Trio
11. The Lesson of Euthanasia,
Virgil C. Blum and Charles J. Sykes / 159
12. Abortion to Euthanasia: A Slippery Slope,
Malcolm Muggeridge / 177
13. From Feticide to Infanticide,
Joseph R. Stanton, M.D. / 185

66670

14. The Murder Case of Dr. Waddill,
    Michael Novak / 199
15. The Killing Will Not Stop, *George F. Will* / 203

IX. The Testimony of Personal Experience
16. There Just Wasn't Room in Our Lives Now for
    Another Baby, *Jane Doe* / 211
17. He (or She) Would Be 23 . . . , *Bill Stout* / 217
18. Abortion: A Nurse's View, *Mary Roe* / 221
19. On Being Alive, *Sondra Diamond* / 225

X. On a Human Life Amendment
20. A Human Life Amendment, *James Bopp, Jr.* / 233

XI. The Testimony of Religion:
Protestant, Catholic, and Jewish Viewpoints
21. Protestants and the Abortion Issue,
    Harold O.J. Brown / 249
22. Stand Up for Life, *Pope John Paul II* / 261
23. Jewish Views on Abortion,
    Rabbi Immanuel Jakobovits / 267

XII. Inspiration and Action
24. A New Birth of Freedom,
    Richard John Neuhaus / 283
25. Grace, Prophecy and Saving Babies,
    Jeff Hensley / 295
26. Handling Tough Questions, *James Manney* / 301

Index / 307

Preface

ON ONE OCCASION in scripture Jesus laments over Jerusalem and her people's hardness of heart.

Today we stand in our cities and cry out. We are deeply saddened by the injustice of abortion, the slaughter of the millions.

Our desire is to cry out with effectiveness, to stem the tide of death. Abortion continues at an undecreased rate since the Supreme Court's *Roe v. Wade* decision of January 22, 1973. In 1982 the figure most frequently heard for abortions annually in the United States is one and a half million. Only a few years ago that estimate was most often quoted at one million a year.

Things are not getting better; they're getting worse.

We then must work to educate people in order to stop the taking of innocent life. To educate others, we must first be well-informed ourselves.

And that is the purpose of *The Zero People,* to provide an up-to-date handbook for those who desire to educate themselves, so they can in turn educate and persuade others.

The Zero People presents some of the best written and best argued factual and persuasive material published on the life issues in the last several years. For that reason, it may be read to inform oneself or given to others who may be straddling the fence to allow them to make up their own minds once they have properly informed themselves.

We must be activists for life. We must be informed, and we must seek to inform and persuade others. We who cherish the lives of the children must be faithful to what is really their cause and not our own.

Because of our proud American heritage of a profound respect for the individual, a heritage that grows from our religious heritage, we have always been on the leading edge of the defense of human life. We must be again.

Few of us will cast deciding votes for life in state or national legislatures or arrive at landmark decisions in courtrooms of importance. But each and all of us can offer information to others in a loving way that will move them toward a deeper respect for the incalculable value of human life.

Let each of us find the small place of service, the small things we can do and do them well. The God who loves both the children and those who abort them will aid our efforts. We will prevail.

I would like to express special thanks to *The Human Life Review* and its publisher, J.P. McFadden, for the use of much of the material in *The Zero People*. Under Mr. McFadden's direction, *The Human Life Review* has done a consistently superb job of addressing the issues surrounding abortion, euthanasia, and infanticide.

Jeff Hensley

Part One

Responding in Love

More than a million unborn children are aborted in the United States every year. This fact staggers the mind. How should we think about abortion? What can we do about it? John Powell, S.J., priest and author, probes the reasons for his own deep commitment to the prolife effort, and helps us confront the enormity of abortion.

ONE

The Silent Holocaust

John Powell

I HAVE SOMETIMES WONDERED why I feel so deeply involved in and committed to the prolife effort. No other issue has ever affected me so strongly. Nothing else has made me feel the loneliness and sorrow I have felt since the Supreme Court legalized abortion in 1973. Nothing else has kept me awake nights as this has. When I look around and see so many other people, good people, who don't share my intense identification with the prolife cause, I naturally wonder why I have responded as I have.

I have thought back over my past trying to answer this question, and I have realized that much of my response to abortion has been shaped by two or three very profound personal experiences. Perhaps I can best communicate the urgency I feel in regard to this issue by describing these experiences.

The first was the birth of a baby boy at St. Thomas Hospital in Akron, Ohio, where I served for two months as chaplain shortly after my ordination. I was in the delivery room at the

John Powell, S.J., is the author of several bestselling books, including *Why Am I Afraid to Tell You Who I Am?* and *Unconditional Love.* Widely known as a prolife speaker, he is professor of theology at Loyola University in Chicago, Illinois. This article is reprinted from *New Covenant* magazine.

insistence of a retired nursing sister. She had stopped me one day in a corridor and said, "Before you leave here you've got to see a baby delivered." Despite my reluctance I was ushered into a delivery room the very next morning.

Everything was very casual and chatty until the baby was ready. Then the room got very still, and a baby boy came into the world. The doctor cleared away the mucus with suction tubes and rubbed the baby's chest and back. The little boy cried.

When I heard that first wail of life, something happened to me that had never happened before—not on my ordination day, not on any of the other momentous days of my life. I simply turned numb. The doctor was explaining about the afterbirth, the drops in the eyes, but I didn't hear much. I was utterly overwhelmed by the beauty and sacredness of that moment.

I thought later of what I had learned in theology classes—that God didn't come to know you and me at our conception or birth. He has known us from all eternity. He had waited from all eternity for that little boy to be born.

I saw a lot of things for the first time in my two months at the hospital. But nothing affected me as much as the birth of that baby boy.

Soon after my stint at the hospital, I was sent to Europe to study theology and to explore that bottomless pit of a language called German. I spent some time traveling around Germany to get practice with the language. One place I visited was Dachau, the Nazi death camp.

I entered with a group of tourists under a sign explaining that West Germany keeps Dachau open as a memorial to the six million people who died in death camps during World War II, in the hope that what happened there may never happen again in the course of human history. "Never again!" the sign read. Inside, a guide passed out brochures with the grimmest pictures I had ever seen—emaciated prisoners, stacks of corpses, mutilated children; unbelievable things.

Our guide took us through the oblong building where the extermination was done. We saw the hooks where people were told to hang up their lice-ridden clothing. We saw the showers, where they waited for water from dummy shower heads while poison gas came up through false drains. We saw the room where corpses were stacked while teeth with gold and silver fillings were pried from their mouths.

Then we came to the ovens. There were eight of them, thickly covered with rust. The slides were pulled out, as if in readiness for the next bodies to be burned.

For the second time in my life, I turned numb. This was the other end of the spectrum. If the birth of the baby had been too beautiful to take in, this was too cruel. I didn't want to believe it. I couldn't take it in.

When we finally left Dachau, I looked back at the sign over the gate. My last memory of the death camp is the line: "That what happened here may never in the course of human history happen again." "Keep us remembering," I thought. "Don't let us ever fall into this darkness again."

When my German was fairly good, I took a job as chaplain in a convent outside Cologne, Germany. Here I met an elderly nun, Sr. Rutilia, who volunteered to practice German conversation with me. Sr. Rutilia always looked very sad when we talked. At first I thought it was my German. After three weeks, however, she was still looking so sad that I finally asked, "Is something hurting you? Do you want to talk about it?"

The good sister burst into tears. "Yes," she sobbed. "What you don't know is that our building here was once a home for retarded children. Our sisters cared for them; that was our life work. We were warned what would happen, but we didn't believe it until the day the vans came. The soldiers walked right in. They took our babies, they threw them in their vans like sacks of garbage. They took them all away to kill them because they were retarded.

"Most people don't realize," she went on, "that the death camps weren't set up for the Jews—not at first. They were for the unwanted life of Germany—the crippled life, the unproductive life. They were killed, all of them."

I really didn't know at that time if this sister had her facts right. Later I read an article titled "Medical Practice under a Dictatorship," published in the *New England Journal of Medicine* in 1949. It was written by Leo Alexander, a psychiatrist who served as an observer at the Nuremberg trials.

Dr. Alexander documented the fact that in the 1920's, before Hitler's rise to power, German medical practice laid the groundwork that made the death camps possible. Many doctors were advocating the Hegelian principle of pragmatism—what is useful is right. They proposed that the insane, the crippled, and the terminally ill be killed because their lives served no useful purpose.

When Hitler took power, he signed decrees allowing doctors to begin killing off anyone who wasn't "functional." These doctors, all of whom had pledged in the Hippocratic oath to protect life, willingly became social executioners for the Third Reich. They went after the insane first, then the crippled, then the aged. They killed deformed and retarded children. By the time the killing of the Jews began, the Nazis and their doctors had killed more than a quarter million Germans, all people who were somehow unproductive, unable to serve the state, unwanted. Then, with all the mechanism of death in place, Hitler was ready to undertake his final solution of the so-called Jewish problem.

When I got back from Europe and thought about all I had experienced there, Dachau and Sr. Rutilia always stood out. The terrible memories of what happened when a people accepted the killing of innocent human beings as the solution to social problems. Then on January 22, 1973, as I was driving through Chicago, I heard a radio announcer say, "The Supreme Court of the United States has today legalized abortion on demand."

A thousand shock waves pounded through my heart and mind. I thought of the little boy I had seen born in Akron, Ohio, and how God has loved each of us from all eternity. I thought of the death camp at Dachau, and the horrible principle that "what is useful is right." The end justifies any means. I remembered the tears Sr. Rutilia wept for her little children.

Since that day of January 22, 1973, I have felt lonely and troubled in my own country. If I had acted purely on my emotions, I would have left. I really wanted out. How can one live in a country where this is happening? Can one be an innocent bystander at killing?

Then the day came when a young woman I knew well walked into my office and said, "Father, I've had an abortion. What do you think of me now?"

I stood up and put my arms around her. "I'll always love you," I said. "But I have to say that I'm very sad you had an abortion."

I wasn't prepared for what she said next.

"I know I've killed my baby. I know. I even asked the nurse if there was some way to baptize the baby before we killed it. But she told me to shut up. She said, 'Shut up, you bitch. We don't need you. You need us.'"

So my young friend lay there quietly, listening to another woman explaining that she was having an abortion because she wasn't going to let a "goddamn pregnancy" interfere with her skiing trip to Aspen. "I put my hands over my ears," she told me. "I didn't want to hear that."

"I asked another nurse—not the one who yelled at me—for a glass of water. I poured it over my belly and I said, 'Baby, it's the best I can do for you. I baptize you in the name of the Father, and of the Son, and of the Holy Spirit.'"

"Wait a minute! Please!" I interrupted her. "Listen to me." And I pleaded with her to accept God's forgiveness, not to destroy the rest of her life. But she left my office with a sad look and terrible, throbbing guilt inside her.

Later another girl came in who had just the opposite reaction. She was pregnant, she told me. Her boyfriend had insisted, "Get rid of the kid! It's like using a vacuum cleaner. I'll pay for half." I could tell from her expression, her voice, the way she sat—all the things you pay attention to when you're counseling— that those words didn't bother her. They really didn't. I thought, "If that doesn't bother you, what *would* bother you? What have we done to our young people? How could we so mislead them?"

It so bothered *me* that I wrote that night to my Jesuit superior, the president of my university, and the head of my department, asking for a year off from teaching to travel around the country and speak to people about abortion and the right to life.

Before my year of speaking began, I went to people involved in the prolife movement. I asked them to explain the abortionist position so I would be prepared to debate it. Did abortionists claim not to know whether they were taking a human life?

"No," I was told. "Nobody says that anymore. The evidence that abortion is the destruction of human life is conclusive."

"Then how do they justify themselves?"

"You'll hear variations on the Planned Parenthood theme: every child has a right to be born if he or she is wanted. In other words, only a wanted baby has a right to live. If a baby will be an embarrassment or a psychological problem or an inconvenience, he or she should be killed. It solves a problem."

I couldn't quite believe that abortionists themselves would be quite so blunt about it. So I began reading their own statements. Here's a sampling:

Mary Calderone, M.D., a former medical director of Planned Parenthood: "Fertilization, then, has taken place; a baby has been conceived."

Neville Sender, M.D., who runs an abortion clinic, Metropolitan Medical Service, in Milwaukee, Wisconsin: "We know it is killing, but the states permit killing under certain circumstances."

Warren Hern, M.D., of the Boulder Abortion Clinic in Boulder, Colorado: "There is no possibility of denial of an act of destruction by the operator. It is before one's eyes. The sensations of dismemberment flow through the forceps like an electric current."

Abortionists at a New York City hospital, as quoted by psychologist Magda Denes in her book, *In Necessity and Sorrow*:

"Even now I occasionally feel a little peculiar about it, because as a physician I'm trained to conserve life and here I am destroying life."

"I dare say any thinking, sensitive individual can't not realize that he is ending life or potential life."

"You know that there is something alive in there that you're killing."

Then I actually began debating abortionists and found that not one ever questioned my assertion that every abortion kills an innocent human being. One doctor whom I debated simply said, "When you solve in some other way all the problems I can solve by abortions, I'll be on your side."

I asked another doctor, a Christian who will nevertheless perform an abortion when amniocentesis tests reveal a defect in the baby, if I could rephrase one of his own statements. "Is this a fair way to express what you just said, doctor? You tell the mother, 'Because your baby is defective (and one in fourteen babies has some kind of defect), you have the right to kill it or not to kill it. If you choose to kill it, I'll do the killing.'"

"Of course," he said. "That's what I just said. There's no other way to say it and still be honest."

When I realized that the doctors who perform abortions know that they are ending human lives, know that the fetus is not just a blob of protoplasm, I told myself that America is already operating on the principle of pragmatism. We have bought the idea that you can end a human life to solve a problem.

Where will this principle take us? Down the same road as the doctors of Hitler's Germany? Down some equally terrible road, but one disguised as the "protection of personal freedom"? Albert Schweitzer once stated, "If a man loses reverence for any part of life, he will lose his reverence for all of life." By looking around at what is happening in our own country, in the wake of legalized abortion, we can see this prophecy come true.

Already in some American cities there are more abortions than live births every year. Already, two state legislatures have seriously considered a bill allowing people to have themselves killed for any reasons they want to stipulate—if they're paralyzed, or become senile, or simply lose their hair. According to one proposal, they could name anyone they wanted to do the killing, provided the person be 14 years old or older.

Already, two Nobel prize winners have suggested that no baby be declared legally alive until three days after birth, so that defective babies who escape abortion can still be killed. Already, there are cases like the one at Johns Hopkins hospital, in which a newborn baby was denied routine intestinal surgery for an easily treated problem and was put aside to die because he was afflicted with Down's Syndrome. It took that baby 16 days to die of dehydration, and the doctors actually filmed a dramatization of the process.

I see these things happening, and I want to cry out, "Is anyone there? Does anyone see what I see? Does anyone care?" These things aren't happening in secret; they're reported in the press; everyone knows about them. In the United States every day 4000 babies are killed by abortion. But when I look around for people to speak out, I find a great deal of indifference. "I'm not going to have an abortion. I don't want to get involved with that. I'm not a fighter anyway."

My plea, then, to my Christian brothers and sisters, is to please do something about abortion. We are the priestly people of God. We are supposed to be bringing the world to God and God to the world, not playing the innocent bystander. Four thousand babies will be killed *today*. Over seven million babies have been killed in the United States since 1973. If we are really Christ's witnesses in the world, we've got to speak up.

Let's be sure to speak up out of love, however, not out of judgment or hatred toward those who perform or who have had abortions. I have been involved with a lot of prolife work, and I'm convinced that one thing that could short-circuit this whole movement would be for it to become infected with vindictiveness or hate. If we want to stand up for the sacredness of human life, we have to speak up out of love—love for the babies who won't see life, and for the frightened women who often don't understand what they're going through, and even for the abortionists who somehow believe that the killing is necessary. We can judge the action of abortion and say loudly and clearly that it is terribly wrong, but we should not take on ourselves God's role in judging the subjective responsibility of individuals.

When I look around for the people who are speaking up about abortion, I find one man in particular who is a real inspiration— Victor G. Rosenblum, a Jewish lawyer with the American Civil Liberties Union. I once watched a television interview with Dr. Rosenblum, during which he was asked, "Dr. Rosenblum, you certainly would permit abortion if the doctor told us the baby was going to be defective, wouldn't you? Or retarded?" The questioner obviously did not know that Dr. Rosenblum has a retarded child, whom he very much loves.

Dr. Rosenblum said, "Oh no, no, no." Then he asked a question of his own. "Do you believe in love?" he said. "Not just the lip service of love. Do you really believe you are called to love? If you do, you don't say, 'I'll love *you,* because you have your mental faculties, and *you,* because you're wealthy, but not *you,* because you only have one arm.' Love doesn't discriminate.

"If we found out that a baby would be born without arms, and we really believed in love, we would say, 'Baby, we're going to love you. We'll make arms for you. We have a lot of skills at that now. And listen, baby, if those arms don't work, we will *be* your arms. We'll take care of you, don't worry, because we love you. You are one of us, a member of our human family.'"

The interviewers didn't know what to do with that. What do you do with someone who really knows what it is to love? So they said, "Well, Dr. Rosenblum, if enough people have abortions and talk openly about them and defend them, this furor will eventually die down, won't it?"

I remember well how this great, good man dropped his head. "Yes," he said, "yes, it will. And that will be the saddest day in all of American history."

Part Two

Roe v. Wade, *and*
Some Implications

The Supreme Court legalized abortion on demand in the United States with two decisions issued on January 22, 1973. *Roe v. Wade*, the better known of these two rulings, overturned state laws regulating abortion. Writing within months of these decisions, John T. Noonan, a professor of law at the University of California (Berkeley), offered an analysis of the Court's reasoning in a now-classic essay, "Raw Judicial Power." The Court did not act in an intellectual or a political vacuum. An editorial that appeared in *California Medicine* in 1970, often quoted after *Roe v. Wade*, describes the "new ethic" that the Court adopted a few years later.

TWO

Raw Judicial Power

John T. Noonan, Jr.

O N JANUARY 22, 1973, the Supreme Court of the United States deciding *Roe v. Wade* and *Doe v. Bolton* announced that a new personal liberty existed in the Constitution—the liberty of a woman to procure the termination of her pregnancy at any time in its course. The Court was not sure where the Constitution had mentioned this right, although the Court was clear that the Constitution had not mentioned it explicitly. "We feel," said Justice Blackmun for the majority, "that the right is located in the Fourteenth Amendment's concept of personal liberty," but he thought that it also could be placed "in the Ninth Amendment's reservation of rights to the people" (*Wade*, pp. 37-38). Vague as to the exact constitutional provision, the Court was sure of its power to proclaim an exact constitutional mandate. It propounded a doctrine on human life which had, until then, escaped the notice of the Congress of the United States and the legislators of all fifty states. It set out criteria it said were required by the Constitution which made invalid the regulation of abortion in every state in the Union, the District of Columbia, the Commonwealth of Puerto Rico, and the City of New York. No one of these bodies had read the Constitution right.

John T. Noonan, professor of law at the University of California (Berkeley), is the author of *Contraception* and editor of *The Morality of Abortion*. This article first appeared in *National Review*.

Wherever the liberty came from in the Constitution and however recent its discovery was, it was of a very high rank. It deserved to be classified as "fundamental" and as "implicit in the concept of ordered liberty" (*Wade*, p. 37). With these characterizations, the right took its place with such foundations of civilized society as the requirement of fair, public trials. Justice Blackmun seemed to sense no incongruity in giving so basic a position to a demand which had, until his opinion, been consistently and unanimously rejected by the people of the United States. He did not pause to wonder how the nation had survived before January 22, 1973, in steadfastly repudiating a right implied in the concept of ordered liberty.

Some of the legislation affected was old, going back to the mid-nineteenth century, some was recent, reflecting the wisdom of the American Law Institute or containing explicit statements of intent to protect the fetus. Some of the legislation had been confirmed by recent popular referenda, as in Michigan and North Dakota; some of the legislation was in the process of repeal, as in New York. Old or new, compromise or complete protection from conception, passed by nineteenth-century males or confirmed by popular vote of both sexes, maintained by apathy or reaffirmed in vigorous democratic battle, none of the existing legislation on abortion conformed to the Court's criteria. By this basic fact alone, *Roe v. Wade* and *Doe v. Bolton* may stand as the most radical decisions ever issued by the Supreme Court.

That these opinions come from a Court substantially dominated by appointees of a President dedicated to strict construction of the Constitution, that they should be drafted by a Justice whose antecedents are Republican, are ironies which do not abate the revolutionary character of what the Court has done in the exercise of what Justice White, in dissent, calls "raw judicial power." In rhetoric, the style is that of a judicial body. In substance, the opinions could have been authored by Paul Ehrlich or Bella Abzug.

Radicalism marks not only the Court's treatment of the states and its preference for the views of an elite to the results of democratic contests. Radicalism is also the mark of the Court's results. In October 1963 Glanville Williams, the spiritual father of abortion-on-demand, put the proposition to the Abortion Law Reform Association that abortion be made a matter between woman and physician up to the end of the third month. His proposal was voted down by the then most organized advocates of abortion. In less than ten years the Supreme Court has written into the Constitution a far more radical doctrine. By virtue of its opinions, human life has less protection in the United States today than at any time since the inception of the country. By virtue of its opinions, human life has less protection in the United States than in any country of the Western world.

The Court's Holdings

Did the Court really go so far? Here is what it held:

1. Until a human being is "viable" or "capable of meaningful life," a state has no "compelling interest" which justifies it in restricting in any way in favor of the fetus a woman's fundamental personal liberty of abortion (*Wade*, p. 48). For six months, or "usually" for seven months (the Court's reckoning, p. 45), the fetus is denied the protection of law by virtue of either the Ninth Amendment or the Fourteenth Amendment.

2. After viability has been reached, the human being is not a person "in the whole sense," so that even after viability he or she is not protected by the Fourteenth Amendment's guarantee that life shall not be taken without due process of law (*Wade*, p. 47). At this point he or she is, however, legally recognizable as "potential life" (*Wade*, p. 48).

3. A state may nonetheless not protect a viable human being by preventing an abortion undertaken to preserve the health of the mother (*Wade*, p. 48). Therefore a fetus of seven, eight, or nine months is subordinated by the Constitution to the demand for abortion predicated on health.

4. What the health of a mother requires in any particular case

is a medical judgment to be "exercised in the light of all factors—physical, emotional, psychological, familial, and the woman's age—relevant to the well-being of the patient" (*Bolton,* pp. 11-12).

5. The state may require that all abortions be done by licensed physicians, that after the first trimester they be performed in licensed "facilities," and that after viability they be regulated so long as "health" abortions are not denied (*Wade,* p. 49). The state is constitutionally barred, however, from requiring review of the abortion decision by a hospital committee or concurrence in the decision by two physicians other than the attending physician (*Bolton,* pp. 17, 19). The Constitution also prohibits a state from requiring that the abortion be in a hospital licensed by the Joint Committee on Accreditation of Hospitals or indeed that it be in a hospital at all (*Bolton,* pp. 14-15).

With belated misgivings, Chief Justice Burger concludes his brief concurrence in Justice Blackmun's opinion with the sentence: "Plainly, the Court today rejects any claim that the Constitution requires abortion-on-demand." Here is a desperate effort to recapture in a sentence what the Court has given away in its list of criteria mandated by the Constitution. Plainly, there cannot be the slightest argument that for the first six to seven months of fetal existence, the Court has made abortion-on-demand a constitutional right. Opposed to the mother's "fundamental personal liberty," the embryo or fetus is valued at precisely zero. His or her very existence seems to be doubted by the Court which refers to the state's interest here not as an interest in actual lives but as an interest in a "theory of life" (*Wade,* p. 47). The woman's right is treated as an absolute, abridgeable only for her own sake by the requirements as to licensed physicians and facilities.

Abortion-on-demand after the first six or seven months of fetal existence has been effected by the Court through its denial of personhood to the viable fetus, on the one hand, and through its broad definition of health, on the other. Because the seven-month-old fetus is not a person—cannot be a person as long as it is a fetus—because it now bears the label "potential life," the fetus is not a patient whose interest the physician must consult. In the Court's scheme, the physician has one person as patient, the mother.

When the doctor considers the mother's health, he is to think in terms of the extensive definition of health first popularized by the World Health Organization (WHO). According to the WHO declaration, health is "a state of complete physical, mental, and social well-being, not simply the absence of illness and disease." The Supreme Court now affixes a seal of approval to this definition, substituting "familial" for "social," but essentially equating health with well-being. What physician could now be shown to have performed an abortion, at any time in the pregnancy, which was not intended to be for the well-being of the mother? What person would have difficulty in finding a physician who, in full compliance with the Court's criteria, could advise an abortion if the patient's emotional demand was intense enough? Never before in British or American law has a baby in the last stages of pregnancy been so exposed to destruction at the desire of the parent.

The Court's Reasoning

How did this Supreme Court reach this extraordinary result? In part through an inept use of history, in part through a schizophrenic style of judicial interpretation, in part through a conscious response to the needs of technocracy.

Let us look at the history. Justice Blackmun's opinion in *Wade* contains a copious gob of it (*Wade*, pp. 14-36). By and large it is a conscientious if pedestrian review of the relevant literature. But it is a history that is undigested—better said, it is history that has been untasted. It has afforded no nourishment to the mind of the judge who set it out. He has not let it engage his spirit. He has not felt the pressure of loyalty to the persons of the past who have shaped our culture. He has not responded as a person to their perceptions.

Justice Blackmun describes with clarity the reason the American Medical Association led the fight in the nineteenth century for statutory protection of the embryo—"the popular ignorance of the true character of the crime—a belief, even among mothers themselves that the fetus is not alive till after the period of quickening"; the consequent "unwarrantable destruction of human life" before the fifth month. He concludes, "The attitude of the profession may have played a significant role in the enactment of stringent abortion legislation during that period" (*Wade,* pp. 26-27). But the unimpeachable facts are apparently forgotten when Justice Blackmun discusses the claim that the purpose of American statutory law was not to protect the fetus, but to protect the mother from sepsis or other risks attendant on abdominal surgery in the unsanitary hospitals of the day. The Justice does not ask why the statutes then bar abortion by drug, or why this kind of surgery alone should have been made subject to the criminal law and customarily classed among "Crimes against the Person."

If Justice Blackmun can read the history, cite the American Medical Association jeremiads, and trace the development of the law, and yet be uncertain as to the law's intent, it must be that he has failed to grasp, failed to integrate, the purposes which animated our ancestors in laying down a thick wall of protection about the baby in the womb. History for him has not been the evocation of persons in fidelity to their fundamental purposes. It has been a charade which is shuffled off the stage when the display of learning is completed.

What of the schizoid style of judicial interpretation favored by the Justice? On the one hand, he declares the Fourteenth Amendment, enacted in 1868, refers to a personal liberty which had escaped attention for over a century—a liberty which, as Justice Rehnquist observes in dissent, would, if noticed, have invalidated the state statutes on abortion in force in 1868. Needless to say, not a single word of history is adduced to show that the framers of the Fourteenth Amendment, the Congress which proposed it, and the states which passed it, intended to

legitimize abortion. In this branch of his opinion, Justice Blackmun is an evolutionist. Constitutions must be reinterpreted or remade to speak to the times. If liberty means one thing in 1868 and something entirely different in 1973, it is what one must expect of a basic document exposed to a variety of times and conditions. As Justice Blackmun says in an oblique reference to the process which he has followed, his holding is consistent "with the demands of the profound problems of the present day" (*Wade*, p. 50).

On the other hand, in determining the meaning of "person" in the Fourteenth Amendment's guarantee, the Justice is curiously wooden. He looks at what person meant literally at the time of the adoption of the Constitution. He notes what person must have meant in other clauses of the document. He observes that fetuses are not enumerated in the census. But he does not ask if the new biological data on the fetus compels the Court to be as evolutionary in its definition of person as it is in its definition of liberty. He refrains from looking squarely at the facts of fetal existence. He takes the term person as if its meaning had been frozen forever. Contrary to the radical substance of the rest of his opinion, he is here, uniquely, a strict constructionist.

Neither the use of history nor the method of construing the Constitution explains why the Court reached the result it did; and the Court has been so curiously circumspect about revealing its reasoning that a commentator is forced to fall back on hints and to resort to inferences. Four features of the opinions are suggestive:

1. Justice Blackmun in an excusatory preamble states that he is aware of "the sensitive emotional nature of the abortion controversy" and concludes with an admonition from Holmes that judges should not brand a statute unconstitutional merely because it embodies opinions which to them are "novel and even shocking" (*Wade*, pp. 1-2). Would it be rash to suppose that Justice Blackmun saw the appropriateness of this advice, even as he did not follow it, when he encountered the opinion

that a fetus is a person? To one vocal segment of American thought, few things could be so novel or shocking as the suggestion that a fetus has human rights. If Justice Blackmun accepted the viewpoint dominant in the media, he could readily have been shocked at the postulates underlying the statutes on abortion.

2. "Population growth, pollution, poverty, and racial overtones" are mentioned by name only on one page of *Wade* as matters "tending to complicate the problem." They then disappear from view only to be embraced in the vague but comprehensive self-justification of the Court's holding: It is "consistent with" the "demands of the profound problems of the present day" (*Wade,* p. 50). Studiously ignored is the recommendation of the Rockefeller Commission that abortion be used as a secondary form of population control. Studiously ignored is the comment of black leaders like Jesse Jackson that what is being prepared by the welfare bureaucrats is a program of genocide in the womb. And yet the Court, looking back as it were on its handiwork, says its holding responds to profound problems of the present. What problems fall within the court's solution but the problems of controlling population growth, the problems of the welfare bureaucracy curtailing welfare rolls?

3. The Court declares that if those trained in medicine, philosophy, and theology are unable to arrive at a consensus as to when life begins, then "the judiciary is not in a position to speculate as to the answer" (*Wade,* p. 44). Incompetence in the area is avowed.

Three pages later, Justice Blackmun describes the abortion statute of Texas as "adopting one theory of life" and rejects that theory as a ground for regulating abortion. Is this the judiciary "speculating as to the answer" or is it not? How can Texas—and the other states with comparable statutes—be wrong in protecting fetal life against arbitrary extinction unless the majority of the Court knows better when life begins. The pretense of incompetence seems to be humbug.

Beneath the avowal of incompetence is a commitment to a

particular theology or theory of human life. Life is an interest worthy of state protection when it acquires the characteristic of "viability" or "the capability of meaningful life outside the mother's womb." At this point, state protection has "both logical and biological justification" (*Wade*, p. 48). At this point, in short, life has characteristics that other humans may recognize. At this point, functionally, the Justice says human life begins.

As both a logical and biological matter, however, viability depends entirely on the relation of a human being's capacities to the environment in which he or she is placed. As Andre Hellegers has pointed out, an adult stripped naked and placed on the North Pole suddenly becomes nonviable. Analogously, a fetus ripped from his mother's womb suffers a sudden loss of the capability to survive. In the environment in which he or she had been existing, however, the fetus was as viable as any of us in our houses.

Neither logic nor biology seems to help in explaining why Justice Blackmun chose the point in the continuum he picked for recognition. But he has thrown out another phrase for our guidance—"capability of meaningful life." Here, it may be, lies the heart of the matter. What it is appropriate for the state to protect is not a human being, but a human being with the "capability of meaningful life." Human life is defined in terms of this capability. Qualitative standards of the life worthy of protection are to prevail, as Joseph Fletcher is reported to have joyously greeted the decision. Our old way of looking on all human existence as sacred is to be replaced by a new ethic more discriminating in choosing who shall live and who shall die. The concept of "meaningful life" is at the core of these decisions.

4. Who shall make the judgment that life has meaning or the capability of meaning? On this key point, it is not, perhaps, unfair to suspect Justice Blackmun of being an elitist, or, if one prefers, a technocrat.

The twin opinions breathe an extraordinary respect for the medical profession. Their explicit presupposition is that a "conscientious physician" using his best professional judgment—not "degraded" by having his judgment reviewed by colleagues (*Bolton*, p. 16)—will determine whether the fetus shall live or die. Turning the community's protection of human life over to the judgment of the technician who will perform the operation, Justice Blackmun goes as far as one judge could go to bring about the technocratic utopia so wittily and so unsparingly described in *Brave New World*.

A large irony of the opinions is this: The Fourteenth Amendment, made necessary by an earlier Supreme Court's attempt to make it legally impossible to protect the personal rights of a free black, is here made the source of holdings which made it legally impossible to protect the personal rights of a fetus. Forever denied the status of person "in the whole sense of the term," forever subordinated to the psychological health of his mother, the baby in the womb has been deprived of the possibility of protection by state or federal law. It would be a waste of valuable energy to exert any effort at amending the abortion laws to achieve in the last two or three months of fetal life the uncertain protection which the Court does not outlaw.

A second major irony is that the Court's alternative authority for the right to abort is the Ninth Amendment. This Amendment reads: "The enumeration in the Constitution, of certain rights, shall not be construed to deny or disparage others retained by the people." The people had already spoken on abortion through the legislatures of fifty states. In Michigan and North Dakota, crushing majorities of the people had, as recently as November 1972, rejected the demand that abortion be allowed on five-month-old fetuses. Who would contend that what Justice Blackmun and his six colleagues legislated could be passed as law in Congress or in any popular referendum? How could the rights of the people be more effectively "disparaged" by an elite than for seven members of a court to pronounce their efforts at controlling assaults on life to be unconstitutional?

These ironies suggest that the solution must be drastic. A majority which will mock the people with the doctrines of technocratic elitism will not stay its hand if confronted with new legislation not conforming to its sovereign mandate. The root of the problem must be reached. Two lines of attack are possible. They could be pursued concurrently:

First. The Court could be expanded from nine to 15. This solution could be labeled "The Abraham Lincoln Solution." It is the idea he put forward in the famous Lincoln-Douglas debates, when Douglas insisted that *Dred Scott* was the law of the land. Douglas, he observed, had been one of five new judges added to the Supreme Court of Illinois, "to break down the four old ones." Was not, he implied, a change in membership in the Court a constitutional way of correcting a bad decision?

In many minds sensitive to the Court's place in our institutional structure there must be reluctance to change the traditional number in response to a particular decision. The "court-packing" plan of Franklin D. Roosevelt and the strong opposition it engendered come to mind. Nonetheless, there is reason why an expansion of the Court may be considered at this time as more than an ad hoc answer to a decision. A committee appointed by the Chief Justice himself (the "Freund Committee") has proposed that the Court be relieved of many of its burdens by the creation of a national appellate body which would decide what cases are appropriate for adjudication by the Supreme Court itself. The plain implication of the proposal is that nine justices are far too few to handle the enormous modern increase in the Court's business. Expansion of the Court to 15 would meet this problem directly without the disadvantage of bifurcating the functions of the highest tribunal. Expansion can be rationally justified as a functional necessity at the same time that it affords a vehicle for restoring the rights of the people.

Expansion has a practical basis. Its political attractiveness does not need underlining. It is, still, however a temporary response. It does not meet the moral issue at its deepest level. It does not provide constitutional protection for human life in the future.

The second possible course, then, is to follow the approach actually taken to overturn *Dred Scott*: Amend the Constitution. Under *Wade* and *Bolton* the fetus can never be a person within the Fourteenth Amendment, the people can never vote to give effective protection to the fetus. Very well, let the people defend the fetus by a new amendment.

The people might go further. They might defend not only humans in the womb, but all nonviable humans—all humans threatened with possible classification as being lacking the "capability of meaningful life." The infant suffering from genetic deficiencies, the retarded child, the insane or senile adult—all of these potential victims of a "quality of life" mystique could be defended by a Human Life Amendment to our Constitution.

THREE

A New Medical Ethic

THE TRADITIONAL WESTERN ETHIC has always placed great emphasis on the intrinsic worth and equal value of every human life regardless of its stage or condition. This ethic has had the blessing of the Judeo-Christian heritage and has been the basis for most of our laws and much of our social policy. The reverence for each and every human life has also been a keystone of Western medicine and is the ethic which has caused physicians to try to preserve, protect, repair, prolong, and enhance every human life which comes under their surveillance. This traditional ethic is still clearly dominant, but there is much to suggest that it is being eroded at its core and may eventually even be abandoned. This of course will produce profound changes in Western medicine and in Western society.

There are certain new facts and social realities which are becoming recognized, are widely discussed in Western society, and seem certain to undermine and transform this traditional ethic. They have come into being and into focus as the social by-products of unprecedented technologic progress and achievement. Of particular importance are, first, the demographic data of human population expansion which tends to proceed uncontrolled and at a geometric rate of progression; second, an ever growing ecological disparity between the numbers of people and the resources available to support these numbers in the manner to which they are or would like to become accustomed;

This editorial is reprinted from *California Medicine,* 113:67-68. September, 1970.

and third, and perhaps most important, a quite new social emphasis on something which is beginning to be called the quality of life, a something which becomes possible for the first time in human history because of scientific and technologic development. These are now being seen by a growing segment of the public as realities which are within the power of humans to control and there is quite evidently an increasing determination to do this.

What is not so clearly perceived is that in order to bring this about hard choices will have to be made with respect to what is to be preserved and strengthened and what is not, and that this will of necessity violate and ultimately destroy the traditional Western ethic with all that this portends. It will become necessary and acceptable to place relative rather than absolute values on such things as human lives, the use of scarce resources, and the various elements which are to make up the quality of life or of living which is to be sought. This is quite distinctly at variance with the Judeo-Christian ethic and carries serious philosophical, social, economic, and political implications for Western society and perhaps for world society.

The process of eroding the old ethic and substituting the new has already begun. It may be seen most clearly in changing attitudes toward human abortion. In defiance of the long held Western ethic of intrinsic and equal value for every human life regardless of its stage, condition, or status, abortion is becoming accepted by society as moral, right, and even necessary. It is worth noting that this shift in public attitude has affected the churches, the laws, and public policy rather than the reverse. Since the old ethic has not yet been fully displaced it has been necessary to separate the idea of abortion from the idea of killing, which continues to be socially abhorrent. The result has been a curious avoidance of the scientific fact, which everyone really knows, that human life begins at conception and is continuous whether intra- or extra-uterine until death. The very considerable semantic gymnastics which are required to rationalize abortion as anything but taking a human life would be ludicrous if they were not often put forth under socially impeccable auspices. It is suggested that this schizophrenic sort of subterfuge is necessary because while a new ethic is being accepted the old one has not yet been rejected.

It seems safe to predict that the new demographic, ecological, and social realities and aspirations are so powerful that the new ethic of relative rather than of absolute and equal values will ultimately prevail as man exercises ever more certain and effective control over his numbers, and uses his always comparatively scarce resources to provide the nutrition, housing, economic support, education, and health care in such ways as to achieve his desired quality of life and living. The criteria upon which these relative values are to be based will depend considerably upon whatever concept of the quality of life or living is developed. This may be expected to reflect the extent that quality of life is considered to be a function of personal fulfillment; of individual responsibility for the common welfare, the preservation of the environment, the betterment of the species; and of whether or not, or to what extent, these responsibilities are to be exercised on a compulsory or voluntary basis.

The part which medicine will play as all this develops is not yet entirely clear. That it will be deeply involved is certain. Medicine's role with respect to changing attitudes toward abortion may well be a prototype of what is to occur. Another precedent may be found in the part physicians have played in evaluating who is and who is not to be given costly long-term renal dialysis. Certainly this has required placing relative values on human lives and the impact of the physician to this decision process has been considerable. One may anticipate further development of these roles as the problems of birth control and birth selection are extended inevitably to death selection and death control whether by the individual or by society, and further public and professional determinations of when and when not to use scarce resources.

Since the problems which the new demographic, ecologic and social realities pose are fundamentally biological and ecological in nature and pertain to the survival and well-being of human beings, the participation of physicians and of the medical profession will be essential in planning and decision-making at many levels. No other discipline has the knowledge of human nature, human behavior, health and disease, and of what is involved in physical and mental well-being which will be needed. It is not too early for our profession to examine this new ethic, recognize it for what it is, and will mean for human society, and prepare to apply it in a rational development for the fulfillment and betterment of mankind in what is almost certain to be a biologically oriented world society.

Part Three

The Population Bomb Fizzles

Fear of the "population explosion" underlies the "quality of life" ethic that dominates so much contemporary thinking about life issues. It is thought that the world will run out of resources if the growth of the world's population is not drastically reduced. In this context some see abortion, infanticide, and euthanasia as tools to limit population and remove dependent groups. Abortion removes the unwanted; euthanasia removes the unproductive; infanticide eliminates the defective and deformed. "The Population Bomb Threat" examines the facts upon which this gloomy scenario has been built.

FOUR

The Population Bomb Threat: A Look at the Facts

Jacqueline R. Kasun

I N RECENT DECADES, torrents of books, articles, news stories, and programs have poured forth to the American public a message of alarm about the "population explosion." Despite the long decline in the U.S. birthrate and the large decrease in numbers of children, the alarm continues. However, although libraries have been filled with doomsday warnings, there has been a notable shortage of facts on the subject. What, then, are the facts?

The first is that there is a notable shortage of facts regarding the size and rate of growth of world population. The best population information exists for the developed and industrialized countries, which probably hold only one-third of the world's people. In these developed countries, rates of population growth are very low. As Ansley J. Coale, director of the Office of Population Research at Princeton University, states: "Of the 31 countries that are usually listed as highly developed, 21 now have birthrates below replacement."[1] Coale points out that, in the U.S.,

Jacqueline R. Kasun is Professor of Economics at Humboldt State University, Arcata, California. This article is reprinted from *Intellect*, June 1977. Copyright 1977 by Society for the Advancement of Education.

by the time the Zero Population Growth movement came along, fertility was in the midst of its steepest decline in history—50% in 16 years. We are below replacement now and are continuing to grow only because of the age distribution of the population. If the downtrend continues, we will begin to have a shrinking population not long after the end of the century.

Compared with many other countries, both population density and rate of growth are relatively low in the U.S. There are about 22 persons per square kilometer in the U.S., compared with between 100 and more than 300 for various countries in Western Europe. The rate of natural increase in the U.S.—0.6% in 1974—is below the average for developed countries.[2]

Thus, there is no population explosion in the U.S. or in the other developed countries. Population scholars estimate that rates of growth are higher in the less-developed world, but also note evidence of declining growth rates in a majority of the countries for which data are available.

The most widely reported estimate, based on fairly good data for about one-third of the world and guessing about the rest, is that world population presently numbers about 3,900,000,000 people, and is increasing at an annual present rate of not quite two per cent. What does this portend for world economic welfare? Can world resources support a population of this size estimated to be growing at this rate?

The Facts About Food

Certainly, our first concern is food. On this point, the facts about recent world food production are in surprising contrast to the gloomy warnings of certain population tracts. The fact is that, between 1962 and 1972, world food production increased 31%, while world population is estimated to have increased only 21%.[3] *Some of the most spectacular increases occurred in regions which have excited the most handwringing. Rice production in Asia increased 40% during the decade of 1960's, while population in that area increased only 25%.*[4] Wheat production in India more than doubled between the late 1960's and 1974.

However, can we expect these trends to continue, or must the increases in population inevitably outrun the world's food-raising capability? On this question of the world's food-raising potential, a number of major studies have reached a common conclusion, which does not support the view that mass starvation is imminent. This conclusion is that there is a *very large, unused potential for world food production.*

For example, in 1974, the University of California published the results of a major survey of world food resources showing that the *world presently uses less than half of its available arable land.*[5] This means that the world could feed twice its present population by using all of its arable land at present average yields. The percentages of unused farm land vary among different regions of the world—for example, Asia uses 74% of its arable land, while Africa uses only 29%—but there is unused potential in every major world area.

Thus, the University of California report concludes that adequate land is available to feed twice the world's present population without increasing average yields. Other studies have estimated how much food could be raised if farmers were to improve their methods. For example, Colin Clark, former director of the Agricultural Economic Institute at Oxford University and noted author of many books on population-resource questions, classified world land types by their food—raising capabilities and found that, if all farmers were to use the best methods now in use, enough food could be raised to provide an American-type diet for 35,100,000,000 people, almost 10 times as many as now exist! Since the American diet is a very rich one, Clark found that it would be possible to feed three times as many again—or 30 times as many people as now exist—at a Japanese standard of food intake. Nor would these high levels of food output require cropping of every inch of available land space. Clark's model assumed that nearly half of the earth's land area would remain conservation areas. The noted city planner, Constantin Doxiadis, arrived independently at a similar estimate of the world's ability to feed people and to provide conservation areas.

Nor does any shortage of fertilizers, irrigation water, or energy threaten world food production, in the view of Clark and the University of California investigators. Supplies of these inputs will be adequate for agricultural purposes throughout the foreseeable future, they say.

It is of some interest at this point to compare the current UN forecast of the eventual size of world population—between 10 and 16,000,000,000 at the end of the 21st century—a figure viewed with extreme alarm in some quarters, with the carefully estimated world capability of feeding between 35 and 100,000,000,000 people, using presently known methods.

The Outlook for Other Resources

However, man does not live by bread alone. He also requires houses and dishwashers and TV sets and cars, especially if he is an American, plenty of gasoline. Does population growth threaten to exhaust world supplies of the material needed to produce these things?

Over the past decades, there have been recurrent predictions of the imminent exhaustion of all energy and basic metals, but the facts have not borne out these prophecies—and indeed they should not. It is a familiar chemical principle that nothing is ever "used up"—materials are merely changed into other forms. Some of these forms make subsequent recycling easier, while others make it more difficult. Thus, it is cheaper to obtain some usable metals from the city dump than from their original ore, but, once gasoline has been burned, it can not be reused as gasoline. Economists gauge the availability of basic materials by measuring their price changes over time. A material whose price has risen over time (when allowance is made for changes in the average value of money) is becoming more scarce, while one whose price has been falling is becoming more abundant, relative to the demand for it. Two major economic studies of the availability of basic metals and fuels found no evidence of increasing scarcity over the period 1870-1972.[6]

What about the future? As Coale points out, insofar as metals are concerned, they exist in tremendous quantities at lower concentrations. Geologists know that going from a concentration of six per cent to one of five per cent multiplies the available quantities by factors of 10 to 1,000, depending on which metal is concerned.

In the case of fuels, the U.S. is currently in the position of having exhausted its own sources of low-cost petroleum. This is not correctly described as a "crisis," however, since higher-cost petroleum supplies are still available in this country and extremely large deposits of coal remain, to say nothing of the possibilities for substitutes such as solar energy. Furthermore, the U.S. has tremendous, unexploited opportunities for economizing in the use of energy. A reduction in U.S. energy consumption to one-half of its present level would still leave us consuming as much per person as the people of Western Europe, whose living standards are as high as ours, and would deliver our environment from the heavy pollution load created by our excessive energy use.

Pollution and Population

This leads us to a consideration of pollution. Some people believe that pollution is chiefly the result of overpopulation and must increase proportionately with population.

However, Barry Commoner, professor of plant physiology at Washington University in St. Louis and director of the Center for the Biology of Natural Systems, explains that the environmental damage found in modern industrial societies is primarily the result of highly polluting technologies which have been recently adopted, rather than a consequence of population growth. He points out that, between 1947 and 1970, population in the U.S. increased 40%, but pollutants due to the use of synthetic pesticides increased 267%; nitrogen oxides in motor fuel increased 630%; inorganic fertilizer nitrogen increased

648%; and detergent phosphorus increased 1,845%.[7]

What these figures mean is that the only hope for cleaning up the environment lies in a direct attack on the polluting technologies responsible for the damage. The fact that the anti-population-growth movement is so heavily subsidized by the leaders of some very polluting industries[8] suggests that the population panic may be intended to deflect sincere environmentalists from attacking the real roots of pollution.

Unemployment Problems

Further, there are the unemployment arguments. It is sometimes claimed that the existence of unemployment "proves" that the population is too large and is growing too fast. Here again, the claims fly in the face of the facts, which are that the causes of unemployment lie in bad public economic policies. Quite simply, through the device of investment tax credits, our government pays employers to lay off workers and replace them with machines, even when people are without jobs. High payroll taxes, minimum wage laws, and unrealistic union wages reinforce this tendency. As long as these policies continue, unemployment will be a problem, whatever the size of the population.

People and Congestion

Finally, one argument for limiting population growth is so seemingly indisputable as to claim everyone's support. This is the fact of congestion, which is so prominent a part of modern life. In fact, however, despite the congestion near the urbanized sea-coasts, most of the planet is still largely empty. As Felice points out, "We could put the entire world population in the state of Texas and each man, woman and child could be allotted 2,000 square feet [the average home ranges between 1,400 and 1,800 square feet] and the whole rest of the world would be empty."[9]

The reason we feel so crowded in our entire modern milieu is

that we use space inefficiently, especially in our transportation systems. The typical American or European now transports himself everywhere in a personal vehicle which requires on the average as much space at its various destinations as we provide in housing for the average family of four. What these figures mean is that each additional automobile in the community creates congestion equivalent to that of several extra people. Thus, during the decade of the 1960's in the U.S., while the human population increased by a modest 13%, we acquired 34,000,000 additional cars, creating as much additional congestion as if we had added more than 100,000,000 people, or more than 50%, to the human population!

As in the case of many other problems mistakenly blamed on "overpopulation," congestion can only be reduced by a direct approach. The simple expedient of moving about in buses, trains, and trolleys, or on foot, instead of in personal automobiles would reduce congestion, as well as urban air pollution, by 90%.

In closing, it should be noted that children are not merely claimants on social resources. Children do not diminish, but add to, the welfare of those who have them, just as truly as material possessions do, and they create far fewer environmental pressures than do the ubiquitous vehicles of the so-called "advanced" societies.

Admittedly, we live on a finite Earth and, if world population growth were to continue for many centuries at the two per cent rate estimated for the present, problems could be expected. History shows, however, that, when countries begin to modernize, an initial stage of rapid population growth is followed by a spontaneous reduction in fertility. This happened in Europe and North America and can now be observed in most less-developed countries.

Therefore, since the so-called "population crisis" is more truly a myth and an alibi than a fact, and since, in any event, population growth slows down spontaneously as economic development proceeds, there seems to be no reasons for alarm or for draconian measures of control.

Notes

1. Figures appearing in *Population and Family Planning Programs: A Factbook,* a publication of the Population Council, December, 1974.

2. Based on estimates by the U.S. Bureau of the Census and the Population Council.

3. Derived from Population Council figures appearing in *Population and Family Planning Programs: A Factbook,* a publication of the Population Council, December, 1974.

4. Population figures from the Population Council. Rice output figures from University of California Division of Agricultural Sciences. *A Hungry World: The Challenge to Agriculture,* July, 1974, p. 68.

5. University of California Divison of Agricultural Sciences, *op. cit.,* p. 72.

6. H.J. Barnett and C. Morse, *Scarcity and Growth: The Economics of Natural Resources Availability* (Baltimore: Johns Hopkins Press, 1963); and V. Kerry Smith, "Re-Examination of the Trends in the Prices of Natural Resource Commodities, 1870-1972," distributed at the 87th Annual Meeting of the American Economic Association, San Francisco, December, 1974.

7. Barry Commoner, "The Environmental Costs of Economic Growth," in Robert Dorfman and Nancy Dorfman, eds., *Economics of the Environment* (New York: Norton, 1972).

8. The Rockefeller fortune, largely derived from interests in oil and chemicals, heavily subsidizes organizations dedicated to reducing the rate of population growth, including the Population Council and Planned Parenthood. According to the *Washington Post* of Aug. 10, 1975, the General Motors fortune has also been heavily devoted to

promoting population control. The Ford fortune is also channelled very importantly to population research and control.

9. Francis P. Felice, "Population Growth," *The Compass*, 1974.

Part Four

A Doctor Who Saves Babies

Three years after abortion became legal in the United States, an eminent surgeon from Philadelphia delivered this wide-ranging speech to the Christian Action Council. Dr. C. Everett Koop, later to become Surgeon General of the United States, brought unique qualifications to his subject. As a physician, he describes fetal development and the techniques abortionists use. As a student of public policy, he examines the effect of abortion on our society. As a leading Christian layman, he outlines the moral challenge abortion presents.

The Right to Live

C. Everett Koop

I WOULD LIKE TO SUGGEST to you that we are a schizophrenic society. We will fly a deformed baby four hundred miles by airplane to perform a series of remarkable operations on such a youngster, knowing full well that the end result will be far less than a complete cure. We will stop a cholera epidemic by vaccine in a country unable to feed itself so that the people can survive cholera in order to die of starvation. While we struggle to save the life of a three-pound baby in a hospital such as mine, next door in the University Hospital obstetricians are destroying infants yet unborn.

So it is not unpredictable in this society that we should be considering the pros and the cons of abortion and euthanasia.

My assignment today is of gigantic proportions. I will assume that you each know bits and pieces of what I have to say but that you will bear with me if I start at square one. It is my intention to tell you of my own credentials to speak on this subject, to give

C. Everett Koop, M.D., Sc.D, was appointed Surgeon General of the United States in November, 1981. He was formerly Surgeon-in-Chief at The Children's Hospital in Philadelphia, and professor of pediatric surgery at the University of Pennsylvania School of Medicine. This article, adapted from an address to the Christian Action Council, appeared in *The Human Life Review* in 1975, and formed the basis for *The Right to Live, The Right to Die,* published by Tyndale House. The article has been slightly revised by the author for publication here.

you some background on abortion, to describe the development of an unborn baby, and to briefly acquaint you with the several techniques for performing an abortion. Then I must tell you what the current situation is legally, what this means in practice, and then recount for you—now that the sides are drawn—the arguments you will hear in favor of abortion. I will attempt to answer these briefly. Finally, I would like to assume the role of prophet and outline for you the implications of the Supreme Court's decision on abortion in reference to the future of this country and in reference to your life and mine as well as the lives of our children.

Professionally, I do not speak on this subject in a vacuum. For more than a quarter of a century, I have been engaged in the surgical care of children, and perhaps that for which I am best known professionally is the operative procedures on newborn babies who are born with defects which are incompatible with life, but nevertheless, can be corrected by the proper surgery at the proper time. These are youngsters who are born with no esophagus with which to swallow, or have their abdominal organs out in the umbilical cord, or up in the chest, or have one of many varieties of intestinal obstruction. Each one of these defects is correctable. Many of them take years of rehabilitation before a youngster is able to return to society, and some of these children, in spite of all that we do for them, are never what society calls normal.

I could not have taken care of thousands of these babies and their families without seeing the joy and the triumph of a life saved, but also the heartbreak of a surgical success somewhat less than perfect. I know the economic burden on the family, I know the problem of chronic illness for the family, for the child, and for the community. I know the psychological burden on such a youngster as he grows up as well as the problems that the family has to face as he goes to school, encounters new friends and tries to achieve a position in the community socially and economically.

Permit me to say that the whole question of the right to live presents anyone who considers it with a number of dilemmas; I have lived through many of them. Let me give you an example; I could have a telephone call any day from an outlying hospital saying that they had just delivered a baby who has no rectum, whose abdominal organs are out in his umbilical cord and who has a cleft spine with an opening in his back so that you can see his spinal cord, and, in addition, his legs are in such a position that his feet lie most comfortably next to his ears. Now, every one of those things that I have mentioned is correctable. But think of the cost! I am not simply talking about money, but think of the cost in anxiety for the family, for the hospital staff, for me; think of the emotional drain on all the people concerned, think of the emotional problems for that youngster in the six or seven years it will take before these defects are corrected. Now the dilemma that is presented to some people in such a situation is, "Should we operate or should we not? Should we let this baby die, unattended, or should we do the things that we know how to do best and let him live?" Dilemma is defined as, "a perplexing predicament, a necessary choice between two equally undesirable alternatives." I am not sure that everyone here would agree that the two alternatives I have mentioned are equally undesirable. Yet everyone talks about rights these days and I would like to ask you whether you think this baby has the right to live. Does this family have the right of a choice? Do I, as the baby's surgeon, have a right of choice? Do I have the right or privilege to try to influence the family to think the way that I do?

In 1776, in Philadelphia, Thomas Jefferson wrote, "We hold these Truths to be self-evident, that all Men are created equal, . . . that they are endowed by their Creator with certain inalienable Rights, that among these are Life, Liberty and the Pursuit of Happiness." Now think about that for a moment. Think about the baby's right to life. Think about the family's right to happiness. Think about my right to the liberty of choice and think about the baby's right to all of those things.

When I speak to an audience such as this on the right to live, I acknowledge at the outset that God is the author and the giver of life and that you and I as His servants have no right to destroy it. And I am speaking of human life, not animal life, and I am not speaking of that perverted doctrine of Albert Schweitzer of the reverence for life. The Bible tells us that man was made in the image of God and at least one meaning of that statement is that like God each of us is a trinity. I am a soul, I inhabit a body and I have a spirit. Everything I read in the Word of God tells me that my soul is immortal and like it or not, you and I will be conscious beings throughout all eternity.

We are not the first society to wonder about these things. Some ancient societies before the Greeks and the Romans practiced infanticide. This is how they controlled their population, took care of their food problem and their economics. Among the Greeks, a people who have such respect in philosophical circles, many—including great philosophers—believed that society should get rid of the frail, the deformed, and the aged. The Romans considered that infanticide was a prudent form of household economy.

In eighteenth-century Philadelphia it was the practice on Sunday afternoons to go down to 8th and Spruce Streets to the first hospital in our country to see the insane who were chained in dungeons. One could buy for a half-penny a willow wand and poke it through the bars to torment them and see their response. It was only after 1800, with the spread of literacy and the Gospel and the Christian compassion that went with it, that hospitals came into prominence, that people were concerned enough to build orphanages, homes for the aged and for the insane. It is only a little more than a hundred years since the first medical missionary left one land and went to another to carry the Gospel of Jesus Christ along with the healing of men's bodies. I believe that the sanctity of human life is part of that Gospel.

The sanctity of human life begins, as I see it, with the various covenants between God and man. The first of these was after Abel had been killed by Cain and Cain was cursed by God. God was very careful to point out that there was to be no blood feud and if there were, His punishment would take place sevenfold.

After the flood, God spoke to Noah and told him that whoever sheds man's blood, by man shall his blood be shed. Many believe that was the mandate from God for capital punishment. After that came the Ten Commandments, and one of those was, "Thou shalt not kill." (It is very clear from the context that the commandment, "Thou shalt not kill," had nothing to do with capital punishment or with manslaughter or with war, but it had to do with murder.) All of these covenants, if you read them carefully, were based upon one thing: man's uniqueness in having been created in the image of God.

It is obvious that Jewish religion held life to be precious to God. Christian doctrine is based upon Judaism plus the teachings of Jesus. Jesus claimed that His teachings were in harmony with the teachings of the Old Testament. He said further that the moral law was immutable and unchanging. He showed how learned men, such as the Pharisees, could misinterpret the law. You will recall on one occasion He said to them, "You are pleased with yourselves because you keep the law and have not murdered anyone, but you have missed the spirit of the law." In the final analysis, as a Christian, I believe in the sanctity of life because I am God's by creation and also God's by redemption through Jesus Christ and His sacrifice on the cross in my behalf.

The liberalization of abortion laws has brought the whole problem of sanctity of life into focus. I am opposed to abortion but let me say that no one has a greater claim on my compassion than an unmarried, pregnant girl. There are other alternatives, particularly Christian alternatives, to that girl's predicament other than abortion. My reasons against abortion are logical as well as theological.

Let me speak first about the logic. It is impossible for anyone to say when a developing fetus or embryo or baby becomes viable; that is, has the ability to exist on its own. The logical approach is to go back to the sperm and the egg. A sperm has 23 chromosomes and no matter what even though it is alive and can fertilize an egg it can never make another sperm. An egg also has 23 chromosomes and it can never make another egg. So we have eggs that cannot reproduce and we have sperm that cannot reproduce. Once there is the union of sperm and egg, and the 23 chromosomes of each are brought together into one cell that has 46 chromosomes, we have an entirely different story. That one cell with its 46 chromosomes has all of the DNA (Deoxyribonucleic acid), the whole genetic code that will, if not interrupted, make a human being just like you with the potential for God-consciousness. I do not know anyone among my medical confreres, no matter how pro-abortion he might be, who would kill a newborn baby the minute he was born. My question to my pro-abortion friend who will not kill a newborn baby is this: "Would you kill this infant a minute before he was born, or a minute before that, or a minute before that, or a minute before that?" You see what I am getting at. At what minute can one consider life to be worthless and the next minute consider that same life to be precious? So much for the logic of permissive abortion.

Although there are ample reasons for the non-religious individual to be frightened about the implications of the Supreme Court's decision on abortion, I do believe that most of those opposed to abortion lean heavily upon religious convictions in coming to their pro-life position. Although I realize that there are others here who will speak today on the theological reasons against abortion, I feel I must say a word so that you will know how I have come theologically to the position I now hold. Two of the Christian doctrines which I cherish most are the sovereignty of God and the infallibility of Scripture. By sovereignty I mean that even though God as apparently given man free will, that free will is nevertheless within the sovereignty of God. God is accountable to no one for His decisions. Even the breath that men use to blaspheme God is a gift from God Himself. As I read the Bible, it seems to say from cover to cover that life is precious to God. I can find no place in the Bible which clearly states when a fetus might be viable but there are some passages which are extremely significant.

In the 139th Psalm, David writing about himself says, "Yes, the darkness hideth not from thee; but the night shineth as the day: the darkness and the light are both alike to thee. For thou hast possessed my inner parts: thou hast covered me in my mother's womb. I will praise thee; for I am fearfully and wonderfully made: marvellous are thy works; and that my soul knoweth right well. My substance was not hid from thee, when I was made in secret, and curiously wrought in the lowest parts of the earth. Thine eyes did see my substance, yet being unperfect; and in thy book all my members were written, which in continuance were fashioned, when as yet there was none of them."

I am also impressed that when the Bible speaks of man in the womb, it also speaks of the whole sweep of the creation and of God's sovereignty from then until the end of time. In the 44th chapter of Isaiah, we read, "Yet now hear, O Jacob my servant; and Israel, whom I have chosen: Thus saith the Lord that made thee, and formed thee from the womb, which will help thee." And then the prophet goes on to quote Jehovah in reference to the creation, the pouring out of his spirit, his blessing upon Israel, the forgiveness of their transgressions, and then goes on to say, "Thus saith the Lord, thy redeemer, and he who formed thee from the womb, I am the Lord that maketh all things; that stretcheth forth the heavens alone; that spreadeth abroad the earth by myself."

Having already mentioned the union of sperm and egg to give 46 chromosomes, let me give you a capsule review of the development of a baby. I do not want to get technical, but perhaps you do not know what happens and when. By the time that a baby is 18-25 days old, long before the mother knows that she is pregnant, the heart is already beating. At 45 days after conception, you can pick up electroencephalographic waves from the baby's developing brain. At 8 weeks, there is a brain. By 9-10 weeks, the thyroid and adrenal glands are functioning. The baby can squint, swallow, move his tongue, and the sex hormones are already present. By 12 weeks, the fingerprints on the hands have already formed and, except for size, will never change. At 13 weeks, he has fingernails, he sucks his thumb, and he can recoil from pain. In the fourth month the growing baby is

8-10 inches in height. In the fifth month there is a time of lengthening and straightening of the developing infant. Skin, hair, and nails grow. Sweat glands arise. Oil glands excrete. This is the month in which the movements of the infant are felt by his mother. In the sixth month the developing baby responds to light and to sound. He can sleep and awake. He gets hiccups and can hear the beat of his mother's heart. Survival outside the womb is now possible. In the seventh month the nervous system becomes much more complex, the infant is 16 inches long and weighs about three pounds. In the final eighth and ninth months there is a time of fattening and of rounding out.

There are three commonly used techniques of abortion; each may have its variations. The technique that is used most commonly for early pregnancies is called the D&C, or dilatation and curettage. In this technique, which is carried out between the seventh and twelfth weeks of pregnancy, the uterus is approached through the vagina. The cervix is stretched to permit the insertion of instruments. The surgeon then scrapes the wall of the uterus cutting the body to pieces and scraping the placenta from its attachments on the uterine wall. Bleeding is profuse. An alternate method to be used at the same time is called suction abortion. The principle is the same as the D&C. A powerful suction tube is inserted through the open cervix. This tears apart the body of the developing baby and his placenta, sucking them into a jar. These smaller parts of the body are recognizable as arms, legs, and head. More than 75% of all abortions performed in the United States and Canada are done by this method.

Later in pregnancy when the D&C or suction abortion might produce too great a hemorrhage on the part of the mother the second most common type of abortion comes into being. This is called the salt poisoning abortion, or "salting out." This method is carried out after sixteen weeks of pregnancy when enough fluid has accumulated in the sac around the baby. A rather long needle is inserted through the mother's abdomen directly into the sac surrounding the baby and a solution of concentrated salt is injected into it. The baby breathes in and swallows the salt and is poisoned by it. There are changes in osmotic pressure; the outer layer of skin is burned off by the high concentration of the salt; brain hemorrhages are frequent. It takes about an hour to slowly kill the baby by this method. The mother usually goes into labor about a day later and delivers a dead, shriveled baby.

If abortion is decided upon too late to be accomplished by either the D&C or salting out procedures, there is left a final technique of abortion called hysterotomy. A hysterotomy is exactly a caesarean section with the one difference, namely, that in a caesarean section the operation is being done to save the life of the baby whereas in the hysterotomy the operation is being done to kill the baby. These babies look very much like other babies except that they are small, weighing, for example, about two pounds at the end of a 24-week pregnancy. These babies are truly alive, and they are allowed to die through neglect or are deliberately killed by a variety of methods. A Boston jury found a physician guilty of manslaughter for killing the product of this type of abortion.

What is the current legal situation in reference to abortion? The Supreme Court has been making decisions in recent years and months which must be of vital concern to every person. First there was the ruling against prayer in public schools. Now if you are for strong separation of church and state, that might have been to your liking, yet a related decision virtually eliminates Bible reading in schools, *even as literature,* and a generation will now grow up in this country knowing more about the writings of Hemingway and Sartre than of St. Paul. Subsequently, the Supreme Court dealt with pornography, or perhaps it would be better to say that they failed to deal with pornography. They sounded such an uncertain note that pornography is still undefined in this country, court cases pile up, but what you and I call pornography still flourishes throughout the land. Next, the Supreme Court ruled that capital punishment was an extraordinary and cruel punishment. It is not my purpose to debate capital punishment here, but it does seem to me that the Supreme Court was overly concerned about the humane treatment for the three murderers killed in the previous six years and had little thought for the effect upon society made by the 78,000 murders that took place in that same period of time. These three actions of the Supreme Court differ remarkably from each other. The prayer decision is in conformity with the post-Christian spirit of our age, but it sets the stage for the erosion of other things that are dear to you and me. Pornography from the Christian perspective may be lawful, but for the Christian it is not expedient. Capital punishment is thought by many to be a divine precept from the covenant given to Noah in the Old Testament as I have already said, but whether this is your interpretation or not, the abrogation of capital punishment by the Supreme Court may very well endanger your life.

It is not my primary intention to undermine your faith in the Supreme Court, but I would like to examine with you this area where the laws of the United States and the laws of God are not in accord, to sharpen your thinking to be critical of civil authority, and finally to show you some of the natural consequences which I believe will affect your lives in days to come as the morality of this nation is constantly eroded.

In 1959, in the Declaration of Human Rights, the United Nations stated: "The child, by reason of its physical and mental immaturity, needs special safeguards and care, including appropriate legal protection before as well as after birth." That was the United Nations in 1959. On January 22, 1973, the Supreme Court of the United States, *Roe v. Wade* and *Doe v. Bolton* announced that a new personal liberty had been found in the Constitution—the liberty of a woman to procure the termination of her pregnancy at any time in its course on demand. It is interesting that the Supreme Court was not sure in its decision where the Constitution had provided this right for a woman; indeed, the Supreme Court was very clear that the Constitution did not mention it explicitly. In spite of the fact that the Court was extremely vague as to where this provision is in the Constitution, it was not the least bit unsure that it had the power to proclaim a specific constitutional mandate. It propounded a new doctrine on human life. It rendered invalid the existing regulation of abortion in every state of the union. Some of this legislation went back to the middle of the last century. Other legislation which was overthrown was recent and was an indication of the concern of lawmakers in this country for the protection of the fetus. Some of the legislation previously valid had been confirmed by popular referenda as recently as November, 1972, in Michigan and North Dakota.

The Supreme Court rulings went far beyond the most optimistic hopes of the pro-abortionists. In 1963 Glanville Williams, one of the earliest activists in reference to abortion-on-demand, proposed to the Abortion Law Reform Association that abortion be a matter between woman and physician up to the end of the third month. His proposal was voted down by the then most radical advocates of abortion. Yet in fewer than ten years the Supreme Court has written into our laws a far more radical doctrine.

Here are some of the specifics of the Supreme Court's ruling:

1. Until a developing baby is "viable" or "capable of meaningful life" (whatever that means), a state has no "compelling interest" which justifies it in restricting abortion in any way in favor of the fetus. For six or seven months (*not* clearly defined!) the fetus is denied the protection of law explicit in either the 9th or the 14th amendments.

2. Even after viability (still not clear) has been reached the developing baby is not a person "in the whole sense" so that even after viability the growing baby is not protected by the guarantee that you and I have in the 14th amendment that life shall not be taken without due process of law.

3. A state still may not protect a viable human being by preventing an abortion undertaken to preserve the health of the mother despite the fact that the Court recognized that even a developing baby, though not a person in "the whole sense," nevertheless is legally recognizable as having "potential life." By this statement a fetus as old as nine months, that is, just before delivery, is placed in a position by

the decision of having his right to life subordinated to the demand for abortion predicated on health. Let me digress here and say that up until the Supreme Court's decision in January of 1973, the definition of health had already been expanded to ludicrous proportions. The slightest upset in the emotional state of a woman contemplating the continuation of a pregnancy was defined as an impairment of health.

4. The state may require that all abortions be done by licensed physicians, that after the first trimester of pregnancy they be performed in "licensed facilities," and that after viability (still not defined) of the fetus abortions may be regulated so long as "health" abortions are not denied. The state was forbidden the previous customary safeguard of requiring review of the abortion decision by a hospital committee or alternatively the concurrence in the decision by two physicians other than the expectant mother's attending physician. In the lesser known decision, the Court also prohibits the state from requiring that the abortion be done in a hospital licensed by the Joint Committee on Accreditation of Hospitals or indeed that it be in a hospital at all. In other words a freestanding abortion clinic without any of the safeguards that medicine has built into policing itself need not be required.

Justice Blackmun, who wrote the majority opinion, made it abundantly clear that if any religion was to be a guide to him it would be paganism. He alluded to the practice of the Persians, the Greeks, and of the Romans, but he ignored Christianity. The Hippocratic oath which has been taken by physicians for the past 2,000 years specifically prohibits abortion and the suggestion of it. Justice Blackmun laid this aside as having no relevance today.

The decision takes some comfort in its wording in the fact that the mortality of abortion is even lower than the mortality for live births. The reference, of course, can only apply to the mother; the baby's mortality is 100%. (History may prove these statements to be incorrect in reference to maternal mortality as statistics on abortion are accumulated.)

Here are some of the direct quotations from the majority opinion of the highest court in our land: "If the state is interested in protection of fetal life after viability it may go so far as to proscribe abortion." It is incredible that the Court would have such a low regard for life, state its callousness so crudely, and to do so while exceeding its own constitutional obligation, if not its authority.

It is further absolutely astounding to me that Justice Blackmun could have included the following sentence in his decision. "We need not resolve the question of when life begins." Indeed need we not! Where does this lead? It leads to infanticide and eventually to euthanasia. If the law will not protect the life of a normal unborn child, what chance does a newborn infant have after birth, if in the eyes of a Justice Blackmun, he might be less than normal?

The Chief Justice of the Supreme Court, Justice Burger, said, "The vast majority of physicians . . . act only on the basis of carefully deliberated medical judgments relating to life and health. . . ." The simple fact of the matter is that the Chief Justice does not know physicians as well as I do, nor does he appreciate how few physicians it takes to make abortion-on-request equivalent to abortion-on-demand.

Finally, in referring to the woman's right of privacy, Justice Blackmun wrote: "This right of privacy . . . is broad enough to encompass a woman's decision whether or not to terminate her pregnancy."

Where does this leave us practically at the moment? At this moment unborn infants have no protection at all anywhere in these United States. There is not the slightest doubt that in the first six to seven months of fetal existence abortion-on-demand is a constitutional right of a woman. There is not the slightest doubt that the value of an embryo or a fetus is absolutely nothing. Abortion-on-demand after the first six or seven months of fetal existence has been effected by the Court because it has denied personhood to the viable fetus on the one hand and through its broad definition of health on the other. If the seven-month-old fetus is not a person (and the Supreme Court has said it cannot be a person as long as it is a fetus), the physician only has one patient, namely, the mother. This is in contradistinction to medical understanding throughout the ages. Now when the physician considers the mother's health, he has to do so in reference to the definition of health given by the World Health Organization: "a state of complete physical, mental, and social well-being, not simply the absence of illness and disease." Obviously, this gives any physician complete license to perform an abortion and complete protection under the law because he could always hide under the umbrella of the World Health Organization's definition of health in that he was working for the well-being of the mother. In short, unwanted-ness can be a death sentence for the baby.

I believe that most people have not thought much about their attitude toward abortion; even those who are vigorously opposed to it sometimes do not have good reasons. Last year I had the privilege of preaching at two Roman Catholic masses at Villanova University. It was a tremendous opportunity to speak to about 1,300 young people. I said to them essentially what I am saying to you. Afterwards, hundreds of those boys and girls came to me and said exactly the same thing: "I have always been against abortion, but now I know why."

The abortion question is argued on four grounds: medical, social, personal and theological. I have already told you some of the medical things you should know about the development of a fetus and the way in which it is killed by abortion. The next thing you should know medically is that the idea that abortion is not killing is a new idea. Five years ago, everybody agreed that abortion was killing an unborn baby. Now we have been brainwashed (and I will have more to say about this brain-washing later) so that words do not mean the same things that they used to mean. For example, you find that the abortionists do not talk about babies in the womb except when they have a slip of the tongue. They do not even like to refer to them as fetuses. When they call the developing baby "the product of conception" it ceases to have a personality and its destruction could not possibly mean killing. As recently as 1967, at the first international conference on abortion, a purely secular group of people, said, "We can find no point in time between the union of sperm and egg and the birth of an infant at which point we can say that this is not a human life." Now if that had been a theological group it would have been easy to understand the statement. But when one considers that this was a secular group of people representing thoughts from many cultures all over the world, that doctrine is worth listening to.

In the *Journal of California Medicine* in 1970 the following remarkable quotation appeared: "The result has been a curious avoidance of the scientific fact which everyone really knows that human life begins at conception and is continuous whether intra- or extra-uterine until death. The very considerable semantic gymnastics which are required to rationalize abortion as anything but taking a human life would be ludicrous if they were not often put forth under socially impeccable auspices." [This editorial is reprinted as Chapter 3 of this book—Ed.] I would add to that that a great many of the medical statements which are pro-abortion come from academically impeccable sources—a tragic circumstance in American medicine today. In countries that have gone the way of abortion-on-demand that we are now embarked upon, there have been developments from which we can learn. Japan is one of these countries. They liberalized abortions just about the way that we did but they did it twenty years ago. In the first eight years they had 5,000,000 abortions. Their experience indicates that as people became used to abortions, as it no longer was a shocking thing to talk about, as people talked about the products of conception rather than talking about an unborn baby, abortions took place later and later in pregnancy. By 1956 26,000 abortions in Japan were at five months, 20,000 were at six months, and 7,000 were at seven months. In 1972 the Japanese government decided to revise legislation to prevent women from having abortions purely for economic reasons. The prime minister said that something must be done about his country being known as a haven of abortionists.

Poland has had a very liberal abortion law for many years but recently the government reversed itself because they realized they were facing genocide. So many people were having abortions in Poland that the population had fallen well below the "population zero" fertility rate. We reached that same rate two years ago.

The Supreme Court's decision enabling freestanding abortion clinics to exist has made it very difficult to keep records in the United States on how many abortions are being carried out and what the complications might be. The National Health Service in Great Britain keeps excellent records and they have been in the abortion-on-demand business for about six years. The liberal pro-abortionists in this country in the days before the Supreme Court's decision told us of how there would be a reduction in illegitimacy, prostitution, venereal disease, and other social ills. Unfortunately, the excellent records of the first five years of liberalized abortion under the National Health Service in Great Britain have revealed an increase in incidence of the following: illegitimacy, venereal disease, prostitution, later sterility of the previously aborted mother, pelvic inflammatory disease from gonorrhea, and subsequent spontaneous abortions or miscarriages. Ectopic pregnancies—that is where the egg is implanted not in the uterus but up in the fallopian tube requiring an emergency abdominal operation—have doubled since abortion has been liberalized. Prematurity in women who had a previous abortion has increased in Great Britain by 40%. No one has done a study on the emotional reaction or the guilt of the woman who has had an abortion and now desperately wants a baby that she cannot have.

The Czechoslovakian government tightened its abortion regulations because they could not afford their special education expenditures. The number of retarded children associated with the high incidence of prematurity in pregnancies involving mothers who had previously aborted children was the reason.

What records we do keep in this country as published in a medical journal in January of 1974 indicate that the maternal mortality rate for saline abortions rose from 9 per 100,000 in the first year to 22.2 per 100,000 in the second year underscoring the greater risks of second trimester terminations of pregnancy. In states like New York before the liberalized abortion laws the mortality rate for mothers was 52 per 100,000 live births. This was not true, however, for states like Rhode Island that do not have the problems of black and Puerto Rican immigration. In the last two years before the liberalized abortion laws there was not a single maternal death at childbirth in the state of Rhode Island and many other states have similar low maternal mortality rates.

The three medical questions that are usually asked of someone in my position who is anti-abortion have to do with rape, suicide and handicapped children.

As horrible a bit of violence is rape, it very seldom results in pregnancy. A study in Minneapolis of 3,500 rape cases revealed not a single pregnancy. The same is true of maternal suicide. A study over seventeen years in Minneapolis revealed that suicides in reference to pregnancy were part of generalized psychoses and in the rare instance where it did occur did so after pregnancy rather than during. Finally, studies on handicapped children have indicated that their frustrations are no greater than those experienced by perfectly normal children. To this latter I can attest. My life has been spent with children who are less than one would consider totally normal and I have considered it a privilege to be involved in extending life to these youngsters. In the thousands of such circumstances that I have participated in I have never had a parent ask me why I tried so hard to save the life of their defective child. Now that I am seeing children I operated upon years ago bring me their children for care, I have never had an old patient ask me why I worked so hard to save his or her life.

It is in the social arena that the abortion question is most ardently debated. Here a small minority of pro-abortion "liberals" have altered our vocabulary, misrepresented statistics, reprehensibly made false associations—and with such great success that they influenced the Supreme Court to perpetrate on the American People, who are fundamentally pro-life, the legalized murder of millions of babies in the name of progress and social reform. You will be told that the Gallup poll has found that "two out of three Americans now favor legal abortion." Dr. Gallup compared the results of a poll taken in June 1972 with his previous polls on abortion. However, he was not honest enough to state that he had changed the questions. Dr. Gallup polled Americans on abortion in 1962, 1965, 1968 and 1969. In all of these polls, he asked identical questions. The record shows that in the years 1965, 1968 and 1969, 68% to 74% of all Americans opposed abortion done solely for the reason of family economic distress. In similar fashion 79% to 91% of all Americans questioned disapproved abortion for the reason of pregnancy being unwanted. Then in June 1972, Dr. Gallup changed his question and framed it in terms of abortion being a private matter. He did not ask the same question as in the previous polls but nevertheless proclaims a vast shift in public opinion. I suspect that Dr. Gallup is framing public opinion rather than sampling it. In November of 1972 Michigan citizens voted on a proposal allowing abortion on demand up to twenty weeks (not the much more liberal interpretation of the Supreme Court). This was rejected by a 62% vote. Parenthetically, let me say that just a few weeks before the polls in that state indicated that abortion legalization would win by 25 points. The vote in the opposite direction was probably tremendously influenced by a statewide educational program undertaken by a coalition of pro-life forces. (A 1975 poll by the Sindlinger organization shows that almost 60% [59.4] of all Americans oppose abortion on demand.)

You will be told that doctors favor abortion on demand. As a back-up to this statement you will be told that the AMA approves abortion. Perhaps you do not know that only 42 percent of our nation's 386,000 doctors pay dues to the AMA.

You will be told that abortion reduces maternal deaths and along the same lines that unwanted pregnancy produces psychoses in pregnant women. The late Dr. Alan Guttmacher, one of the most ardent pro-abortionists, wrote as long ago as 1950s: "Today it is possible for almost any patient to be brought through pregnancy alive, unless she suffers from a fatal illness such as cancer or leukemia, and if so, abortion would be unlikely to prolong, much less save life." And then in reference to psychosis, Guttmacher said: "There is *little* evidence that pregnancy itself worsens a psychosis, either intensifying it or rendering a prognosis for full recovery less likely." Dr. Guttmacher was an obstetrician at Mt. Sinai Hospital in New York City, and president of Planned Parenthood-World Population.

You will be told that already the liberalized abortion laws have reduced infant deaths. This is like suggesting amputation of the leg in normal men to prevent ankle fractures while skiing. It is not possible to save one child's life by killing another. Obviously if one does 1,000,000 abortions, none of those fetuses will ever become infant deaths since none of them will ever live to be infants.

You will be introduced to situational ethics from academic sources considered to be above reproach. Dr. Mary Ellen Avery, professor of pediatrics at Harvard University and physician-in-chief of Boston Children's Hospital, writing in the *New England Journal of Medicine,* suggests that if on abortion the infant is large enough to survive the extraordinary care provided by an intensive care unit, the physician should decide about caring for the child or not caring for the child on the basis of whether the parents wish the child to survive. In other words, wantedness is the test for survival. Incidentally the Boston Children's Hospital is now in the ludicrous situation of having one of the world's most sophisticated intensive care units for premature babies with an enviable record in survival while across Longwood Avenue, at the equally famous Boston Lying-In Hospital, babies the same age and size are having their lives terminated. One team of doctors is spending fantastic amounts of time, money and energy to save a three-pound life while across the street another team is destroying an almost identical human being.

In all of these social discourses you will be introduced to the war of semantics. In 1974, in December, Donald P. Warwich, chairman of the Department of Sociology and Anthropology of York University, Toronto, wrote on the "Moral Message of Bucharest," which was a report on the International Congress on Population. He called attention to the fact that "population studies" is a euphemism for family planning research; "family planning," a cover for birth control; abortion (itself a euphemism for feticide) is called a "retrospective method of fertility limitation."

Semantics can be the preparation for accepting a horror. The most flagrant manipulative use of semantics occurred when the American College of Obstetrics and Gynecology changed the definition of pregnancy to mean from implantation of the fertilized egg to delivery instead of from conception to delivery, which pregnancy had always meant. This was to make the use of the IUD (intra-uterine device)—which is not a contraceptive but an abortifacient—more palatable to American women.

How much easier to kill the product of conception than to kill an unborn baby. The term gender identity is less shocking than lesbianism or homosexuality. How much more acceptable is a pregnancy advisory service when compared to an abortion clinic. A mature relationship means going steady for the past week, and the age of consent has come to mean puberty or before.

There are countless other social misrepresentations that you may be presented with but the ultimate one will have to do with overpopulation. Overpopulation is certainly a major concern but it is not overpopulation that is our problem; it is the distribution of the world's population. I would suggest that when someone talks to you about this subject that you ask: "What country are you most concerned about?" He will practically always answer: "India." Then you can introduce an interesting statistic. New Jersey is twice as crowded as India and it will take two hundred years of population growth such as the United States was experiencing five years ago before these United States will be as uncomfortably crowded as New Jersey.

I began these remarks by suggesting that our society might be schizophrenic. As further indication that this is not far from the case, remember that the Supreme Court has declared the unborn baby to be a non-person. Yet, a paternity action can be brought by a pregnant woman as soon as she knows she is pregnant; some states have statutes on their books that say that the abortionist must make every effort to resuscitate the baby he has just aborted; an unborn baby can be injured in an accident and at a later date, after he is born, can sue the person who injured him; a fetus can inherit an estate and take precedence over a person who is already born as soon as that fetus is himself born.

In any discussion in a social realm concerning abortion you will be exposed to some smoke screens; things that people set up so that they can talk about abortion. One of these will be a discussion of meaningful life. Who can say whose life is meaningful? You must be careful that some critic does not come along and consider our lives to be "without meaning." Think of people such as Franklin Roosevelt, Napoleon, Helen Keller, or perhaps someone in your own family who might have been thought at one time not to have a meaningful life, yet with the passage of time made a remarkable impact on history. You will be told that restrictive abortion laws work to the detriment of the poor. Yet, in the first year that abortion was liberalized in New York City, the majority of women who were aborted were middle-class white women who wanted their abortions for reasons of convenience that were non-medical. The women's liberation movement is frequently wrapped up around the abortion issue and whether you are for or against women's lib, do not get the baby and the bath water mixed up. Eventually the old argument that restrictive laws were merely made to be broken and therefore should be removed will be brought to your attention. There are two answers to that. The first is that we have laws against murder which people break but that does not mean that the laws against murder should be removed. Secondly, if a legal abortion cannot be obtained and it is assumed that criminal abortion will be substituted for it, the answer is that you do not fight one crime with another crime.

You will recall that the Supreme Court invoked the "right of privacy" as the telling argument in making its decision. Along these lines, the first among the personal arguments that is frequently reiterated is the woman's declaration, "I want the right to my own body." Apart from the obvious suggestion that the right to her body begins considerably before the need for an abortion, there are other concerns. Total sexual freedom leads to the demand for abortion but without consideration of the rights of the product of that freedom, namely, the unborn baby. The fact of the matter is that the child in the womb is not a part of the woman's body, subject to her absolute control. She provides the environment and the sustenance but this sustenance does not go to a subhuman creature devoid of human rights. For example, if the baby were part of the mother it would have the same blood type—which it does not always have.

Abortion is surely the worst choice we can offer to a frightened pregnant woman who for a variety of reasons does not see her way clear to having a baby. Here the challenge lies, especially the Christian challenge as an alternative to abortion. Parenthetically, let me say that since the liberalization of abortion there are countless childless couples who no longer are able to adopt from the pool of unwanted but born human beings that formerly existed.

It is interesting that women claim that they are personally exploited when a man gets them pregnant. Yet these same women do not realize that abortion exploits them still more. Abortion provides a new business in another kind of feminine prostitution. So says Mary R. Joyce, who claims that the sexual revolution is yet to begin. She claims that when women prostitute themselves to what is called the "baby scrambler," the suction machine for abortion, they give the money to men more often than not. She further quotes that in New York City alone, doctors in hospitals made approximately $140,000,000 in the first year-and-a-half of New York's liberalized abortion laws (without counting the abortion clinics). Mrs. Joyce is convinced that if women were not so intellectually passive, they would be able to see through their new so-called liberation very clearly.

I have already spoken of the simple theology which leads me to my position. I am distressed that the major denominations in the Protestant faith in our country with the exception of the Missouri Synod Lutherans have been brainwashed along with the rest of our population concerning abortion. The right of privacy has been stressed by the Supreme Court. A United Presbyterian committee said, "Abortion of a non-viable fetus is not a legal matter. A woman, her doctor, her minister or counselor should decide." Now, that is so private that they left the father out of consideration. The Methodists said: "Abortion and sterilization are the decision of those most concerned." But the Methodists forgot the baby.

I have talked of the law and I have certainly talked of life. Now I would like to say a few things about the days ahead. There are natural consequences of sin, even for the Christian. You may kill your enemy and immediately repent of this act, and ask God's forgiveness on the basis of the sacrifice of Jesus Christ and you will be forgiven. But in the process, the police siren is heard approaching nevertheless. There are natural consequences of sin that cannot be escaped. So it is with the liberalization of abortion. A few months after the Supreme Court decision was made, I was asked to address the graduating class at Wheaton College. I wrote my remarks in early May and gave the commencement talk in early June. In my talk I said there were ten things that you and I would see because of the Supreme Court's decision. Between the time of writing in May and the time of delivery in June, three of these things had happened and since then I think the other seven have happened as well.

First of all I said that the law would look ridiculous. Several weeks after I wrote that, a young woman boarded an airplane in Pittsburgh and flew to Youngstown, Ohio, a flight of thirty-two minutes. During that time she delivered a baby and left it in the restroom of the airplane. Now, if she had had an abortion in Pittsburgh, before she got on the plane, she would have been the darling of Planned Parenthood. But thirty-two minutes later, with a natural birth of a premature baby in the state of Ohio, she was sought on two charges, child abandonment and attempted murder. Since then it has been ruled that a minor female may have an abortion on demand without the consent of her parents; yet the law also requires that her parents be responsible for the bill. And even more ridiculous from the point of view of the law is the fact that the unborn baby being a non-person is nevertheless eligible at his mother's request for welfare. A minor may have an abortion without parental consent, but not have her ears pierced for earrings!

Second, I said that liberty would lead to license. And within a week of the decision of the Supreme Court, the New York Medical Society took a stand in reference to the patient's right to die but at the discretion of the patient's family, not at the discretion of the patient. Now, you can imagine what that can lead to.

Third, the right to die leads to the right to kill in mercy. In March of 1973, two months after the Supreme Court decision, a Dutch jury found a physician guilty of killing her mother when she had terminal cancer. Now, the victim of the mercy killing was not in pain, but she was just tired of it all. The sentence was a one week suspended sentence in prison. Since that day there have been nine or ten mercy killings that I know of; there have been no convictions for murder to my knowledge.

A fourth effect of the action of the Supreme Court in

reference to abortion is that it will contribute first to the process of depersonalization and secondly to the process of dehumanization. There are a number of episodes in the history of man of which we are all ashamed. Indeed, if we had the chance to act otherwise, we would do so if given that opportunity. Yet, at the time, not only were these things legal, but they were accepted by the people and were even proved to be logical to those few who complained. Jews were considered to be non-persons in Nazi Germany. Indians were not thought to be persons in the United States. The same Supreme Court to which I have referred so frequently, in the Dred Scott decision in 1857, declared the Negro to be a piece of chattel property. They would have been more honest if they had said non-people. Lt. Calley expressed the opinion that the Vietnamese were not human beings. Now, the Supreme Court tells us that unborn babies are not persons in our society. So, we regard the unborn baby today in the way we once looked at the Indian and the Negro slave and in the same way that the Nazis saw the Jews. In all of these areas, if persons had treated other persons as persons and if they had stood for the preservation of life, there would have been no slavery, no Dred Scott decision, no Wounded Knee and no Nazi Germany guilty of atrocities against Jews.

Fifth, there will be enormous numbers of abortions. Because we do not keep accurate records, I cannot give you the exact number of abortions that have taken place in this country in thirty months, but using the statistics of the abortionists, it is over 3,000,000.

Sixth, there has been and there will continue to be a change in sexual attitudes. You cannot have over a million abortions taking place every year without everybody knowing about the process. It seems to me inevitable that the social attitude of the young will change. There will always be a way out if contraception does not work or if it is not used. Already here in our community, the advertising media make pregnancy a loathsome thing. As you leave the airport in Philadelphia and drive into the center of town, you see on billboards and on the tops of taxicabs the following sign: "Pregnant? For abortion information, call number - - - -." The week after the Supreme Court decision, there appeared this headline in the Philadelphia Bulletin: "Abortion Study to Be Included in the New Girl Scout Program." The article went on to say the Girl Scouts were planning a new merit badge, a section of which recommends that older scouts visit an abortion clinic and familiarize themselves with birth control. The President of the Girl Scouts of Philadelphia said the badge was "relevant and proper education for the youngsters." These were girls in the seventh to tenth grades.

Seventh, I believe the door is open to a number of things that like abortion are disturbing to a large segment of our population. You may not be immediately aware of the fact that it has been the custom in this country when some private activity was repugnant to the moral sensitivity of the American people, there was legislation against it. That is why we have laws against such seemingly private engagements as homosexuality, sodomy, prostitution and adultery. Did you realize that there are also laws prohibiting activities quite lawful in other countries today and in our country in days gone by? I refer to gambling, the taking of addictive drugs, cockfighting and dueling. There are even laws against suicide! Some of these things are done essentially in private. But they are outlawed because they offend other people who know about them.

Eighth, the newborn infant who is not perfect is probably the next target. Remember the Supreme Court left the decision between feticide and infanticide very hazy by refusing to come to grips with the time that life begins. In May of 1973, in the *Johns Hopkins* magazine, right after the Supreme Court decision, the following was set out in a box in large type for emphasis, "If the family and the medical staff agree not to treat a child, assuming he is going to die anyway, then why not make sure he dies quickly and painlessly as possible. I think there is little difference between euthanasia and passive euthanasia." And later the same month, *Time* magazine reported a quotation by a Nobel Prize winner, James D. Watson, the same man who discovered the double helix DNA in the genetic code. *Time* quoted Dr. Watson's statement that appeared in *Prism* magazine, a publication of the American Medical Association: "If a child were not declared alive until three days after birth, then all parents could be allowed the choice only a few are given under the present system. The doctor could allow the child to die if the parents so choose and save a lot of misery and suffering. I believe this view is the only rational, compassionate attitude to have"—so said the winner of the Nobel Prize.

Ninth, abortion is back in the hands of abortionists. The pro-abortionists use, as I said a moment ago, as one of their chief arguments, the terrible plight of those who had abortions at the hand of illegal abortionists in their offices, back rooms, etc. Now, the less publicized decision of the two that the Supreme Court made, the Georgia one, threw out the safeguards of having abortions in a hospital that is accredited and in the mainstream of medical practice. Freedom to establish independent abortion clinics now exists. You probably have read in the papers how Philadelphia was rocked with scandals ranging from kickbacks for referral, to the willingness of a freestanding abortion clinic to do an abortion on a reporter from the *Evening Bulletin* who was not even pregnant. It is again inevitable that abortions will largely be done legally by those who recently did them illegally. I recently saw a title in one of the opinion magazines entitled, "Suddenly, I'm a legal abortionist."

Tenth, and finally, the phrase of the pro-abortionists that angers me almost as much as the phrase, "the female's right to her own body," is the term "meaningful life." It was said that non-viable babies had no meaningful life. Well, they do. For these small living products of abortion that look just like you and me were used for scientific experiments until recent legislation forbid it. Would they have been used if they were "meaningless"? Obviously not.

The implications go far beyond these ten prophesies which

have already come true. The trouble begins when there is acceptance of the idea that there is such a thing as a life which is "not worthy to be lived." The abortion movement in Germany began about 1900 and it had the significant support of intellectuals in that country by 1911. Then the overpopulation psychology that we are now being exposed to here began to develop there at that time. After the defeat of World War I, there was a collapse of social and moral values in Germany (just as we are experiencing here) and abortion, although still illegal, became rampant and the euthanasia movement was launched about 1920 against "worthless" people, but such "mercy killing" was not performed at that time. By the time Hitler came, the stage was set. Physicians suggested the value of euthanasia to Hitler. His first program in mass killing was able to take place *only* because abortion had become an accepted thing. Hitler first exterminated 275,000 people, *not* Jews, but the frail, the infirm, and the retarded. Eventually, as World War II approached, even amputees from World War I were eliminated because they were of no service to the Reich! It is significant that it was the medical profession, for "social reasons," that started the movement, not Hitler.

What can we expect from a society that can rationalize away the most fundamental of human values, the value of life? What will become of us if we permit our society, through our courts, to legalize murder as a solution to a personal problem? Our problems are great because we fight perverted power in high places. The Rockefeller Commission, the Ford Foundation, the Sunnen Foundation, and the Scaife Foundation are all heavily involved in pushing abortion and those things which follow as the night, the day. The Rockefeller Commission, for example, recommended not only abortion but sex education and contraceptives for teenagers without parental consent, widespread sterilization of males and females, and government-subsidized child care centers for all families wishing to make use of them. Is this very far from Hitler's Germany?

Here is what your children might well read in their college biology textbook (*Life on Earth* by Wilson *et al*): "Abortion is the most effective method of population control. . . . At what point a fetus becomes a human being is a controversial, biological, and ethical question. The moral dilemma is further complicated by the knowledge that in many cases a particular fetus will be seriously defective or unwanted by its parents. Born with such a handicap a child is likely to lead a troubled life and to add a heavy burden on an already overpopulated society . . . abortion has always been one of the most popular methods of birth control throughout the world." Magnificent misrepresentation spoken with great authority.

It is said that social reform seldom moves backward. The only way that the horror I have been recounting can be corrected is by a constitutional amendment or an act of Congress which declares that life begins at conception and thereby gives the unborn the protection of the Constitution. It can be done; it will take a tremendous united effort. Remember that it was only the indignant protest of concerned citizens that eliminated the indiscriminate use of the living unborn and born human fetus in scientific experimentation. The fact that the conscience of American people working through the pro-life movement brought about this change is historically significant and should not only not be minimized or discounted but should be a source of encouragement to us.

It should be obvious that as soon as one questions the value of human life there really is nothing to prevent him from considering what human beings under what circumstances should rightfully be exterminated. It takes almost nothing to move from abortion which is killing of an unborn baby in the uterus to the killing of the retarded, the crippled, the sick, the elderly.

Take heed, you who do not fit into someone's ecological ideal in form and function. That day may not be very far off when a death selection committee declares that you are no longer a person.

Part Five

Abortion and Women

Most feminists have adopted the right to abortion as a feminist issue. In "Abortion as a Feminist Concern," Janet E. Smith issues a dissent: abortion is rather an assault on women's fundamental identity. In "Complications of Legal Abortion" a physician offers a disturbing report on a women's issue that does not get much attention—the fact that abortion is dangerous.

SIX

Abortion as a Feminist Concern

Janet E. Smith

FOR THE MOST PART abortion has been included in a package of "women's issues" and as one of the "rights" or even "goods" which women have been denied. Indeed, the U.S. Supreme Court based, at least in part, its opinion of January 1973 on what it perceived as a woman's right to privacy. I argue that such a view is a fundamental misunderstanding of women's rights and, even more importantly, that behind pro-abortion thought there lies a confusion about what it means to be a woman. I argue that abortion is an act which will, on analysis, prove to be harmful to the woman.

Rather than being a "right" of women, abortion is a great disservice to women, one which reflects both a growing lack of appreciation among women for those powers and capacities which are distinctly theirs as women and a growing despair that women are willing and able to be full participants in society and to make the sometimes noble sacrifices demanded of individuals for the good of society. Seeing abortion as solely a matter of women's rights assumes that the fetus has no rights or that the rights of the woman are unquestionably superior. But abortion,

Janet E. Smith is a graduate student at the University of Toronto. This article was adapted from an address she gave at the University of Manitoba and originally appeared in *The Human Life Review* (150 E. 35th St., New York, NY 10016.)

no matter where it fits into the scheme of the rights for women, is a violation of the right to life for another human being.

You may be surprised to learn that, in our law, although the fetus is currently without the right to life, it does have some rights. For instance, under civil law the unborn child has the right to inherit part of his father's estate should his father die before he is born, and he has the right to sue his mother, or a doctor, for injuries sustained while in the womb.[1] In fact, before 1973, when the Supreme Court declared unconstitutional the laws forbidding abortion in the states, the law had given ever more protection to unborn human beings. Such increased legal protection reflected the medical scientists' growing knowledge that the care a fetus receives—or doesn't receive—affects the developing child. It may also be surprising to learn that there is precedent in law for respecting the rights of the fetus *over* those of the mother. In 1964 the New Jersey Supreme Court ruled that a woman who had religious objections to blood transfusion must submit to such a procedure for the well-being of her unborn child.[2] We might ask why such legislation exists, why such decisions were made. Clearly because life and hence certain rights do not begin at birth. As biology tells us, life begins at conception. It is information well-known to anti-abortionists, though perhaps news to the general public, that the fetal heart begins to beat 18-25 days after conception—that is, before a woman even knows she is pregnant; that brain waves have been recorded as early as 40 days, and that at 12 weeks all organs are present and functioning. From this point fetal development is largely a matter of growth in size and sophistication. This information is not hard to come by, but many are genuinely ignorant of it; others evidently choose to ignore it.

What then excludes the fetus from the right to life granted to other humans? Its size? Its stage of development? The fact that it receives its food and oxygen in a manner different from the rest of us? Or is it its inability to defend itself? What rights of a mother or a father or even the state, for that matter, can supersede the right of another human being to life?

I once gave a talk to seventh graders (who had no trouble at all in perceiving that abortion was the killing of a baby); a youngster asked: "If all that you say is true, how could our government permit abortions?" I asked myself, "How *does* one account for seven men of the Supreme Court trivializing a value basic to Western civilization—right to life for all men regardless of race, color, creed, and, might I add, size and age?" It seemed to me that her question amounted to wondering why mankind does evil. I responded that mankind in general, our society in particular, seems inclined to choose the easier way. It is difficult to be loving and caring. It is challenging, demanding, exhausting, and expensive to provide the care and support needed by women in distress. It is much easier, quicker, and cheaper to send a woman to an abortionist. Unfortunately our society seems to be so insensitive and materialistic that we would rather kill life than find the means to support it.

But we are not concerned here with the reasons why the Supreme Court and the society which it guides permit abortions, but with another even more perplexing question. So abortion is killing, so that killing is now legal. Still, why are over a *million* women a year in the U.S. aborting their own children? And given the fact that they *are* doing this, what does it tell us about the conception which women have of themselves? Is it a true view of what it is to be a woman?

Some would have us believe that the women who are having these abortions are poor and uneducated, and/or that their health is threatened by childbirth. But such claims are demonstrably false, for most are young and healthy, and childbirth has never been safer. Furthermore, a large portion of women having abortions are college-educated and have greater prospects for attaining material success and "self-fulfillment" in this world than their parents and grandparents ever dreamed of. True, most of the women getting abortions are unmarried, but the stigma attached to single parenthood and even that of unwed parenthood has very nearly disappeared. And never before have there been so many couples waiting to adopt children; but what are their chances when in some communities the number of abortions has already surpassed live births? And at the risk of promoting what is an appalling possibility, I can inform you that a woman could sell the baby that she chooses to abort for $15,000 on the black market. So the situation today is that an unmarried pregnant woman has unparalleled access to assistance and considerable assurance of acceptance by society should she choose to bear her child; she could be an unknown but willing benefactor to a couple who desperately want to adopt a child; or, if she were willing to deal with the syndicate, she could be rich.

If women are getting abortions for reasons other than poverty, shame, and lack of alternatives, what are their reasons? What accounts for the epidemic of abortions in the U.S. since 1973? Several explanations come to mind. A complete analysis would require a lengthy critique of our culture, of the values of our society. I prefer, though, to use a technique employed by my favorite teacher; that of parables and subsequent analysis. I shall begin with the biblical story of Solomon whose fame as a wise man, for most of us, is best known through the story demonstrating his understanding of women.

Solomon made his judgment based upon his recognition of a certain "instinct" in women. You know the story: two prostitutes bore children at the same time. One woman's child died and she laid claim to the other woman's baby. This case of disputed motherhood was brought before Solomon, the wisest of judges. Since he had no means of establishing who was the rightful mother, he offered to cut the baby in half. He depended upon the love of the real mother for her child. He was proven right: the real mother, willing to lose her child to save its life, begged Solomon to give the child to the other woman. Now, these women were not pillars of virtue; they were prostitutes. Even so, Solomon was sure he could depend upon the maternal instinct to determine who the real mother was. Would Solomon be able to use the same method today? Are today's women women?

Do women today have this maternal feeling, this "instinct" or tendency—or whatever term one wishes to apply to this special love for their children? Possibly I should phrase the question differently. For indeed, if it is an instinct or tendency inherent in all women, today's women *must* have it. But since even naturally good tendencies and talents need to be developed and nourished, perhaps the question should be: are today's women and the society in which they live failing to encourage and foster this tendency in women? Or has it been weakened by those "modern" ideologies which argue for "self-fulfillment"? Do we want, as women, as we pursue other goals, to sacrifice anything—even our children—for these goals? Do we want to lose the ability to be mothers and motherly? It does seem that women today have such an underdeveloped or diminished maternal instinct that they are not only unwilling to make sacrifices for their children but are also willing to kill them.

Certain conversations which I have had with women recently have made me realize that women today are indeed gravely confused about what it means to be a woman. These conversations have convinced me that behind women's demands for unlimited access to abortion lies a profound displeasure with the way in which a woman's body works and hence a rejection of the value of being a woman. Whereas one might hope that the women's movement would be based on the assertion that it is great to be a woman and that women would endeavor to promote the powers and qualities which are theirs, the popularity of abortion indicates quite the opposite. Abortion is a denigration of women, a denial of one of the defining features of being a woman—her ability to bear children. Now some may deny that this is a defining characteristic of women. But is there any more certain criterion? A woman is a woman because she can bear children.

Traditionally, the most admirable qualities have been associated with motherhood. Throughout the ages good women, both mothers and non-mothers, have been portrayed as warm, sensitive, loving, and generous. The source of these qualities is the love for one's children—and those whom a woman succeeds in some way in viewing as her children. These qualities are allied with a woman's willingness to make loving sacrifices in behalf of both her physical and adopted children.

I should like to relate four recent encounters I've had with women which I consider vivid illustrations of the fact that we are losing the view of women which enabled Solomon to demonstrate his wisdom. To me, they reveal that some women have a distressing lack of appreciation for being women. I realize that the women in these stories hold fairly extreme and certainly not altogether representative views. But that which is normal or usual, "the middle way," can best be ascertained by looking at the extremes. Women who are willing to die for their children are an extreme of goodness; women who kill their children so that they might obtain a certain self-centered "lifestyle" are another extreme. The following conversations should help any woman to locate herself on the spectrum.

The first woman would surely have robbed Solomon of his title as a wise man. She was certainly very different from the usual characterization that pro-abortionists provide of the women seeking an abortion. Attractive, healthy, college-educated, about 20, she approached me one day (at a university) to argue that women had a "right" to abortion. I countered, as usual, with information about prenatal life, to demonstrate that the fetus is in fact a living human being. I chose this line of argument because I like to believe that people who support abortion do not believe that it is the taking of a human life—thus, perhaps, a demonstration of the humanity of the unborn would be sufficient to change their views. But this girl cut me short; she readily agreed that the fetus was a human being; she demanded the right to abort anyway. Such an admission, sad to say, seems common now among those who argue for abortion. I then proceeded to ask what reasons she considered legitimate for taking another's life. We went through a series of the usual reasons. With some success I argued that killing babies is not a good solution to the supposed population crisis; that it's better to want the unwanted than to kill them. I even managed to argue, again with some success, that the child whose father is a rapist has no fewer rights than one whose father is a loving man. But then she stumped me. She said: "Well, everything you say is right, but if I became pregnant I would have an abortion. I don't want stretch marks." I repeated: "Stretch marks?" She answered: "Yes. If I carried the child to term I might get stretch marks and then I could not wear a bikini." And then—would you believe?—she said: "Vanity is a very important part of my life." She agreed that she would be killing a baby were she to have an abortion but she was still willing to do so simply because of her vanity. On reflection, I realized that her case fell in the most extreme category used to justify abortion—that of abortion to save the life of the mother. Now I do not mean her biological life (a medical necessity doctors tell us is quite rare) but her life in a perverted sense. To her, to be a woman is to be a sex object. As a self-admitted sex object she had been completely drawn in by the modern hedonistic philosophy which tells us that unless you are young, beautiful, slim, and without stretch marks your life is not worth living. Pregnancy was a threat to her "life," perceived as the possession of an attractive body. This young woman was not a freak, but simply a very frank product of our times.

One indication that the cries for abortion are the cries of those who view women as sex objects is the fact that *Playboy* magazine contributes generously to the pro-abortion lobbies. Nor has this connection gone unnoticed. John T. Matthews (in *The Human Life Review*, Winter '76) observed: "To state the paradox—if it is one—the same ladies who protest so vehemently that men should stop treating them as 'sex objects' also demand abortion: which can only be required, one would imagine, if in fact they are sex objects."[3] The young girl so concerned about stretch marks is an extreme example: she saw a baby as a hindrance to her desire for self-fulfillment—i.e., being a desirable *sex* object. *Nothing,* today is supposed to stand in the way of devotion to the newly-enshrined god (or is it goddess?) of "self-fulfillment," not even babies. But isn't it true that women have the potential to bear children, and to fulfill one's potentials is fulfillment? The vague and elusive dreams of self-fulfillment seem to have gained precedence over the more basic, immediate and literal fulfillment of childbirth. Beware the exhortation to self-fulfillment! Women must make certain that in trying to find themselves they do not *lose* themselves in a sense quite contrary to the Biblical injunction to lose one's self in order to find one's self.

Abortion is a denial of one of those powers which make women women. Childbearing is basic to them. We might expect that deliberate and violent denial of such a potential may be devastating. Some women argue that the fetus (be it a human being or not) is part of their bodies and that they may do with it what they will. In one sense—a very different sense—the argument is true. Pregnancy and childbearing are perfectly normal conditions for women, and hence a part of their physical and psychological makeup. To have an abortion is to destroy part of one's self. It is normal for a woman to carry the children she conceives to term. To remove that child forcibly interrupts and harms the healthy functioning of her body. To put it bluntly, an abortion amounts to a mutilation of the woman's body and to a denial of her nature. Studies documenting the frightening physical and psychological dangers of abortion corroborate this interpretation that abortion does violence to the woman. The physical dangers include increased chances of sterility, of subsequent spontaneous abortion and an inability to carry future pregnancies to term (with the attendant increased likelihood of retarded or handicapped children.[4] These dangers are not insignificant. Moreover, statistics always do represent *actual women*. That means us. In the psychological sphere percentages are harder to compute, but studies[5] have found that among the psychological aftereffects are recurrent nightmares about the fetus, even a feeling of repulsion for sex and for children. Both physically and psychologically one's "femininity" has been impaired. If the young lady so concerned about her attractive body ever has an abortion, she may well avoid stretch marks, but she will not retain her appealing womanhood; she will be less of a woman.

The second young woman told me that as long as there is no 100% effective form of birth control, abortions must be available as a "back-up." Now, many people are appalled at the notion of abortion as a means of birth control, but, of course, for those who really believe abortion is only the removal of extraneous tissue, such abhorrence is irrational. Abortion is indeed being used not only as a "back-up" to failed birth-control but *instead of* birth control. The Badgley Report, a government study in Canada,[6] reported that 85% of the women who had abortions in 1975 were "contraceptively experienced." They had full knowledge of birth control but chose not to use it, for a variety of reasons: too dangerous, too unaesthetic, or simply a hinderance to spontaneity. Abortion could always "take care of" any unwanted pregnancies.

To this woman who argued that abortion is necessary as long as methods of birth control are imperfect, I answered that there is one infallible means of birth control—abstinence, either total or periodic. To this she laughed. Our society has taught us that sexual activity is essential to our happiness. The principle that one should engage in an act only when one is willing to accept all consequences of that act is unpopular with our irresponsible age. Yet the demand for abortion as a "back-up" for birth control is a residue of the "daddy will fix it" attitude. If something has gone wrong (how twisted we have become: "going wrong" now means that one has conceived a child) then it must be fixed

Many of those who have been involved in the anti-abortion movement for a long time maintain that there are definite links between the attitudes fostered by birth control and the current popularity of abortion. If man (and I use the term generically) has done all that he can to prevent conception, any conception which happens is by definition an accident, not a blessing from God, as in Judeo-Christian teaching. The use of contraception implies that man can control conception; that he can "plan" parenthood. I argue that the phrase "planned parenthood" is misleading. One can only create conditions favorable or unfavorable to conception but one cannot *plan* a pregnancy. There are too many women who have been trying to conceive for years without success, and too many women who have conceived contrary to their intentions to make any talk of "planned parenthood" accurate.

There are those who say that more and better birth control will eliminate the "need" for abortions. In fact, all the evidence shows that the increased use of contraceptives corresponds to the increased numbers of abortions; failure of contraception, you see, produces that fearsome "unwanted" child. Studies tell us that in England in 1949, couples who used contraception had 8.7 times the number of abortions as the other couples and "in Sweden after contraception had been fully sanctioned by law, legal abortions increased from 703 in 1943 to 6,328 in 1951."[7] When man feels he has control over creation he believes that he has the right to destruction also. A far cry from the consoling thought "Only God can give life, only God can take it away."

Yet back to my interlocutor. Her argument for the imperative of a perfect means of birth control or as "back-up" had another disturbing twist. She argued that as long as men could engage in sex without the "danger" of becoming pregnant, women should have this "right" also: otherwise the sexes would not be equal. Thus women should go to the extreme of killing their offspring in order to gain so-called "equality" with men. It seems to me that feminists should find this a very "unliberated" attitude. At root this argument suggests that the manner in which a male's body functions is better than that of a woman. The argument amounts to an admission that a woman would rather be a man and that she is willing to tamper with her natural body chemistry to have sex on a man's terms, not on a woman's.

Now, while abortion and birth control are on very different moral planes (one is the taking of a human life already begun, the other is preventing life from beginning), they are alike in that they interfere with the natural functioning of a woman's body. Some women apparently consider their bodies imperfect in that they, on occasion, are able to conceive. A woman who uses birth control rejects this ability, which is evidently considered to be an imperfection. In seeking to correct this imperfection, a woman takes measures which are customarily prescribed only for illness or defect. But can a woman who is able to conceive be said to be in need of medicine or corrective devices? Is not her body operating as a woman's body ought to operate? In using birth control, women render useless one of the properties which define their womanhood. In a sense, these women become more men than women, since they now operate like men; they can engage in intercourse without the possibility of conceiving.

You will not be surprised to hear that many in the woman's movement are disturbed about the way in which the most "popular" forms of birth control work, and the effects they have on women. Recently, in Winnipeg, where I spoke at a feminist conference, I had the pleasure of being entertained by Germaine Greer. She, perhaps the most famous of feminists, spoke adamantly against birth control. She argued that women are relatively infertile creatures—fertile for only a short period each month, which is, in fact, easily calculable. Thus, she argued, it is foolish for women to put lethal devices into their bodies or to take massive doses of drugs (all the dangerous side effects of which remain unknown) to combat a condition—fertility— which is not a disease. She also maintained that present methods of birth control are not suitable for "liberated"women. Birth control makes women more open to exploitation by men—they can't say "no" so easily. More importantly, the use of contraceptives fails to acknowledge the difference between the sources of female and male sexual satisfaction. So in her view, once again, women are ruining themselves; they are interfering with their natural body chemistry, for the sake of the pleasure of men.

Ms. Greer has even advanced the startling suggestion that women actually *refuse* to engage in intercourse if better contraceptives are not devised. I make a simpler suggestion; that is, that women "make love" only to men whom they love and with whom they are willing to share responsibility for any "products" of that love.

All this suggests that women ought to reconsider their acceptance of the pill as the great "liberator." They must reflect upon what it does to their bodies, to their relation to men and to their status as women. Moreover, if the use of contraceptives makes women and society more receptive to abortion, not to say insistent upon it, we ought to be extremely wary of considering birth control as a good. To consider it as an *answer* to abortion becomes positively ludicrous.

The third woman with whom I spoke reinforced my impression that our age puts a very low value on human life, that we now value our feelings above the good of others, and that women, in asking for abortion, reveal that they wish to place their own desires above the good of society. Instead of being the transmitters of life and a warm source of love and generosity, women now are willing to kill life growing within them in order to spare themselves some real or imagined pain, physical or psychological.

In my speaking tours of high schools I have found increasing numbers of students who do not grant immediate assent to the notion that all human life is valuable and deserving of protection. A perplexing question from a young lady reveals in a striking way this growing indifference to life.

During one particular session I completed a lengthy presentation about prenatal life and abortion in which I had been careful both to enumerate the alternatives to abortion and to praise the nobility of those women who have the courage and generosity to carry a child to term and then to give it up for adoption. A girl then asked a question which threw me. She asked, "What really is the difference between having an abortion and giving a child up for adoption?" At first I missed her point and answered that most fundamentally the difference was between a dead and a live baby, the difference between a couple which is able to adopt a child and one which can not. She repeated again, "I still don't see the difference." She was referring, you see, to the difference for herself; either way she was without the child. It made no difference to her whether it was dead or alive. Only with the aid of a philosopher friend could I discover the root of her confusion. He reminded me that we live in a society in which man is considered to be a combination of chemicals, differing only from rocks, plants and other animals in his chemical makeup. Hence one should be able to dispense with any combination of chemicals as easily as with another. Ours is, after all, the disposable society. When something displeases us we simply dispose of it. We can't, as of yet, legally dispose of all other humans who annoy us, but I begin to think this is only because they may protest. The unborn babies can hardly cry foul. The social contract into which most of us enter—I will respect your rights and life if you will respect mine—is denied the aborted baby. We are living in a society which is not generous enough to extend such rights to the unborn (or, increasingly, to the "unwanted" of any age). For some the "might" of the born makes "right" over the unborn. Thereby all of our rights are less secure since all humans are not granted the right to life, only those who have qualified. Presently this means all those who are born; but we all know we only need a mad man like Hitler to come along and insist on further qualification.

My philosopher friend helped me further. He maintained that unless we view man as being made in the image of God we might well ask why we respect human life. Unless the right to life is inherent and possessed by all, our hold on it is tenuous. Viewing children as a gift from God is not a silly sentimental view. It happens to be the one view which *requires* that we respect another's gift of life—because it is God's will that the person live; *we* are not empowered to decide otherwise.

A woman who sets her rights, the supposed right to privacy or right over her own body, above the life of another human being is saying that a woman's rights are superior to human rights. She has put herself above the human race, she has made herself the executor over life and death. *Is* that a woman's right?

In refusing to see the difference between an abortion and putting a child up for adoption, my young friend had effectively removed herself from society. The only will she needed to consider was her own; not the baby's, not her lover's, not society's, not God's. She had become a unit, an island unto herself. She holds a view I have heard other women expound.

Many girls have told me that they could not live with the memory that they had given up a child for adoption. They would always wonder what had happened to that child. They prefer the finality of abortion. One needn't be reminded of one's past, or leave reminders of former mistakes. Yet women fail to realize that one cannot "unconceive." A woman is a mother at the moment she conceives. She cannot erase the fact that new life has begun in her. She either allows that life to continue or she "terminates" it. Psychologists tell us that some women, even if they do not physically carry their children to term in their wombs, carry their children to term in their heads. A woman will most likely be aware of the projected due date for her child and may be as aware as a mother who has given her child up for adoption of the age her child would be over the years. The difference between abortion and adoption for the woman herself is *not* that one action allows her to forget her pregnancy and the other does not. After abortion she must live with the fact that she has asserted her will over the life of another; in giving the child up for adoption she respects the life of another; she recognizes rights beyond her own.

Although some believe that it is easier to live with an abortion than with giving up a child for adoption, increasing numbers argue that abortion is always an agonizing, bitter experience. One woman poignantly revealed to me the nagging sorrow which women can feel. She came and stood quietly by the side of the "pro-life" table I was tending. Her eyes clouded with tears, she whispered: "I am certainly glad to see you here. I had an abortion 20 years ago and have regretted it ever since. I do not want young girls to go through what I have." You may say that this is only one woman's response, that many women can be found who think the abortion they had was the "right thing to do." I do not doubt that such women can be found. But I ask: What ought to be the response of a woman to her action of destroying life growing within her? Is the apparent ability of some women to go through abortion without regret indicative of a certain callousness? Is it possible that the woman who experiences intense and lingering sorrow over an abortion is having the correct response? At least those women who are sorry can be forgiven—what is our response to those who kill and experience no sorrow?

Let us beware, lest we think feeling sorrow excuses the action. Magda Denes, in her book *In Necessity and Sorrow*,[8] records her visits to an abortion clinic and the terrible effects which the endless killing has on doctors, nurses, and the "patients" too. The author has had an abortion herself, and argues that abortion is necessary but that it should be done in sorrow. You see, she admits that abortion is killing but she claims that it is necessary and suggests that the sorrow felt in some way excuses the killing. First, I ask, necessary for what? Certainly not for the well-being of the child. Then for the well-being of the mother? But if pregnancy is not a disease (though the U.S. Center for Disease Control in Atlanta has classified unwanted pregnancy as a *veneral disease*) but rather is perfectly normal for a woman's body, how can the surgical procedure of abortion be said to be necessary? Surgery is properly used to correct malformations or imperfections, and, as a branch of medicine, is supposed to heal. So if there is no healing to be done, how can abortion be necessary? But if Ms. Denes is correct, why should the "necessary" treatment of abortion need to be done in sorrow? I suppose that I can hardly disagree with her that killing should be done in sorrow, but, truly, isn't it rather that killing of the innocent ought not to be done at all? As with any other killing, do we not think that the killer is harmed as well as the victim? Those who kill, whether justifiably (as in war) or not, suffer from the act of killing. Do we not think that in a sense the "humanity" of killers is lessened? Have we not argued for ages that war is dehumanizing? And since a woman, by nature, is a giver of life, isn't the killing of life—especially of the life growing within her—isn't it bound to cause a severe diminishing of her "humanity" or more specifically her "womanhood?"

As a member of the human genus, a woman who aborts her child has committed a violation of a fundamental human right. She has taken a human life. As a member of the female sex, she has violated her own nature; she has snuffed out that marvelous maternal instinct of which all of us were beneficiaries. A woman does society great harm, and herself as well, in having an abortion.

The fourth and final woman about whom I am going to speak did meet the "usual" description given by pro-abortionists. She was in her sixth month of pregnancy with her second child. She was twenty-seven, mother of a four-year-old, divorced, abandoned by the father of the second child—and trying to finish her college education. As we spoke she told me that absolutely everyone who knew she was pregnant had advised her to have an abortion: her doctor, the nurse, her friends. They all told her that it was irresponsible for her to bring another child into this world. She was poor, unmarried, and still unemployed and untrained. Others had told her that it took a great deal of money to raise a child. Her answer was that no one handed her a check as she emerged from the womb.

This woman was resolute in her determination to have her child. She said that since she had borne one child there was no chance of her having an abortion—no one could convince her to kill what she knew was life. She said she knew it would be hard but why should the child pay with its life for her mistake? Here was a woman willing to assume her responsibilities but who was being told that she was irresponsible. How many women could withstand such pressure? More important, why did her friends respond in such a fashion? Why was it *assumed* that she should not have the child? Why, instead of asking how they might help her keep her child, did her friends urge her to commit an act she knew to be killing? The answer, it seems to me, is based on two primary assumptions: that happiness depends upon a certain present and potential financial status, and that a mere woman could not cope with such adversity, i.e., we no longer believe that old maxim "love will find a way." I reject both assumptions.

To holders of the first assumption, I address the question: are the poor necessarily unhappy? Furthermore, should we *kill* the poor rather than help them? It is popular nowadays in the U.S. to point out how costly it would be for the taxpayers to support the babies of welfare women if we do not pay for their abortions. So life does indeed have a price tag. And is our society really so impoverished that we are not able to assist the poor—that we would prefer that they abort their offspring rather than strain our pocketbooks? What kind of people have we become? Do we value human life so little, and, more in keeping with my argument here, why do we underrate our women so?

As to the second assumption: Why is it that we assume women are incapable of dealing with the adversity of an unwanted pregancy by any other means than that of destroying life? Is this a flattering view of women? Is this a true view of women? Are women so weak psychologically that they cannot deal with what I so often hear referred to as the "trauma" of an unwanted pregnancy? I argue that by allowing women to abort their unwanted pregnancies we are telling them that we have a very low opinion of them. Isn't a mark of a mature and responsible person the ability to face problems squarely? Does not the mature person have the ability and the desire to consider the well-being of all those who are involved in a situation which presents problems—not just herself?

In fact, I take the legalization of abortion to be an indication that as a society we expect less of our women than we do of our men. After all, society has traditionally in times of war asked men to risk their own lives. But we are unwilling to ask women to offer a few months of their lives in order to give life. Why is it that we expect men to be able to risk their lives for the well-being of us all, while we do not ask a woman to give a few months to protect a life she is responsible for creating?

In this day of unparalleled opportunities for women, when women pride themselves on their ability to fend for themselves, when many agencies are designed for helping women in distress—why do we assume that women who become pregnant when inconvenient for them are not resourceful enough to find a way to nourish the life they have conceived? Or is it not a lack of resourcefulness—but a lack of love? And, as I have been arguing, a lack of love not only for the unborn child in whose creation the woman has played a part—but also of love for oneself for what she is; that is, a lack of love for being a woman and for the power which belongs exclusively to women, that of bearing children.

A popular saying in the women's movement claims that "women hold up half the sky." I would like to take the sentiment further and suggest that *only* women can hold up one particular half of the sky and thus it is necessary that women remain women. We cannot deny one important fact; women are the bearers of life, and thus it follows that they are entrusted with the protection and care of life, which, we might say, is their half of the sky. One of my male friends is fond of saying that his pregnant wife considers him merely a donor. In a very real sense, the future of humanity is in the hands of women, or, more specifically, in their wombs. We ought not, as women, to be demanding a world in which we may destroy freely the life we are capable of creating. Rather we ought to demand and work toward the goal of a world where life is safe for all.

Notes

1. *Swain v. Bowers,* 91, Ind. 307, N.E. 598, 1927, and *Torrigan v. Watertown News Co.,* 352, Mass. 446, 225 N.S. 2nd 926, 1967.

2. *Fitkin v. Anderson,* 421, 201 A. 2nd 537, 1964.

3. John T. Matthews, "Reflections on Abortion," *The Human Life Review,* Winter 1976, Vol. II, No. 1.

4. For further information on the physical dangers see Dr. and Mrs. J.C. Wilke's *Handbook on Abortion,* revised edition citing the *Nursing Times,* London, 1971, pp. 90-97, and *Spontaneous and Induced*

Abortion, report of World Health Organization Scientific Groups, Technical Report Series No. 461, p. 37. See also by M. and A. Wynn, *Some Consequences of Induced Abortion to Children Born Subsequently,* London Foundation for Education and Research in Childbearing.

5. For psychological dangers see a study by L.K. Gluckman, "Some Unanticipated Complications of Therapeutic Abortion," *New Zealand Medical Journal,* August 1971.

6. *Badgley Report,* p. 341.

7. John T. Noonan, Jr., *Contraception* (Belknap Press: Cambridge Press, 1966), p. 519.

8. Magda Denes, *In Necessity and Sorrow: Life and Death in an Abortion Hospital* (Basic Books, Inc., 1976). Excerpt in *The Human Life Review,* Winter 1977, Vol. III, No. 1.

SEVEN

Complications of Legal Abortion: A Perspective from Private Practice

Matthew J. Bulfin, M.D.

A DOUBLE TRAGEDY recently occurred in Atlanta, Georgia, as an aftermath of legal abortions in two teenage girls. A 19-year-old died after seven days in a coma following her abortion. The second teenager, a 15-year-old, suffered such severe cardiac and cerebral anoxia that she lapsed into a most precarious condition with an extremely poor outlook.

It is incongruous that these two catastrophes should occur on the same day in the same clinic in Atlanta. Atlanta is the home of the Abortion Surveillance Branch of the Center for Disease Control, which is a division of the Department of Health, Education and Welfare of the United States government. The Abortion Surveillance Branch repeatedly maintains that abortion is safer than childbirth, that the serious complication rate for legal abortion is less than 1 percent, and that the safest

Matthew J. Bulfin is in private practice in obstetrics and gynecology in Lauderdale-by-the-Sea, Florida. This article is reprinted from *New Perspectives on Human Abortion,* edited by Thomas W. Hilgers, et. al, published by Aletheia Books, copyright © 1981, University Publications of America, Inc., Frederick, Md.

method of birth control is one that uses abortion as a backstop for contraception failures.

The Abortion Surveillance Branch may be missing vital input for its mortality and morbidity studies by not seeking information from the physicians who see the complications from legal abortions—emergency room physicians and the obstetricians and gynecologists in private practice. The doctors who do the abortions and the clinics and centers where abortions are done should not be the only sources from which complication statistics are derived.

In 1976 the United States reported the highest number of legal abortions in the world—a total of 988,267.[1] Of those countries which reported abortions by woman's age, the United States had the highest percentage of teenagers (32 percent) who obtained legal abortions. In contrast, only 2 percent of Japanese women who obtained abortions were teenagers. Clearly, the American teenager should be given the facts about abortion complications.

Never before have women undergone abortion operations in such vast numbers. In 1972, as a gynecologist in private practice, I began seeing a marked increase in the number of patients who had undergone legal abortion operations. With this increase, I also began seeing patients with significant complications—both mental and physical—following their legal abortions. Because of this concomitant occurrence I began keeping an office log listing the patient's name, age, and type of complication.[2]

From January 1972 to June 1979, I saw 802 patients who had undergone legal abortions. Of these 802 women, 159 (19.9 percent) suffered mental or physical complications of such magnitude or duration as to be considered significantly disabling. Even though 643 patients (80.1 percent) had essentially negative findings upon examination and review of medical history, my impression is that the great majority of these women viewed their experience as painful, traumatic, and one that they would like to forget.

The following table summarizes the diversity of complications seen in this group of women following their legal abortions.

Classification of Types of Complications in 159 Patients Following Legal Abortions

	No.	%
Sepsis, peritonitis, endometritis, salpingitis, abscess	41	25.79
Mental and psychologic sequelae	23	14.47
Hemorrhages: recurrent and disabling	20	12.58
Infertility: repeated miscarriages	14	8.81
Re-operations: laparotomy, hysterectomy and D&Cs	13	8.18
Uterine and cervical trauma: perforations, lacerations	12	7.55
Second trimester syndrome (fetus expelled: patient unattended)	8	5.02
Menstrual dysfunction: oligomenorrhea and amenorrhea	8	5.02
Pelvic pain syndrome	8	5.02
Abortion done: patient not pregnant	4	2.52
Hysteria following expulsion of recognizable fetal parts	3	1.89
Marital breakup	2	1.26
Severe kidney damage	2	1.26
Resection of ileum: colostomy	1	.63
Total	159	100.00%

Sepsis, Peritonitis, Endometritis, Salpingitis, and Pelvic Abscess (41—25.79 percent)

The above type of problems represented 25 percent of all significant complications seen. Ascending infections from lack of asepsis or inattention to strict surgical technique gave rise to many of the near-fatal complications.

A 17-year-old patient required complete extirpation of her reproductive organs because of far advanced pelvic abscesses intractable to antibiotics and medical management. Following her "lunch hour" abortion she had become critically ill with endometritis and peritonitis from a perforated uterus.

Another 17-year-old was hospitalized for five days for a 105 degree fever with sepsis and peritonitis following her clinic abortion in which the uterus had been perforated. The serious medical problem was compounded by the patient's total concealment of the true nature of her illness from her parents, and her expectation that I, as her physician, would not divulge the cause of her problem to her parents. Fortunately I was able to keep this confidence because of her recovery.

Mental and Psychologic Sequelae (23—14.47 percent)

Among these patients there were all stages of distress, anxiety, and remorse. Several of these patients became pregnant again within one year after their abortion to help expunge the guilt which they felt so deeply.

A 32-year-old with three children was coerced by her husband and mother to undergo an abortion because of a nervous breakdown a year previously. The trauma she felt from "destroying her baby" never left her, and her psychiatric problems became greatly aggravated by the experience. She has suffered loss of self-esteem and has feelings of hostility toward her husband and mother.

Hemorrhages: Recurrent and Disabling
(20—12.58 percent)

A 23-year-old suffered a hemorrhage the day after a clinic abortion in a nearby city. She instructed me, as I was making arrangements for her hospitalization, not to tell her husband the true nature of her problem as "he would kill her" if he found out she had had an abortion; he had had a vasectomy two years previously. Fortunately, she required only blood replacement—no re-operation was necessary.

Infertility (14—8.81 percent)

A 16-year-old patient underwent a saline abortion in 1972 at the urging of her mother. The saline abortion was painful and greatly protracted: it lasted 48 hours before the patient expelled the fetus. Complications of fever and endometritis developed, prolonging her hospital stay. The following year she married the boy who had impregnated her, but since then she has suffered three miscarriages and harbors deep resentment toward her mother.

Uterine and Cervical Trauma: Perforations
and Lacerations (12—7.55 percent)

An 18-year-old underwent a suction curettage abortion in her 10th week of pregnancy. After the abortion was seemingly completed, the physician attempted to insert an IUD into the uterus. When the IUD could not be located after insertion, it was determined that the uterus had been torn and that the IUD had been inserted into the abdominal cavity. Laparotomy was necessary for removal of the IUD and repair of the laceration in the anterior uterine wall.

A 19-year-old, 10 weeks pregnant, underwent suction curettage abortion at a clinic in a large metropolitan area. During the procedure she experienced excruciating pelvic pain radiating to her upper abdomen. The physician stopped the operation, instituted antishock measures, and transferred her to a nearby hospital where her condition was deemed critical from internal hemorrhaging—laparotomy was performed. A uterine rupture and laceration of the bowel were found. The uterine rent was repaired, resection of 14 inches of bowel was done and a colostomy was performed. The patient suffered a stormy postoperative course, was hospitalized for 41 days, and required psychiatric care after her release from the hospital.

The patients who had abortions done during the first month of pregnancy often had little or no anesthesia. These patients had great discomfort and tended to experience endometritis and residual pelvic pain for months afterwards.

A high percentage of the patients I saw with serious complications evidently had the length of the pregnancy underestimated by the doctor doing the abortion, with resultant cervical lacerations, hemorrhaging, uterine perforations, and retained placental and fetal tissue. Some of these patients thought to be under 12 weeks pregnant were actually in their 14th to 16th week, and the fetal size caused serious problems through retained limbs and skull fragments. Determining gestation age can be much more of a challenge than would be suspected: it is apparently just as easy to err in estimating fetal size at the time of abortion as it is in guessing the weight of the baby before delivery. The complications associated with a miscalculated abortion can be life-threatening for the mother.

Assembly-line abortions tend to be associated with a higher rate of retained tissue, fetal parts, hemorrhage, and infection necessitating hospitalization and prolonged postoperative management. Antibiotics, blood transfusions, and repeat curettage were often needed by patients suffering these complications.

Some of these patients confided to me the great lengths to which they went in order to conceal their true identities. Eleven of these patients admitted to giving false names and addresses at the abortion clinic, as they in no way would risk the chance that their true identities might be learned.

Discussion

The experiences of the author in dealing with abortion complications are really not much different than the experiences of those physicians who actually do the abortions. At the annual meeting of the Planned Parenthood Physicians in 1977 at Miami Beach, doctors who do thousands of abortions were gathered together to share experiences and perfect their expertise. These abortionists have seen complications ranging from serious to catastrophic, and they had many words of caution for the neophytes in the audience. They admitted to making errors in clinical evaluations of the stage of gestation; first trimester abortions became second trimester abortions with their increased morbidity and mortality rates. There was genuine fear among them of winding up with a live fetus through miscalculations of stages. They were also apprehensive about using pitocin and prostaglandins in patients who had previous abortions and uterine scar tissue.

Avulsion of the fetal head was one of the more gruesome complications that could and did happen, especially in early second trimester abortions. A fetal skull with its sharp spicules left behind in the uterus created a critical complication.

The Abortion Surveillance Branch of the Center for Disease Control publicizes the increase in abortion complications as pregnancy advances. Second trimester abortions carry higher morbidity and mortality rates and a much higher incidence of adverse mental and psychologic sequelae.[2]

When it is apparent that thousands of women have ceased using birth control pills because of the mandatory disclosure of all the possible side effects and dangers of oral contraceptives, it is only reasonable that these women be given the same information concerning the possible dangers of abortion as well as the actual complications and side effects that occur.

I strongly urge that a more accurate and comprehensive system for reporting the complications of legal abortions be instituted. Abortion clinics should be required to document their mortality and morbidity rates and publicize the rates of their postoperative follow-ups. Many abortion clinics see only 20 to 30 percent of their patients for post-abortion checkups. Obviously, meaningful statistics will be difficult to obtain when the majority of patients having abortions may not report back to the clinic where the abortion was done. It is also most important to know what percentage of women undergoing abortions are actually pregnant; the number who are not pregnant and who undergo abortions needlessly is not insignificant. My own experience in the Fort Lauderdale area causes me to raise this question.

We should be most wary of the rising abortion rates, especially in teenagers. The number of teenage girls who have had to have hysterectomies in the aftermath of severe abortion complications is unfortunately not known, even with improving efforts at abortion surveillance. The number of females who have lost their reproductive capacity because of post-abortion endometritis and sepsis cannot be accurately delineated. It is only recently that meaningful studies have been made on women who have undergone more than one legal abortion; the findings on what happens to these patients' reproductive potentials are not encouraging.

The 1 percent complication rate for legal abortions often cited by the Center for Disease Control may be correct for the university medical center, but their figure could well be challenged by the private practitioners who work in areas where the neighborhood abortion clinics do most of the abortions.

Notes

1. U.S. Department of Health, Education and Welfare, Center for Disease Control, "Abortion Surveillance 1976" (Atlanta: August 1978).

2. The diversity of complications that occurred in 54 teenagers, seen in private practice, following their legal abortions has been described in a recent issue of the *Southern Medical Journal.* See Matthew J. Bulfin: "A New Problem in Adolescent Gynecology," *Southern Medical Journal* 72:967, 1979.

Part Six

Public Policy: Rape, Incest, and Children

Efforts to prohibit abortion run up against the objection that abortion should be available in cases of pregnancy resulting from rape and incest. In "The Most Unwanted Pregnancies" Basile J. Uddo examines this question from a moral, medical, and public policy point of view. Philip G. Ney, a psychiatrist, analyzes another public policy question often mentioned in connection with abortion—its impact on children and family life.

EIGHT

The Hard Cases: Rape, Incest, and Public Policy

Basile J. Uddo

IT MUST BE ADMITTED that whatever consensus exists in opposition to abortion rapidly dissipates on the question of rape and incest exceptions to any anti-abortion legislation.[1] Even among those who identify themselves as pro-lifers, rape and incest cause consternation. In fact, several generally prolife moralists become concerned and accommodating when the pregnancy in question is rape or incest-induced.[2] It seems evident, however, that much of the controversy over rape and incest exceptions stems from misinformation and exaggerated fears of pregnancy. Ignorance about fertility patterns and factors influencing the possibility of conception, along with pro-abortion rhetoric, have created a baseless fear that pregnancy is far more likely than in fact it is.[3] Add to that some faulty moral reasoning about how to respond to these pregnancies, and we have an issue much in need of clarification. This discussion

Basile J. Uddo is professor of law at Loyola University in New Orleans. This article is based on a paper he delivered at the Conference on the Effects of a Human Life Amendment, sponsored by the St. Louis University Medical Center in October 1981. The full paper will appear in *Restoring the Right to Life: The Human Life Amendment* (J. Bopp, ed., Brigham Young University Press), scheduled for publication February 1983.

is an attempt to correct these misconceptions, and to put the issue in proper perspective.

The Nature of the Problem

The interworkings of opposition to abortion and the matter of rape and incest pregnancies raises problems. Usually when discussions of rape and incest exceptions are raised, the major conflict is over whether there should be an explicit recognition that surgical abortion would be legally permitted to terminate an already established pregnancy that resulted from rape or incest. Proposals for such an exception tend to be bold admissions that as a matter of public policy the children of rape or incest should not enjoy the protection that would be afforded other unborn children. Typically, the proposal is less grounded in theory—despite occasional attempts to rationalize the pregnancies of rape and incest as continuing aggression—than in utility. The utilitarian solution being the easy destruction of a growing reminder of a repulsive experience.

A Problem of Distortion Not of Fact

When rape and incest are raised as justifications for abortion of established pregnancies, it is generally done in a context that emphasizes the emotional and prejudicial nature of the subject. This context at least impliedly suggests that the issue is real, and the frequency of rape/incest pregnancies high enough to warrant special exceptions.[4] While this has typically been a successful rhetorical device, it does not correspond to reality. The fact is that rape and incest pregnancies are extremely infrequent occurrences.

The more candid commentators, even those decidedly pro-abortion, have admitted to the unlikelihood of such pregnancies.

A pregnancy conceived by forcible rape would probably head the list as the most often unwanted, *but it is such an unlikely* event that it is not really relevant to an understanding of the reasons why women define certain pregnancies as unwanted.[5]

Clearly the statistics support this conclusion. Great Britain has had legalized abortion long enough to have amassed some fairly dependable statistics. One report found that of 54,000 abortions done in Britain in 1969 only 80 were done as a result of rape.[6] A similar Czechoslovakian study found only 22 allegedly rape-induced pregnancies out of 86,000 consecutive induced abortions.[7]

The American experience confirms these foreign studies. A 1967 study in Chicago reported no pregnancies from confirmed rape in the prior 9 years.[8] Similarly, Washington, D.C., in 1968 reported only 1 pregnancy in more than 300 rape victims.[9] One very recent and excellent treatment of this topic has drawn together much of this data to conclude:

> The findings of pregnancy [from rape] vary from an incidence of none (0) to 2.2 percent of the victims involved. In four of the studies no pregnancies were documented. This included a large percentage of women at risk who for various reasons did *not* take any hormones such as DES. Of interest is the work of Hayman, co-author of by far the largest study— 2,190 female victims; Hayman states that "a very small proportion of patients became pregnant as a result of the assault." Added significance can be attached to Dr. Hayman's not recommending estrogen therapy, on the basis of his experience, as a standard procedure in treating victims of sexual assault. Editorializing in the *Annals of Internal Medicine,* he summarized the statistics as follows: "The probability of becoming pregnant or contracting syphilis or gonorrhea is small, very roughly, from 1 in 200 to 1 in 50."[10]

So overwhelming are the statistics that a New Zealand commission on contraception, abortion, and sterilization, which suggested a significant liberalization of New Zealand's abortion law in 1977, recommended against allowing abortions for rape since the incidence of such pregnancies were too low, and the likelihood of false reports too high to warrant a rape exception.[11]

Why So Few?

The reality of the infrequency of rape-induced pregnancies is grounded in medical fact. There are several very sound reasons why rape so seldom results in pregnancy. Fundamental among these is the relatively low incidence of conception from *any* single unprotected act of coitus. Christopher Tietze places the occurrence of such conceptions between 1 in 20 to 1 in 50 or 2%-4%.[12] Yet rape conceptions would be even lower.

The percentage is even lower in the case of rape because not every legally defined rape—defined as penetration—results in ejaculation. Consequently, legal rape may occur without the presence of sperm. Also militating against pregnancy is the low percentage chance of an attack occurring during the one to three day period in a victim's menstrual cycle when ripe ovum and viable sperm could produce conception. Moreover, even rape on the day of ovulation has only a 1 in 10 chance of pregnancy.[13] In addition to these already scant odds there is reason to believe that the trauma of a sexual assault might inhibit ovulation even if it would have otherwise occurred. This finding was first suggested by a ghoulish Nazi experiment wherein women who were about to ovulate were subjected to realistic mock gas-chamber executions and then examined to see if the experience affected ovulation, which it did, very often inhibiting it altogether.[14]

Two other very significant factors support an incidence of rape pregnancy far below the Tietze data on unprotected coitus. First, large numbers of victims are in fact protected in the sense that they may have been surgically sterilized, had a previous hysterectomy, were using some form of passive contraceptive, or were otherwise infertile.[15]

Second, a growing body of data shows a high incidence of sexual dysfunction among sexual assailants including erective and ejaculatory dysfunction, sufficient to minimize the likelihood of vaginal ejaculation.[16] Given these many and varied obstacles to conception it is easy to understand the extremely low incidence of pregnancies conceived through rape.

The Case of Incest Pregnancies

Thus far the discussion has focused upon the incidence of rape-induced pregnancy without mention of incest. This is true because incest does present a somewhat different problem, primarily because incest might often involve more than a single act of coitus effected under assault circumstances. In fact, some incest relationships could involve numerous acts of intercourse over substantial periods of time.

Yet the logical likelihood of more pregnancies is very difficult to substantiate largely because there simply is not much reliable, pertinent data. The dearth of data is not surprising given the social opprobrium attached to incest, and given the family ties involved. Small wonder that reporting would be inconsistent. Unlike rape, where although reporting may understate the problem there remain enough reported cases to accurately assess the pregnancy problem, reported incest cases are too few to assess. For example, in 1966 in an urban area the size of Chicago's Cook County only twelve indictments were entered for incest.[17] Consequently, much of the data on incest pregnancies is contradictory and largely dependent upon the date and sources of the data and the methods of collection. Despite the contradictions there are several sound studies that suggest an incidence of pregnancy similar to rape in its infrequency.

Dr. George Maloof, for example, reports that "incest treatment programs uniformly marvel at the low incidence of pregnancies from incest."[18] He cites the experience of the Christopher Street program in Minneapolis, which reported a 1 percent pregnancy rate among 400 female incest victims.[19] Similarly, an incest treatment program in Santa Clara County, California, reported a less than 1 percent incidence of pregnancies in 1500 families treated.[20] A Washington State program reported no pregnancies.[21] Yet, as Dr. Maloof admits, some studies have found dramatically higher incidence of incest pregnancies, some as high as 18-20%.[22] Why the contradiction? The answer seems to lie in the age of the study: older studies draw on untreated cases of incest, new figures are coming from incest treatment centers themselves, the point being that current awareness of the problem and efforts to treat the causes have oftentimes succeeded in ending incestuous relationships before pregnancy occurs. The older studies of untreated cases arose in a context where pregnancy was seen by the victim as a way to disclose the relationship and end it, an act of desperation rendered unnecessary by prompt intervention and treatment. Consequently, in the modern treatment context the incidence of incest pregnancies is probably quite low. But even with a higher incidence there are many sound reasons against "treating" these pregnancies through use of abortion. These reasons will be discussed below.

The Case Against a Rape/Incest Exception

Having discussed the infrequency of rape/incest pregnancies and the historical treatment of the problem, how should we, as pro-lifers, respond to the pressure for exceptions. It might be asked, "Is not the absolute prohibition too harsh given the small number of pregnancies involved and the admitted difficulty that even one such pregnancy could produce for the woman involved?" In short, it might be argued that, all things considered, a rape/incest exception might be a tolerable concession on a very controversial point. There are both moral and practical reasons why this argument is without merit. First, and foremost, is the moral consideration. Morally the value of life should not be determined by the context of conception. As repelling as rape and incest are as crimes, the unborn child is not the criminal. As difficult as carrying the pregnancy might be, it is a lesser concern than the protection of life. Bernard Nathanson summarized the issue quite well in *Aborting America*:

If a part of the human community were not at stake, no woman should be required to undergo the degradation of bearing a child in these circumstances, but even degradation, shame, and emotional disruption are not the moral equivalent of life. Only life is.[23]

While Nathanson may ignore creative ways of lessening the "degradation" he is on point concerning the moral principle.

Yet, how can we ask an individual woman actually faced with the problem to accept this moral analysis? How can we ask her to make what she will surely view as a sacrifice—even though it is for a higher good? Has our society ever asked as much? Indeed we have. For much of our history as a nation, with the approval of moralists and the law, we have asked young men to sacrifice their freedom, their convenience, their futures, indeed their lives, to defend their country in times of war. Even those conscientiously opposed to war have been asked—again with moral and legal approval—to give of themselves in some form of national service. Similarly, we have required that parents be bound by child abuse and child neglect laws. Laws that mandate that parents care for and protect their children, despite economic, physical, or psychological hardship—even to the point that a parent cannot prefer his or her life to that of his or her children. The demand is great, but done in service of a higher good—the protection of innocent and defenseless children.

In the practical realm, a rape/incest exception is ill-advised because it would undeniably be the thin edge of the wedge used for permitting many abortions beyond those specified. While the point has been overstated, and has accounted for an unjustified callousness toward rape victims, rape is a difficult crime to establish, especially so when prompt reporting and examination are not made. Consequently, allowing abortion for rape invites a flood of bogus rape abortions.

The willingness of abortion providers to fudge on the indications for abortion has been well documented. Even before

California liberalized its abortion laws, one study demonstrated that a large number of hospitals and physicians would willingly perform abortions if rape was the alleged cause of the pregnancy, despite the fact that these would have been illegal abortions.[24]

This professional malleability was underscored after California liberalized its abortion law and allowed rape as a justification. As one doctor put it: "Forcible rape is a problem at the present time in California because the presentation of false rape cases has increased. This is evidenced by the fact that among applications for therapeutic abortion for forcible rape in California, 19 percent were turned down by the committee in terms of their disbelief in the actuality of the forcible rape itself."[25] Presumably, the rejected cases were only the more blatant ones, and many others could not be filtered out.

It seems quite safe to assume that a rape/incest exception could never be contained, especially given the mind-set of many existing hospital staffs. This mind-set was rather vividly portrayed at a pro-abortion conference held in 1970 where one physician bemoaned the dramatic difference in abortion ratios between ward patients and private patients. His question was: "I am concerned as to whether we are really *recruiting* to make these services available to the poor."[26] Notice the word "recruiting," apparently a common practice as indicated by another conference participant: "Dr. Guttmacher has proudly referred to the nearly equal ward and private abortion rates at Mount Sinai Hospital. I would like to explain that as residents, *we beat the bushes to get cases for that committee so that he could get the ward ratio higher.* "[27] Could one really depend upon these people to carefully apply any kind of an exception, much less one as malleable as rape/incest?

A rape exception would also present another significant problem. That is, how should rape be defined? Forcible rape? Statutory rape? All felonious intercourse, as the infamous Model Penal Code says? There is an enormous difference between concern for the pregnant victim of real forcible rape and the young girl impregnated by her slightly older boyfriend in an act of consensual intercourse. Yet many proponents of a rape exception fail to distinguish between and among these cases.

Also, a rape exception produces the possibility of aborting a child willingly conceived, even between a married couple several days before a rape. Physically there would be no way to determine whether the child was already in existence at the time of the rape or was the product of the rape. Consequently, the child of a wholly licit and loving union could be destroyed under a rape exception.[28]

Another, important point should be considered in this regard. Few would doubt that the traditional difficulty in obtaining rape convictions and in sensitizing the population to the crime of rape has emanated from a suspicion about the veracity of the allegation of rape.[29] It is only recently that critics of these problems have begun to persuade prosecutors, and the public, that rape as a crime must be taken seriously. It is submitted that a rape exception would do damage to the progress made in this area. Such an exception would increase the motivation for and number of false accusations, thereby seriously damaging the credibility of genuine rape victims. This would be an unfortunate result of creating an exception for which there is no justifiable right.

Most of the reasons against a rape exception would apply with equal force to one for incest. Certainly the moral arguments are the same, especially in light of data questioning the evidence of a correlation between incest and genetic defects.[30] The practical problems—false claims, difficulty of proof, etc.—would also be similar. The difference, however, is in the higher incidence of pregnancy due to incest and the evidence that after the fact solutions such as abortion are no solution at all. While at first blush it would seem that an incest exception would be more necessary because of the arguably higher incidence of pregnancy, quite the opposite seems true.

First, despite the greater number of pregnancies, incest-afflicted families are extremely hesitant to admit to the occurrence of incest. Consequently, the view that incest victims will openly seek abortions, if such are allowed, is naive at best.[31]

The second, and more important point, however, is that abortion is never a treatment for incest. In fact, the quick disposal of the evidence of incest could well subject the victim to continued exploitation. What incest demands is intervention and multifaceted treatment. As noted earlier, this approach not only treats causes rather than symptoms, but it actually could prevent pregnancies and negate any need for an incest exception. Recall my earlier comments[32] about the discrepancies between the low pregnancy figures from incest treatment centers as compared with the higher figures from studies where early intervention and treatment seemed not to exist. In Dr. Maloof's opinion pregnancies were more likely "when the community was less sensitive to reacting to a possible incest situation and when treatment programs which allow families to work together were not available."[33] So abortion does not stop the problem, while treatment can. Encouragement to treatment rather than abortion makes good sense.

Finally, incest pregnancies, unlike rape, when they do occur are seldom revealed until the second trimester when abortions become significantly more dangerous. Hence, an incest exception would invite the infliction of greater harm on an already traumatized victim.

The Better Way

Abortion is to rape and incest what morphine is to pain—a superficially appealing, temporarily relieving, woefully inadequate response to something serious. The immediate benefits only mask the deeper wounds which fester to the point of great injury. A physician would never "treat" his patient only with morphine unless his was a hopeless case. To "treat" rape and incest pregnancies with abortion is a way of saying these women are hopeless cases—violated, tainted, damaged goods, for whom abortion is a way to scrub away the "Scarlet Letter,"[34] little more being possible for these "ravaged" victims.

Of course, this need not be the case. As awesome and horrible as these crimes may be, the victim need not be degraded by being asked to take life as a response. These women can be treated with dignity and love. They can be helped as whole persons, not simply as bearers of bad memories that must be extinguished.

Sensitive counselors have dared to suggest that both rape and incest are problems larger than pregnancy which call on us as creative, loving beings to find a better way to treat their victims. That better way seems apparent in a commitment to societal change that can stem the problem, and when it does occur in a commitment to competent counseling, broad-based support—emotional, physical, and financial—and development of dignified alternatives such as adoption.[35]

Conclusion

Rape and incest are among the most controversial issues in the already controversial abortion debate. Yet as has been demonstrated, much of the controversy stems from ignorance and emotion, not from reality. The significant problems that these crimes present are in no way ameliorated by the availability of abortion; in fact, abortion is a hindrance to more sensitive, caring, and integrated treatment. The human response to the real problems of rape and incest is complex and challenging. It requires understanding, care, and compassion; it substitutes life-giving for death-dealing; it treats the women with respect—not embarrassment or revulsion. It accepts the children of these crimes as children, not as monsters; it clothes them with human dignity, not deadly revulsion.

No matter how few are the pregnancies from these crimes they must be viewed as the clearest examples of genuine "problem" pregnancies which our society has not done well in understanding or providing for. A new attitude must emerge that emphasizes that the considerable difficulty involved in helping other human persons is well worth it, especially when, in every case, not only will an innocent woman be spared compounded degradation, but an equally innocent human life will be spared.

Notes

1. A 1974 poll commissioned by the National Committee for a Human Life Amendment showed 74% support for a rape exception. A 1978 Gallup poll showed majority support for a rape exception. These statistics are reported in various memoranda, etc., of the National Committee for a Human Life Amendment.

2. *See, e.g.,* Gustafson, "A Protestant Ethical Approach," and Williams, "The Sacred Condominium" appearing in *The Morality of Abortion,* Noonan (ed.) (Harvard, 1970), p. 107 and 164-67.

3. As a result of responses received from female medical students, McGuire and Stern concluded that "the general tendency in female responses was . . . to overestimate the incidence [of pregnancy]. Similar dynamics [ignorance, fear, and exaggeration] probably account for an escalation of estimates of the frequency of pregnancy resulting from sexual assault. (S. Mahkorn & W. Dolan, "Sexual Assault and Pregnancy," appearing in *New Perspectives on Human Abortion,* T. Hilgers, *et. al,* editors [University Publications of America, 1981] at 188. [Hereinafter cited as *Mahkorn and Dolan.*)

4. *See,* comments of Senator Brooke during Labor/HEW Appropriations Bill Conference Committee Meeting, Sept. 15, 1976, estimating 10,000 rape-induced pregnancies per year in the U.S.

5. N. Lee, *The Search for an Abortionist* (U. of Chicago Press, 1969), p. 149 (emphasis added).

6. Registrar General's "Statistical Review of England and Wales for 1969" (London 1971, H.M.S.O.), *cited in* R. Gardner, *Abortion: The Personal Dilemma* (Eerdmans, 1972) at 169, n. 10.

7. B. Willke & J. Willke, *Handbook on Abortion* (Hayes Pub. Co., 1979), p. 40.

8. Diamond, "ISMS Symposium on Medical Implications of the Current Abortion Law in Illinois," *Illinois Medical Journal* (May 1967), pp. 677-80.

9. Hayman, Stewart, *et. al,* "Sexual Assault on Women and Children in the District of Columbia," *Public Health Reports* (December 1968), pp. 1021-28.

10. Mahkorn and Dolan, *supra* note 6, pp. 187-188 (emphasis added). See also, Fujita & Wagner, "Referendum 20—Abortion Reform in Washington State," in H. Osofsky & D. Osofsky, *The Abortion Experience: Psychological and Medical Impacts* (Harper & Row, 1973). The authors report on 524 women receiving abortions at Haborview Hospital under Washington's then new liberal abortion law. Only 3 or 0.6% were reportedly done to end a rape-induced pregnancy.

11. *Report of the Royal Commission of Inquiry into Contraception, Sterilization and Abortion* (New Zealand, 1977).

12. C. Tietze, "Probability of Pregnancy Resulting from a Single Unprotected Coitus," 11 *Fertility and Sterility* 485-88 (1960).

13. *Mahkorn and Dolan, supra* note 6 at 189.

14. Hellgers, U.S.C.C. Abortion Conference, Washington, D.C., October 1967 cited in Mecklenburg, "The Indications for Induced Abortion: A Physician's Perspective," appearing in *Abortion and Social Justice*, T. Hilgers and Dr. Horan (ed.) (Sheed & Ward, 1972) at 49. See also, D. Granfield, *The Abortion Decision* (Doubleday, 1969) at 112.

15. Mahkorn and Dolan, *supra* note 6 at 189.

16. *Id.* at 188.

17. Mecklenburg, *supra* n. 17 at 50.

18. G. Maloof, "The Consequences of Incest: Giving and Taking Life," in *The Psychological Aspects of Abortion*, Mall and Watts (ed.) (University Publications of America, 1979) at 74.

19. *Id.*

20. *Id.*

21. *Id.*

22. *Id.* at 74-75.

23. B. Nathanson, *Aborting America* (Doubleday & Co., 1979) at 239.

24. Packer and Gampell, *Therapeutic Abortion: A Problem in Law and Medicine*, 11 Stanford Law Review 417, 435-44 (1959).

25. Overstreet, "Abortion and Obstetrics—The Means of Determining the Legitimacy of Requests for Abortion," appearing in

Abortion in a Changing World, J. Hall (ed.) (Columbia U. Press, 1970), vol. 2 at 74.

26. *Id.* at 81 (emphasis added).

27. *Id.* at 81-82 (emphasis added).

28. Rare though it may be this situation does occur. *See* L. Holmstrom and A. Burgess, *The Victim of Rape: Institutional Reactions* (John Wiley & Sons, 1978) at 85.

29. Margolin, "Rape: The Facts," 3 *Women: A Journal of Liberation* 20-21, cited in Sagarin, "Forcible Rape and the Problem of the Rights of the Accused," in *Forcible Rape: The Crime, the Victim and the Offender,* D. Chappell, *et al.* (ed.) (Columbia, 1977) at 155.

30. Comments of Dr. Carl Olstrom in *Medical World News,* February 4, 1967, reported in "Rape and Incest Exception Not Needed and Unwarranted" (National Committee for a Human Life Amendment).

31. This is borne out by the data. "Studies of incestuous pregnancies have invariably revealed that more pregnancies are allowed to go to term than are aborted." (Maloof *supra* note 21.) Of course these figures are not all the product of a fear of disclosure. Oftentimes the pregnant daughter resists abortion despite the wishes of the parents. Maloof, *supra* note 21 at 84-85.

32. *See* notes 18-22 and accompanying text.

33. Maloof *supra* note 21 at 75.

34. The "Scarlet Letter Syndrome" is effectively discussed and criticized in Mahkorn and Dolan, "Sexual Assault and Pregnancy" appearing in *New Perspectives on Human Abortion,* T. Hilgers, et al. (ed.) (University Publications, 1981) at 192.

35. On responses to rape pregnancies *see* Mahkorn, "Pregnancy and Sexual Assault" appearing in *The Psychological Aspects of Abortion,* Mall and Watts (ed.) (University Publications, 1979) at 53. On incest pregnancies see Maloof, *supra* note 21 at 73. *See also* K. Meiselman, *Incest: A Psychological Study of Causes and Effects with Treatment Recommendations* (Jossey-Bass, 1979) at 331 et seq.

NINE

A Consideration of Abortion Survivors

Philip G. Ney, M.D.

WHEN UP TO FIFTY PERCENT of North American pregnancies end by induced abortion,* it is reasonable to consider a live newborn as a survivor. In any situation where a mother, spouse, grandparent or physician has seriously deliberated abortion, the live child has survived a carefully considered option to destroy him. In those few situations where a live aborted infant has been given adequate medical care, he has survived a highly technical assault on his life. Both groups have survived when fifty percent of their kind have not, where they were up against forces they could not influence, where the decision to allow them to live was entirely out of their hands, and where their fate depended largely on their place of residence, sex, intelligence, physical attributes or time of existence. In these respects, survivors of abortion have in common those experiences that are the lot of most disaster

---

*(Although national statistics generally show a 1:4 or 1:3 abortion-live birth ratio, some cities like Washington, D.C., have abortion ratios well above fifty percent of the reported pregnancies.)

Philip G. Ney, M.D., is professor and head of the Department of Psychological Medicine, Christchurch Clinical School, University of Otago, Christchurch, New Zealand. This article is reprinted from *Child Psychiatry and Human Development*.

survivors. This paper raises the question, do abortion survivors have any psychological difficulties known to other types of survivors (1, 2, 3) or are their difficulties unique?

If children who survive abortion are psychologically affected, they are victims and as such must be studied to determine what difficulties they might encounter and what special help they require. The victims themselves should understand the unconscious factors that will influence their attitude toward those who have determined their fate (mothers and physicians), and those who may have attacked them (doctors and nurses), and those who could remind them of earlier conflicts (their own children).

A Child's Awareness

Demographic studies of abortion often cite abortion rates as a percentage of the number of live births but seldom note the prevalence of fertile women or mothers who have had one or more abortions. However, Jekel et al (4) found that of the young mothers (median age 16 years) reporting to the Yale-New Haven Hospital 1967-69 and given comprehensive service and counselling, 34% had an abortion during the follow-up period. The Canadian National Population Survey (5) done four years after the abortion law was liberalized found 46.3% of women 30-49 years had had an abortion. Tietze (6) suggests a lifetime abortion rate of 1000 abortions per 1000 women as a plausible minimum for a country with moderately effective contraception. The lifetime rate per 1000 women in the U.S. was 520 in 1975. With increasing abortion rates, a 50% prevalence rate for mothers is a plausible estimate.

Whether abortion survivors are affected is partly determined by whether they perceive the experience, know of siblings who did not survive, or understand the general social attitude toward them. Though there is evidence that unborn children both perceive and remember their interuterine existence, those children who did survive an attempted abortion death will not be considered further in this paper.

Psychoanalysts have often observed children's accurate

awareness and dramatic reaction to their mother's pregnancy. Cramer (7) noted a 5.1-year-old boy's reaction to his mother's three-month pregnancy: "He asked to taste her milk." Anna Freud (8) discusses the use of new material in a child's psychoanalysis evoked by the child's awareness of his mother's pregnancy. In the analysis of a four-year-old (9) and an eleven-year-old (10) the mother's pregnancy was a very important event. Niederland (11) recorded the dreams of a boy from 17 to 47 months which included pregnancies. Kestenburg (12) indicates that even small children know of their mothers' early pregnancy, partly because of changes in the way they are handled.

Eissler (13) states that Goethe was probably kept constantly in tension and conflict by the bewildering observation and experience of his mother's repeated pregnancies and child deaths. Pearson (14) reports the analysis of an adolescent who stated, "I knew she had two miscarriages and then when I was five years old, she stayed in bed when pregnant with my sister." Kent et al (15) describe the perceptions of depressed women in group psychotherapy who knew of their mother's attempt to abort them and partly because of that aborted their own pregnancies. Mothers are being advised to tell their children what is the reason when they are depressed following a miscarriage (16) and presumably this applies also to abortions. Our clinical observations tend to confirm the reports of others; even young children know of their mother's early pregnancy, (17) abortion and miscarriage. Cavenar et al (18) report the case of a five-year-old boy who became severely disturbed by the knowledge of his mother's abortion which she had when he was two-and-a-half years old.

A seven-year-old patient reported a dream in which three siblings went with him to play in a sand bank. While playing, the undermined bank collapsed and buried his siblings. Who they were he could not tell me but he knew they were brothers and/or sisters. His mother admitted to three early miscarriages but insisted her child could not have known.

Children are jealous of any siblings that could displace them in the parents' affection (19). However, there is no evidence that a child is glad when a sibling is killed. Rather they feel guilty, sometimes because destructive wishes toward a brother or sister seem to have been fulfilled. Bowlby (20) describes how, if there is a loss of a parent, children form strong subsidiary attachments to each other. In a social environment where children have a fifty percent chance of losing a parent or when one parent is already gone, because of separation or divorce, a child may look upon his new unborn sibling as a potential attachment. Since safety lies in numbers, especially in the companionship of familiars (21), children do want siblings.

Three Types of Survivors

In describing the family's reactions to a child's death from carcinoma or accident, Krell (22) notes that because children are egocentric, the surviving children react with a gnawing sense of guilt, wondering "was it my fault?" Children may feel just as guilty about a child destroyed in abortion (23). Krell (22) indicates that a concatenation of parent and child guilt produces a conspiracy of guilt resulting in three possible syndromes. These may also affect abortion survivors.

The "haunted child" survives to live in distrust of what may be in store for him while the parents conspire not to burden him with the facts. The child is haunted by a mystery, knowing and yet not knowing, always afraid to ask for clarification because he may discover something more awful than he expects.

The "bound child" reflects a parental need to control those forces that destroyed his sibling. If an abortion was done for convenience, social pressure or economic necessity, the parents struggle to make sure it cannot happen again. Preconsciously aware of their destructiveness, the parents overprotect the survivor against projected hostilities. As the child is kept from freely exploring the world, so his intelligence, adaptability and curiosity are crimped.

The "substitute child," maybe an abortion survivor, is especially wanted to replace the child that is no more. This child carries a heavy burden of expectation that he may not be able to fulfill. When he is disappointing, the parent may react with enraged frustration. They may have "terminated" the life of one child that could have been all they hoped for. Now this child continually lets them down.

Since almost all legal restriction to abortion in Canada and the United States has been removed, women can choose to abort an unwanted unborn infant. The state will not protect him, the community does not want him, and amniocentesis quickly determines if he is the right kind of child. Children may not be wanted because they are the wrong sex, or deformed, have limited abilities or simply because they arrived at an inconvenient time. Children are becoming increasingly aware of the fact that they exist only because their mothers chose them and chose them only because they were desirable. Since their fate once hung on their desirability, they tend to feel secure only when they are pleasing their parents. Consequently, they try too hard to please. This factor, added to their innate tendency to protect their parents, means they will tend to blame themselves whenever there is family disharmony. Consequently, a large number of children become over-anxious parent-pleasers until they can no longer cope. Then they become self-blaming and depressed or hostile and rebellious. Though parents may fail to recognize the child's depression because of their own pre-occupation with guilt, there is an increasing incidence of depression and suicide (24) among children which may be partly explained by this mechanism.

Future Psychological Difficulties of the Surviving Child

Abuse and Neglect. Lenoski's evidence (25) indicates that ninety percent of battered children are wanted pregnancies. Barker (26) found higher rates of abortion among women who have abused their children and also among siblings of abused children. Our study (27) indicates that child abuse is more frequent among mothers who have previously had an abortion. The mother's guilt or high expectations may be reasons why there is this correlation. A more plausible cause is that because of guilt, there is an antepartum depression that interferes with the mother's ability to bond. Children not well bonded appear to be at a higher risk to a parent's occasional rage or neglect (28).

Recent research indicates that abortion results in depression during a subsequent pregnancy (29) and immediately post-partum (30). This depression from abortion or loss of a previous child appears to delay a mother's preparation for her newborn by diminishing her anticipation. It has long been recognized that a significant personal loss without completed grieving will interfere with subsequent attachments (31, 32). The abortion that occurred in the first pregnancy seems to truncate the mother-infant bonding mechanism so that it does not develop as well in subsequent pregnancies.

Parents have real difficulty adjusting to the loss of their newborn, and grief is not significantly related to birth weight or duration of life of the dead infant (33). Though longer and more intense mourning was seen in mothers for whom pregnancy was a positive experience, mothers grieved whether an infant lived one hour or twelve days, whether he weighed 2,000 grams or a non-viable 580 grams and whether the pregnancy was planned or unplanned (34). Lewis (35) has shown how important it is for parents to mourn the loss of a stillborn. If one twin dies the mother has difficulty attaching to the survivor (34).

To be able to bond well, a mother must have finished mourning the loss of previous babies (36). The depression can be more difficult to deal with when there is ambivalence (37). Mourning is more difficult when there has been a wish for or a contribution to the death of the lost person. When an infant has been aborted there is usually intense ambivalence. Consequently, it is difficult to complete mourning, and the depression which interferes with mother-infant bonding will persist. These less well bonded infants are more subject to abuse and neglect (27).

Mary Ainsworth (38) describes how a child's early physical contact with its mother builds into him confidence to explore the environment and to become independent. Without that, education and maturing may be more difficult. Some mothers who have had an abortion develop an aversion to touching babies. An intelligent young woman told me, "I desperately wanted a baby after my abortion, but when they handed it to me, I handed it right back. I couldn't touch it, something was wrong." Abortion may be a major factor in reducing parent-infant skin contact and therefore the development of the child's intelligence, independence, and maturity.

The ability to parent depends upon a mother and father's ability to recognize the subtle changing needs of their infant children. If that responsiveness is tampered with, the baby's needs will not be met as well. To abort an infant, people must first dehumanize him and ignore those demands his helpless dependency makes upon them. Up to fifty percent of the population of fertile men and women must have learned to deny the reality of their unborn offspring, with his needs for protection and care, before they could consent to his life being terminated. This may make it harder for them to perceive the reality of their newborn baby and respond to his needs.

Under normal circumstances, fathers become increasingly attached to and protective of their child during pregnancy (39). Now that men have no legal right to restrain a woman requesting an abortion (40), they cannot protect their unborn baby. Since their baby might be destroyed at any time, they hesitate to become emotionally involved and attached to that baby. Even when a man and a woman make a joint decision to have a child, the man is never sure that she will not change her mind. Rather than suffer a loss, he remains aloof and unattached. Thus he is more likely to be unconcerned about his child's welfare after it is born.

An Existence that Depends on Being Wanted. Children who are aware of their mother's miscarriages and abortions probably cannot understand why they survived when siblings did not, why they were chosen to live when a brother or sister was "terminated." They could feel guilty for existing and may develop an existential neurosis. Preconsciously realizing that something inhibits the development of their full potential, they become increasingly demanding for freedoms and opportunities. Rather than examine their own inadequacies or their lack of motivation, they escalate their demands of parents and community to provide advantages which will make them a full and mature person. Otherwise, feeling guilty and helpless, they may decide they are unworthy of life and, thus, neglect themselves or commit suicide.

Since a child's father could not protect him and since the state had no law to safeguard his life when he was most vulnerable, the child has a potential to become very angry at paternal or authority figures. Since his existence hung by the thread of being wanted, he may distrust those who did not provide him the security of legal protection. These angry, distrustful children may not willingly work for their community but demand from it more rights and privileges.

Children who exist only because their mothers chose them may feel a deep sense of unpayable obligation to their mothers. In the past, children believed they existed because God created them, or because the state protected them, or because the tribe needed them, and/or the parents desired them. In situations where abortion was seriously considered, children may well know they exist only because their mothers chose not to abort them. Since about fifty percent of fertile women have had abortions, it is likely many more considered abortions. Is it possible that when these millions of surviving children become teenagers, they will want to shed that feeling of obligation? If so, they may rebel more against mother figures and there may be increased discrimination against women.

Before the state gave up its legal protection of children and before contraceptives made it possible for every child to be a "wanted child," few people questioned whether they were wanted. Now they do. Since their security rests in their wantedness, people, especially children, keep checking with each other, "Do you really want me?"

Stateless persons appreciate what it is like to live an existence that depends on being wanted. It demands constant pleasantness but evokes awful anger toward those who should recognize their right to exist whether they are pleasing or not.

Growing Ambivalence Towards Children

It appears that more people are weighing the cost of raising a child against the chance of purchasing a house or a new car (41). Relative to the importance of attaining one's full worth or retaining an enjoyable life style, children seem to be declining in value. The final confirmation of this is that 30-50 percent of them are destroyed in utero. The devaluation by society may result in children devaluing themselves. With diminished self-worth, adolescents care for themselves less well and they are less hopeful. They are more prone to depression which results in suicide, which is now the third major cause of death in adolescents (42).

When children are devalued, they have less confidence they will be cared for and become more demanding. These irritating demands produce an increasingly hostile reaction from the adult world. Children are angry because they cannot count on being cared for but must be continually pleasing or incessantly demanding. Adults are angry because children are so unappreciative and selfish. The net effect is a growing hostility between the generations.

Since abortion survivors had parents who had more difficulty seeing and responding to their needs, they may hesitate to have children or if they have children they may respond poorly to their needs. Adolescents who had poor nurturing may want to have children in order to obtain vicarious gratification by trying hard to meet their infant's needs. This may be why "sex education" has not worked in reducing teenage pregnancies (43).

Abortion may also produce a sense of emptiness which increases the desire to be fulfilled by having a baby. On the other hand, young people who are abortion survivors may not want to have a child because they are afraid the anger they feel toward their mothers will be displaced onto their young.

Abortion may tend to run in families. In an attempt to deal with the anger and anxiety of being chosen, some survivors destroy their young as revenge on their mothers who tried to abort them (15).

When a child's subtle pleas for nurture go unnoticed or when his demands are met with rage, the child suppresses his yearning for love. Children who are not loved have more difficulty loving and thus a vicious cycle of disregard, parents and children for each other, escalates from one generation to the next. Children need personal time and attention, but parents in pursuit of their own pleasures substitute material gifts. The children who still hope now redirect their pleas from parents to those material substitutes. That basic appeal to parents which should evoke an adult's care and concern is becoming an increasingly raucous clamor for material possessions which cannot satisfy them. Therefore, children become both material-istic and destructive.

An Endangered Species

From time immemorial it was taboo to attack the helpless, defenseless, wounded or female in the species. Even in times of terrible unleashed aggression or war, it is an atrocity to attack children. Now society legally sanctions and pays for the destruction, on a massive scale, of helpless life. That taboo has been broken in so many people that they have a suppressed response to protect the unborn and newborn. The breaking of that taboo no longer evokes a social protest. To a threat that may endanger the species, society has become increasingly passive and ineffectively permissive.

Many of those who still could respond, when contemplating rescuing an infant about to be aborted, think first of social ostracism or bureaucratic obstructions. Although the helpless-ness of the baby demands a rescue response, we all become anxious when facing the difficulties. As we turn away from the challenge, we relax. That relaxation reinforces an avoidance response which we soon learn to rationalize as medically expedient or socially beneficial. The voiceless plight of the baby is no longer effective in evoking uniform outrage. So many millions of people have a conditioned avoidance to tackling the problem of unrestrained abortion, the current practice is unlikely to change.

The species may be endangered. Evidence shows that in countries with long periods of unrestricted abortions, the negative population growth is not stopped by tightening the abortion laws (44). Even when monetary incentives have been used in Communist countries, there is a diminishing desire to have children. The continuity of our species may be endangered because abortion interrupts the parent-child mutuality and devalues children.

With the development of prostaglandin suppositories (45), the very wish of some feminists has come true (46). Every woman can now do her own abortion in her own home and attempt it at any stage of pregnancy. There will be many medical complications, and also more psychiatric disorders arising from the impossible conflict of a woman trying to decide whether to flush the struggling live infant down the toilet or rush it to the hospital for resuscitation.

If the government outlaws prostaglandins they will be sold by drug-dealing syndicates on the black market and they will be poor quality. If self-procured abortions remain illegal, women will not want to rush to the hospital and report their incomplete abortion. For these reasons, there will be tremendous pressure on the government to legalize the sale of prostaglandins and to decriminalize self-induced abortions.

If approximately fifty percent of women of childbearing age are procuring abortions, it probably means fifty percent of fertile men are coercing women or colluding in an abortion. While abortions are done under the surgical drapes by a professional who advised the "termination," most people can believe it is only a "conceptus" or "tissue." When people have prostaglandin abortions in their homes they will see that what they just terminated was truly human. Since the greatest crime is to destroy your own helpless offspring, the accumulating guilt will be overwhelming. Men and women may welcome war as a diversion from their own inner suffering. To be killed might be a relief and to kill not be anything new.

Though every human life should have the right to exist independent of its quality or wantedness, we have gone beyond the point where merely tightening abortion laws will save the lives of unborn babies. The best way to gain the community's and individual's desire to protect life is to impress on everyone the fantastic value of every human life. Maybe we will learn before it is too late that our own life is bound with the same life forces that give life to the smallest unborn human. May God grant us sufficient wisdom to see that to allow babies to die is to die ourselves, to kill those most helpless is to make us helpless to the attack of others.

Summary

If these observations and deductions are correct, there is a very large number of abortion survivors. That number is growing by about 60 million each year. These survivors are the indirect victims of the highly technical "termination" of their siblings. The knowledge they have been chosen to live creates peculiar psychological problems which may retard their development, subject them to an increased risk of abuse, neglect, existential guilt, materialism and becoming poor parents. Having been told they must appreciate being alive, they do not complain. Yet, we must wonder what happens in the future when abortion survivors hold in their hands the fate of those aged or enfeebled parents and professionals who regarded them so callously.

The state has abdicated its obligation to protect every life in favor of granting women the power to decide the life or death of their unborn children. Since many people have an ambivalent regard for their own lives, they will regard with equal ambivalence those who granted them a life. As living loses its traditional meaning, i.e., to sustain and enhance the life of others, so more people will question the purpose of their living. A vicious cycle ensues for which the state does not want to be held responsible. It has all too happily handed this onerous obligation to women who have unwittingly accepted an impossible role.

With widespread abortion on demand we are dealing with a potentially species lethal, ecological change. We must carefully study the full and far-reaching implications. I submit we begin with a careful analysis of abortion survivors.

Notes

1. Koranyi, E.K.: Psychodynamic theories of the survivor syndrome. *Can Psychiatric Assoc J,* 14:165-173, 1969.

2. Krell R.: Holocaust families: The survivors and their children. *Comp Psychiat,* 20:560-568, 1979.

3. Des Pres, T.: *The survivor,* New York: Pocket Books, 1977.

4. Canadian National Population Survey in Report of the Committee on the Operation of the Abortion Law. Robin F. Badgley, Chairman, Government Printers, Ottawa, 1977.

5. Jekel, J.F., Tyler, N.C., Klerman, L.V.: Induced abortion and sterilization among women who became mothers as adolescents. *Am J Public Health,* 67:621-629, 1977.

6. Tietze, C., Bongaarts, J.: Fertility rates and abortion rates, Simulation of family limitations. *Studies in Family Planning,* 6:114f., 1975.

7. Cramer, B.: Outstanding developmental progression in three boys. *Psycho Anal Study Child,* 30:15-49, 1975.

8. Freud,A.: About loving and being lost. *Psycho Anal Study Child,* 22:9-14, 1967.

9. Emmry, S.: Analysis of psychogenic anorexia. *Psycho Anal Study Child,* 1:167-184, 1945.

10. Singer, M.B.: Fantasies of a borderline patient. 15:310-356, 1960.

11. Niederland, W.G.: The earliest dreams of a young child. 12:190-208, 1957.

12. Kestemberg,J.: Personal communication, 1980.

13. Einsler, K.R.: Notes on the environment of a genius. *Psycho Anal Study Child,* 14:267-313, 1959.

14. Pearson, G.H.J. (Ed): *A handbook of a child psychoanalysis.* New York, Basic Books, 1968.

15. Kent, I., Greenwood, R.D., Nicholls, W.: Emotional sequelae of elective abortion. *B C Med J,* 20:118-119, 1978.

16. Le Shan, E.: Tell children how you really feel. *Women's Day,* February 18, 1980.

17. Dunn, J., Kendrick D.: The arrival of a sibling: Changes in patterns of interaction between mother and first-born child. *Psychol Psychiat,* 21:119-132, 1980.

18. Cavenar, J.D., Spaulding, J.E., Sullivan, J.L.: Child's reaction to mother's abortion: Case report. *Military Med* 144:412-413, 1979.

19. Levy, D.M.: Studies in sibling rivalry. *Res Monogr Am Orthopsychiat Assoc,* 2, 1937.

20. Bowlby, J.: Attachment and loss. Vol 2, *Separation,* New York: Basic Books, 1973.

21. Bowlby, J.: Attachment and loss. Vol 1, *Attachment.*

22. Krell, R., Rabkin, L.: Effects of sibling death on the surviving child, a family perspective. *Fam Process,* 18:471-477, 1979.

23. Cavenar, J.O., Mallbie, A.A., Sulivan, J.L.: Aftermath of abortion: Anniversary depression and abdominal pain. *Bull Menninger Clin:* 42:433-438, 1978.

24. Holinger, P.C.: Violent deaths among the young: recent trends in suicide. *Am J Psychiatry,* 136:1144-1147, 1979.

25. Lenoski, E.F.: Translating injury data into preventive health care services: Physical child abuse. Dept. of Pediatrics, University of Southern California, unpublished, 1976.

26. Barker, H.: Abused adolescents, advances in research and services for children with special needs. Presented at the International Conference on the Child, University of British Columbia. Unpublished, June 1979.

27. Ney, P.G., Hanna, R.: A relationship between abortion and child abuse. Paper given at Royal College of Physicians and Surgeons, Canada, May 1980.

28. Martin, H.P. (Ed): *The abused child.* Cambridge, Ballinger Publishing, 1976.

29. Kumar, R., Robson, K.: Previous induced abortion and antenatal depression in primiparae: A preliminary report of a survey of mental health in pregnancy. *Psychol Med,* 8:711-715, 1978.

30. Colman, A.D., Colman, L.L.: *Pregnancy: The psychological experience.* New York, Herder and Herder, 1971.

31. Bowlby, J.: Grief and mourning in infancy and early childhood. *Psychoanal Study Child,* 15:9-52, 1960.

32. Freud, S.: *Mourning and melancholia.* Strachey, J. (Ed). Standard Edition, Vol 14, p. 249, Hogarth: London.

33. Benfield, D.B.: Grief response of parents to neonatal death and parent participation in deciding care. *Pediatrics,* 62:171-177, 1978.

34. Klaus, M.H., Kennell, J.H.: *Maternal-infant bonding.* St. Louis, C.V. Mosby Co., 1976.

35. Lewis, E.: Mourning by the family after a still birth or neonatal death. *Arch Dis Child,* 54:303-306, 1979.

36. Lewis, E., Page: Failure to mourn a stillbirth: an overlooked catastrophe. *Brit J Med Psychol,* 51:237-241, 1978.

37. Maddison, D., Walker W.L.: Factors affecting the outcome of conjugal bereavement. *J Psychosom Res,* 13:297-301, 1968.

38. Ainsworth M.D.S.: Infant-mother attachment. *Am Psychol,* 34:932-937, 1979.

39. Lamb, M.E.: Paternal influence and the father's role: A personal perspective. *Am Psychol,* 34:938-943, 1979.

40. Bellottiv, B.: American Supreme Court, 75-73, 1976, and Hummerwadel v. Baird U.S. Supreme Court, 75-190, 1976.

41. Spencer, S.: Childhood's end. *Harpers,* pp. 14-19, May 1979.

42. Tonkin, R.: Mortality in childhood. *B C Med Assoc J,* 21:212, 1979.

43. Hadelson, C.C., Notman, M.T., Gillon, J.W.: Sexual knowledge and attitudes of adolescents: Relationship to contraceptive use. *Am J Obst Gyn,* 55:340-345, 1980.

44. Moore-Caver, E.C.: The international inventory on information on induced abortion. International Institute for the Study of Human Reproduction, Columbia University, 1974.

45. Hefni, M.A., Lewis, G.A.: Induction of labour with vaginal prostaglandin E_2 pessaries. *Brit J Obstet Gynecol,* 87:199-202, 1980.

46. Payne, J.: Speech to CARAL rally, SWAG report, p. 5 (Victoria, B.C.), April 1980.

Part Seven

The Experience of Pain by the Unborn

Abortion is often justified as a humane way to spare the pregnant woman pain and suffering. In "The Experience of Pain by the Unborn," John T. Noonan finds that she may do so only by inflicting pain and suffering on her unborn child.

TEN

The Experience of Pain
by the Unborn

John T. Noonan, Jr.

O NE ASPECT OF THE ABORTION QUESTION which has not been adequately investigated is the pain experienced by the object of an abortion. The subject has clearly little attraction for the pro-abortion party, whose interest lies in persuading the public that the unborn are not human and even in propagating the view that they are not alive. Indeed, in a remarkable judicial opinion Judge Clement Haynsworth has written, "The Supreme Court declared the fetus in the womb is not alive. . . . "[1] Judge Haynsworth's statement is merely a resolution of the oxymoron "potential life," which is the term chosen by the Supreme Court of the United States to characterize the unborn in the last two months of pregnancy.[2] Before that point, the unborn are referred to by the Court as alive only according to one "theory of life"[3]; and as the phrase "potential life" appears to deny the actuality of life, Judge Haynsworth does not exaggerate in finding that, by definition of our highest court, the unborn are

John T. Noonan, Jr., professor of law at the University of California (Berkeley) is a well-known prolife speaker and writer. A version of this article, which is reprinted from *The Human Life Review*, appeared originally in *New Perspectives on Human Abortion,* edited by Thomas W. Hilgers, et al., published by University Publications of America, 44 N. Market Street, Frederick, Md. 21701.

not alive. From this perspective, it is folly to explore the pain experienced. Does a stone feel pain? If you know as a matter of definition that the being who is aborted is not alive, you have in effect successfully bypassed any question of its suffering.

It is more difficult to say why the investigation has not been pursued in depth by those opposed to abortion. The basic reason, I believe, is the sense that the pain inflicted by an abortion is of secondary importance to the intolerable taking of life. The right to life which is fundamental to the enjoyment of every other human right has been the focus. That suffering may be experienced by those who are losing their lives has been taken for granted, but it has not been the subject of special inquiry or outrage. The assumption has been that if the killing is stopped, the pain attendant on it will stop too, and it has not seemed necessary to consider the question of pain by itself. In this respect, those opposed to abortion have been, like most medical researchers, concentrating on a cure not for the pain but for the disease.

There are good reasons, however, for looking at the question of pain by itself. We live in a society of highly developed humanitarian feeling, a society likely to respond to an appeal to empathy. To those concerned with the defense of life, it makes no difference whether the life taken is that of a person who is unconscious or drugged or drunk or in full possession of his senses; a life has been destroyed. But there are those who either will not respond to argument about killing because they regard the unborn as a kind of abstraction, or who will not look at actual photographs of the aborted because they find the fact of death too strong to contemplate, but who nonetheless might respond to evidence of pain suffered in the process of abortion. In medical research it has proved useful to isolate pain as a phenomenon distinct from disease, so it may be useful here.[4]

The Analogy of Animals

The best indication that attention to the pain of the unborn may have social consequences is afforded by the example of humanitarian activity on behalf of animals. Let me offer three cases where substantial reform was effected by concentrating on the pain the animals experienced. In each case it was accepted that animals would die, whatever reform was enacted; an appeal on their behalf could not be based on an aversion to putting animals to death. The only forceful argument was that the way in which the animals were killed was cruel because it was painful to the animals.

The first case is that of trapping animals by gins—traps that spring shut on the animal, wound it, and hold it to die over a probably protracted period. A campaign was launched in England against this method of trapping in 1928, and after thirty years Parliament responded by banning such trapping.[5] A second case is the butchering of cattle for meat. The way in which this was for centuries carried out was painful to the animal being slaughtered. A typical modern statute is the law in California which became effective only in 1968—all cattle are to be rendered insensible by any means that is "rapid and effective" before being "cut, shackled, hoisted, thrown or cast." Or, if the animals are being slaughtered for kosher use, their consciousness must be destroyed by "the simultaneous and instantaneous severances of the carotid arteries with a sharp instrument."[6] A third case: a 1972 California statute regulates in detail the methods by which impounded dogs or cats may be killed. If carbon monoxide is used, the gas chamber must be lighted so that the animal's collapse can be monitored. A newborn dog may not be killed other than by drugs, chloroform, or a decompression chamber. The use of nitrogen gas to kill an older dog or cat is regulated in terms of an oxygen reduction to be reached within sixty seconds.[7] Each of these laws has a single goal: to assure that the animal not suffer as it dies.

It may seem paradoxical, if not perverse, to defend the unborn by considering what has been done for animals. But the animal analogies are instructive on three counts: they show what can be done if empathy with suffering is awakened. They make possible an *a fortiori* case—if you will do this for an animal, why not for a child? And they exhibit a successful response to the most difficult question when the pain of a being without language is addressed—how do we know what is being experienced?

The Inference of Pain

Our normal way of knowing whether someone is in pain is for the person to use language affirming that he or she is suffering.[8] This behavior is taken as a sign, not necessarily infallible but usually accurate, that the person is in pain. By it we can not only detect the presence of pain but begin to measure its threshold, its intensity, and its tolerability. Infants, the unborn, and animals have no conceptual language in which to express their suffering and its degree.

Human infants and all animals brought up by parents will cry and scream.[9] Every human parent becomes adept at discriminating between a baby's cry of pain and a baby's cry of fatigue or of anxiety. How do we distinguish? By knowing that babies are human, by empathizing, by interpreting the context of the cry. We also proceed by trial and error; this cry will end if a pain is removed, this cry will end if the baby falls asleep. But animals, we know, are not human and are, in many significant ways, not like us. How do we interpret their cries or their wriggling as pain reactions if they are silent?

What we do with animals to be able to say that they are in pain is precisely what we do with the newborn and the infant: we empathize. We suppose for this purpose that animals are, in fact, "like us," and we interpret the context of the cry. We also proceed by trial and error, determining what stimuli need to be removed to end the animal's reaction.[10] We are not concerned with whether the animal's higher consciousness, its memory and its ability to understand cause and to forecast results, and different from our own, even though we know that for us the development of our consciousness, our memory, our understanding, and our sense of anticipation all may affect our experience of pain. With animals, we respond when we hear or see the physical sign we interpret as a symptom of distress.

Once we have made the leap that permits us to identify with animals, we do not need to dwell on the overt signs of physical distress. All we need is knowledge that an injury has been inflicted to understand that the animal will be in pain. Consider, by way of illustration, this passage on the cruelties of whaling: "A lacerated wound is inflicted with an explosive charge, and the whale, a highly sensitive mammal, then tows a 300-ton boat for a long time, a substantial fraction of an hour, by means of a harpoon pulling in the wound."[11] The author does not particularize any behavior of the wounded whale beyond its labor tugging the whaleboat, nor does he need to. We perceive the situation and the whale's agony. In a similar way the cruelty involves in hunting seals is shown by pointing to their being shot and left to die on the ice.[12] The pain of the dying seal is left to imaginative empathy.

We are, in our arguments about animal suffering and in our social response to them, willing to generalize from our own experience of pain and our knowledge of what causes pain to us. We know that pain requires a force inflicting bodily injury and that, for the ordinary sentient being who is not drugged or hypnotized, the presence of such a force will occasion pain. When we see such a force wounding any animal we are willing to say that the animal feels pain.

The Nature of Pain

If we pursue the question more deeply, however, we meet a question of a mixed philosophical-psychological character. What is pain? Pain has in the past been identified with "an unpleasant quality in the sense of touch." Pain has also been identified with "an unpleasantness," understood as "the awareness of harm."[13] In the analysis of Thomas Aquinas, *dolor* requires the deprivation of a good together with perception of the deprivation. *Dolor* is categorized as interior *dolor,* which is consequent on something being apprehended by the imagination or by reason, and exterior *dolor,* which is consequent on something being apprehended by the senses and especially by the sense of touch.[14] The Thomistic definition of exterior *dolor,* while general, is not incongruent with a modern understanding of pain, which requires both harmful action on the body and perception of the action. It has been observed that pain also has a motivational component: part of the pain response is avoidance of the cause of the pain.[15] In the words of Ronald Melznack, a modern pioneer in work on pain, "The complex sequences of behavior that characterize pain are determined by sensory, motivational, and cognitive processes that act on motor mechanisms."[16]

Pain, then, while it may be given a general definition, turns out upon investigation to consist of a series of specific responses involving different levels and kinds of activity in the human organism. Melzack has put forward a "gating theory" of pain, in which the key to these responses is the interaction between stimuli and inhibitory controls in the spinal column and in the brain which modulate the intensity and reception of the stimuli.[17] Melzack's theory requires the postulation of control centers, and it is not free from controversy. [18] Yet in main outline it persuasively explains a large number of pain phenomena in terms of stimuli and inhibitors.

To take one illustration at the level of common experience, if someone picks up a cup of hot liquid, his or her response may vary depending on whether the cup is paper or porcelain. The paper cup may be dropped to the ground; an equally hot porcelain cup may be jerkily set back on the table. What is often looked at as a simple reflex response to heat is modified by cognition.[19] To take a more gruesome experience, a number of soldiers severely wounded on the beach at Anzio told physicians in the field hospital that they felt no pain; they were overwhelmingly glad to be alive and off the beach. The same wounds inflicted on civilians would have been experienced as agonizing.[20] For a third example, childbirth without anesthesia is experienced as more or less painful depending on the cultural conditioning which surrounds it.[21]

As all of these examples suggest, both the culture and specific experiences play a part in the perception of pain. Memory, anticipation, and understanding of the cause all affect the perception. It is inferable that the brain is able to control and inhibit the pain response. In Melzack's hypothesis, the gating mechanism controlling the sensory inputs which are perceived as painful operates "at successive synapses at any level of the central nervous system in the course of filtering of the sensory input."[22] In this fundamental account, "the presence or absence of pain is determined by the balance between the sensory and the central inputs to the gate control system."[23]

What is the nature of the sensory inputs? There are a larger number of sensory fibers which are receptors and transmitters, receiving and transmitting information about pressure, temperature, and chemical changes at the skin. These transmissions have both temporal and spatial patterns. It is these patterns which will be perceived as painful at certain levels of intensity and duration when the impulses are uninhibited by any modulation from the spinal column or brain.[24]

The Experience of the Unborn

For the unborn to experience pain there must be sense receptors capable of receiving information about pressure, temperature, and cutaneous chemical change; the sense receptors must also be capable of transmitting that information to cells able to apprehend it and respond to it.

By what point do such receptors exist? To answer this question, the observation of physical development must be combined with the observation of physical behavior. As early as the 56th day of gestation the child has been observed to move in the womb.[25] In Lieley's hypothesis "the development of structure and the development of function go hand in hand. Fetal comfort determines fetal position, and fetal movement is necessary for a proper development of fetal bones and joints.[26] If fetal bones and joints are beginning to develop this early, movement is necessary to the structural growth; and if Liley is correct, the occasion of movement is discomfort or pain. Hence, there would be some pain receptors present before the end of the second month. A physiologist places about the same point—day 59 or 60—the observation of "spinal reflexes" in the child. Tactile stimulation of the mouth produces a reflex action, and sensory receptors are present in the simple nerve endings of the mouth.[27] Somewhere between day 60 and day 77 sensitivity to touch develops in the genital and anal areas.[28] In the same period, the child begins to swallow. The rate of swallowing will vary with the sweetness of injection.[29] By day 77 both the palms of the hands and the soles of the feet will also respond to touch; by the same day, eyelids have been observed to squint to close out light.[30]

A standard treatise on human physiological development puts between day 90 and day 120 the beginning of differentiation of "the general sense organs," described as "free nerve terminations (responding to pain, temperature, and common chemicals), lamellated corpuscles (responding to deep pressure(, tactile corpuscles, neuromuscular spindles, and neurotendinous end organs (responding to light and deep pressure)."[31] But as responses to touch, pressure, and light precede this period, visible differentiation must be preceded by a period in which these "general sense organs" are functioning.

The cerebal cortex is not developed at this early stage; even at twelve to sixteen weeks it is only 30 percent to 40 percent developed.[32] It is consequently a fair conclusion that the cognitive input into any pain reaction will be low in these early months. Neither memory nor anticipation of results can be expected to affect what is experienced. The unborn at this stage will be like certain Scotch terriers, raised in isolation for experimental purposes, who had no motivational pain responses when their noses encountered lighted matches; they were unaware of noxious signals in their environment.[33] But if both sensory receptors and spinal column are involved, may one say with assurance that the reception of strong sense impressions causes no pain? It would seem clear that the reactions of the unborn to stimuli like light and pressure are the motivational responses we associate with pain. We say that a sense receptor is there because there is a response to touch and a taste receptor is there because there is a response to taste. By the same token we are able to say that pain receptors are present when evasive action follows the intrusion of pressure or light, or when injection of a disagreeable fluid lowers the rate of swallowing. Liley is categorical in affirming that the unborn feel pain.[34] His conclusion has recently been confirmed by an American researcher, Mortimer Rosen, who believes the unborn respond to touch, taste, and pain.[35]

While the likelihood of weak participation by the cerebral cortex will work against the magnification of the pain, there will also be an absence of the inhibitory input from the brain which modulates and balances the sensory input in more developed beings. Consequently, the possibility exists of smaller and weaker sensory inputs having the same effect which later is achieved only by larger and stronger sensations.

As the sensory apparatus continues to grow, so does the cerebral cortex: light stimuli can evoke electrical response in the cerebral cortex between the sixth and seventh months.[36] By this time there will be a substantial cerebral participation in pain perception together with the likelihood of greater brain control of the sensory input. If a child is delivered from the womb at this date, he or she may shed tears. He or she will cry.[37] As we do with other newborns, we interpret these signs in terms of their context and may find them to be signs of pain. What we conclude about the delivered child can with equal force be concluded about the child still in the womb in months six through nine: that unborn child has developed capacity for pain.

In summary, beginning with the presence of sense receptors and spinal responses, there is as much reason to believe that the unborn are capable of pain as that they are capable of sensation. The ability to feel pain grows together with the development of inhibitors capable of modulating the pain. By the sixth month, the child in the womb has a capacity for feeling and expressing pain comparable to the capacity of the same child delivered from the womb. The observation sometimes made that we don't remember prenatal pains applies with equal force to the pains of being born or the pain of early infancy. Memory, it must be supposed, suppresses much more than it recalls. If we remember nothing about life before birth or life before three or four, it may even be that some recollections are painful enough to invoke the suppressive function of our memory; life in the womb is not entirely comfortable.

The principal modern means of abortion are these. In early pregnancy sharp curettage is practiced: a knife is used to kill the unborn child.[38] Alternatively, suction curettage is employed: a vacuum pump sucks up the unborn child by bits and pieces, and a knife detaches the remaining parts.[39] In the second trimester of pregnancy and later a hypertonic saline solution is injected into the amniotic fluid surrounding the fetus. The salt appears to act as a poison;[40] the skin of the affected child appears, on delivery, to have been soaked in acid.[41] Alternatively, prostaglandins are given to the mother; in sufficient dosage they will constrict the circulation and impair the cardiac functioning of the fetus.[42] The child may be delivered dead or die after delivery.[43]

Are these experiences painful? The application of a sharp knife to the skin and the destruction of vital tissue cannot but be a painful experience for any sentient creature. It lasts for about ten minutes.[44] Being subjected to a vacuum is painful, as is dismemberment by suction. The time from the creation of the vacuum to the chief destruction of the child again is about ten minutes.[45] Hypertonic saline solution causes what is described as "exquisite and severe pain" if, by accident during an abortion, it enters the body of the woman having the abortion.[46] It is inferable that the unborn would have an analogous experience lasting sometimes two hours, as the saline solution takes about this long to work before the fetal heart stops.[47] The impact of prostaglandins constricting the circulation of the blood or impairing the heart must be analogous to that when these phenomena occur in born children: they are not pleasant. If, as has been known to happen, a child survives saline or prostaglandin poisoning and is born alive, the child will be functioning with diminished capacity in such vital functions as

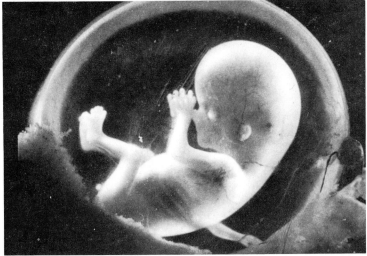

1.

This 48-day-old fetus, though less than an inch long, has all the organs of an adult human being. Many of them already function. His heart has been beating for over two weeks. His brain and muscles function together so well that the babe's whole body will twist and turn away when his upper lip is stroked with a fine hair.

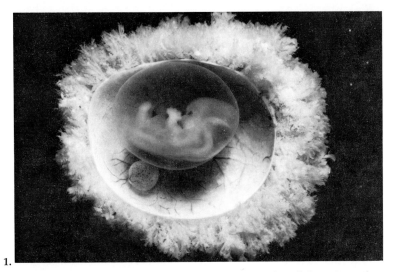

2.

At ten weeks, this boy's adrenal and thyroid glands are functioning. He sucks his thumb and responds to pain. He can kick, curl his toes, and turn his feet. His brain is formed much as it will be in adulthood. And his finger-prints already bear the pattern that is uniquely his. His heart has now been beating for seven weeks — pumping blood that he has made himself. He's a little over two inches long and would fit comfortably in the palm of your hand.

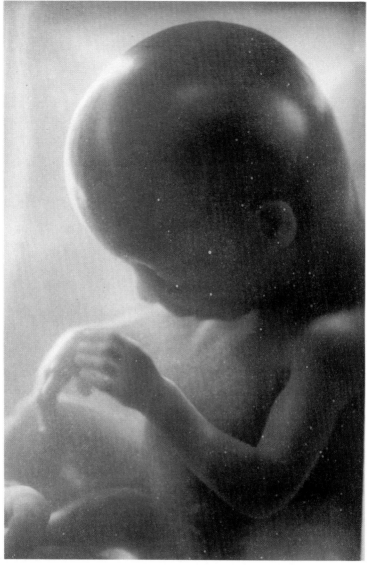

3.

At twenty weeks, the fetus weighs a little under half a pound and is between eight and ten inches long. Fine baby hair grows on his eyebrows and eyelashes and on the top of his head. Sleeping habits now begin to emerge. He moves vigorously at times, is drowsy and sleepy at others.

If he were born prematurely at this stage, he would stand a chance of survival in a well-equipped hospital. Others have survived and thrived.

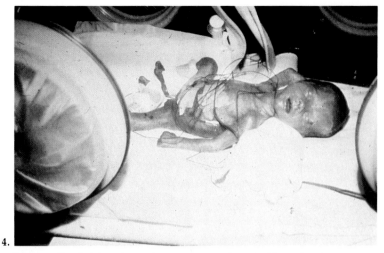

4.

Suzanna South (above) was born prematurely only 19 weeks after conception. The picture below shows her three years after birth.

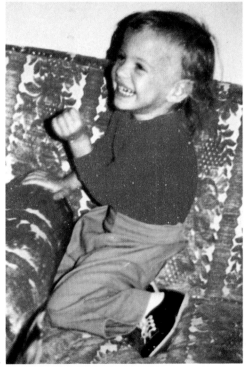

5.

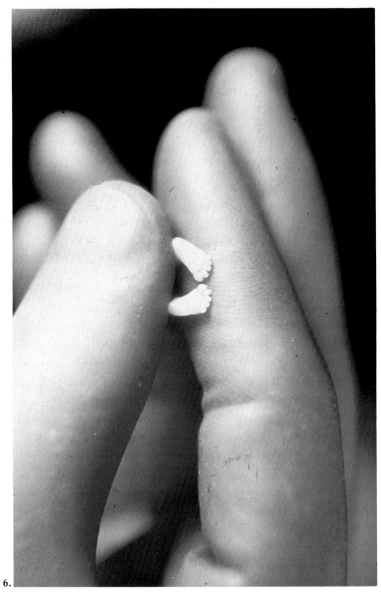

6.
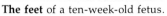
The feet of a ten-week-old fetus.

breathing and cardiac action.[48] Such impaired functioning is ordinarily experienced as painful.

Do the anesthetics the mother has received lessen the pain of the child? It is entirely possible that some drugs will cross the placenta and enter the child's system, causing drowsiness. Anesthesia, however, is not administered to the gravida with the welfare of her child in mind, nor do the anesthetics ordinarily used prevent the mother from serious pain if she is accidentally affected by the saline solution. It may be inferred the child is not protected either. Is it possible that the abortifacient agent destroys the pain receptors and the capability of a pain response earlier than it ends the life of the unborn, so that there is a period of unconsciousness in which pain is not experienced? This is possible in curettage by knife or suction, but it would seem to occur haphazardly, since stunning the child is not the conscious aim of the physician performing the abortion. In saline or prostaglandin poisoning it seems unlikely that the pain apparatus is quickly destroyed. An observation of Melzack is of particular pertinence: the local injection of hypertonic saline opens the spinal gate, he has remarked, and evokes severe pain. At the same time, it raises the level of the inhibitors and closes the gate to subsequent injections.[49] From this it may be inferred that an unborn child subjected to repeated attempts at abortion by saline solution—the baby in the *Edelin* case was such a child[50]—suffers a good deal the first time and much less on the second and third efforts. The general observation of Melzack on the mechanism of pain is also worth recalling: any lesion which impairs the tonic inhibitory influence from the brain opens the gate, with a consequent increase in pain.[51] Any method of abortion which results first in damage to the cortex may have the initial effect of increasing the pain sensations.

From the review of the methods used, we may conclude that as soon as a pain mechanism is present in the fetus—possibly as early as day 56—the methods used will cause pain. The pain is more substantial and lasts longer the later the abortion is. It is most severe and lasts the longest when the method is saline poisoning.

Whatever the method used, the unborn are experiencing the greatest of bodily evils, the ending of their lives.[52] They are undergoing the death agony. However inarticulate, however slight their cognitive powers, however rudimentary their sensations, they are sentient creatures undergoing the disintegration of their being and the termination of their vital capabilities. That experience is painful in itself. That is why an observer like Magda Denes, looking at the body of an aborted child, can remark that the face of the child has "the agonized tautness of one forced to die too soon."[53] The agony is universal.

Conclusion

There are no laws which regulate the suffering of the aborted like those sparing pain to dying animals. There is nothing like the requirement that consciousness must be destroyed by "rapid and effective" methods as it is for cattle; nothing regulating the use of the vacuum pump the way the decompression chamber for dogs is regulated; nothing like the safeguard extended even to newborn kittens that only a humane mode of death may be employed. So absolute has been the liberty given the gravida by the Supreme Court that even the prohibition of the saline method by a state has been held to violate the Constitution.[54] The Supreme Court has acted as though it believed that its own fiat could alter reality and as if the human fetus is not alive.

Can human beings who understand what may be done for animals and what cannot be done for unborn humans want this inequality of treatment to continue? We are not bound to animals to the same degree as we are bound to human beings because we lack a common destiny, but we are bound to animals as fellow creatures, and as God loves them out of charity, so must we who are called to imitate God.[55] It is a sign not of error or weakness but of Christlike compassion to love animals. Can those who feel for the harpooned whale not be touched by the situation of the salt-soaked baby? We should not despair of urging further the consciences of those who have curtailed their convenience to spare suffering to other sentient creatures.

With keener sensibilities and more developed inhibitors than animals, we are able to empathize with their pain. By the same token, we are able to empathize with the aborted. We can comprehend what they must undergo. All of our knowledge of pain is by empathy: we do not feel another's pain directly. That is why the pain of others is so tolerable for us. But if we begin to empathize, we may begin to feel what is intolerable.

We are bound to the beings in the human womb by the common experience of pain we have also known in the womb. We are bound to them as well by a common destiny, to share eternal life. As fellow wayfarers, we are bound to try to save them from a premature departure. We can begin to save them by communicating our knowledge of the suffering they must experience.

Notes

1. *Floyd v. Anders,* 440 F. Supp. 535, 539 (D.S.C. 1977).

2. *Roe v. Wade,* 410 U.S. 113, 162 (1973).

3. Id. at 163.

4. On the usefulness of looking at pain as a separate phenomenon, see Ronald Melzack, *The Puzzle of Pain* (New York: Basic Books, 1973), pp. 9-10.

5. C.W. Hume, *Man and Beast* (London: Universities Federation for Animal Welfare, 1962), p. 214.

6. Cal. Agric. Code S 19 (1967).

7. Cal. Penal Code SS 597 v. and w. (1978).

8. John S. Liebeskind and Linda A. Paul, "Psychological and Physiological Mechanisms of Pain," *American Review of Psychology* 28 (1977):42.

9. As to parentally cared-for animals, see Hume op. cit., p. 45.

10. *Ibid.*, pp. 94-95.

11. *Ibid.*, p. 215.

12. *Ibid.*, pp. 215-216.

13. Edward Boring, *Pain Sensations and Reactions* (Baltimore: The Williams and Wilkins Co., 1952), pp. v-vi.

14. Thomas Aquinas, *Summa Theologica,* I-II, q. 35, art. 7.

15. Melzack, op. cit., p. 163.

16. *Ibid.*, p. 165.

17. *Ibid.*, pp. 158-166.

18. See Liebeskind and Paul, op. cit., p. 47.

19. Cf. Melzack, op. cit., pp. 29-31.

20. *Ibid.*, pp. 29-30.

21. *Ibid.*, p. 22.

22. *Ibid.*, p. 166.

23. *Ibid.*, p. 171.

24. *Ibid.*, p. 158.

25. A. William Lieley: "The foetus as personality," *Australia and New Zealand Journal of Psychiatry* 6:99, 1972.

26. A. William Lieley, "Experiments with Uterine and Fetal Instrumentation," in *Intrauterine Fetal Visualization,* ed. Michael M. Kuback and Carlo Valenti (Oxford: Excerpta Medica; New York: American Elsevier Publishing Co., 1976), p. 75.

27. P.S. Timiras, *Developmental Physiology and Aging* (New York: The Macmillan Company, 1972), p. 153.

28. *Ibid.*, p. 153.

29. Lieley: "The foetus as personality," op. cit., p. 102.

30. Trypena Humphrey, "The Development of Human Fetal Activity and Its Relation to Postnatal Behavior," in *Advances in Child Development and Behavior*, ed. Hayne W. Reese and Lewis P. Lipsitt (New York: Academy Press, 1973), pp. 12, 19.

31. Timiras, op. cit., p. 137.

32. Geoffrey S. Dawes, *Fetal and Neonatal Physiology* (Chicago: Year Book Medical Publishers, 1968), p. 126.

33. Melzack, op. cit., p. 28.

34. Lieley: "Experiments with Uterine and Fetal Instrumentation," op. cit.

35. Mortimer Rosen, "The Secret Brain: Learning Before Birth," *Harper's,* April 1978, p. 46.

36. Timiras, op. cit., p. 149.

37. Paul Mussen, John Congar, and Jerome Kagan, *Child Development and Personality,* 2nd ed. (New York: Harper and Row, 1963), p. 65.

38. Louis M. Hellman and Jack A. Pritchard, eds., *Williams Obstetrics,* 14th ed. (New York: Appleton-Century-Crofts, 1971), p. 1089.

39. Selig Neubardt and Harold Schwelman, *Techniques of Abortion* (Boston: Little, Brown and Company, 1972), pp. 46-47.

40. *Ibid.,* p. 68.

41. Magda Denes, *In Necessity and Sorrow: Life and Death in an Abortion Hospital* (New York: Basic Books, 1976), p. 27.

42. Sultan M.M. Karim, *Prostaglandins and Reproduction* (Baltimore: University Park Press, 1975), p. 107.

43. See *Floyd v. Anders,* 440 F. Supp. 535 (D.S.C. 1977), for a case where the child died after delivery.

44. Andre Hellegers, director of the Joseph and Rose Kennedy Institute, to the author, oral communication.

45. *Ibid.*

46. Neubardt and Schwelman, op. cit., p. 68.

47. Karim, op. cit., p. 107.

48. See A.I. Csapo et al.: "Termination of pregnancy with double prostaglandin input," *American Journal of Obstetrics and Gynecology* 124:1, 1976.

49. Melzack, op. cit., pp. 181-182.

50. *Commonwealth v. Edelin,* —Mass., 359 (N.E. 2d) 4 (1976).

51. Melzack, op. cit., p. 171.

52. Thomas Aquinas, *Summa contra Gentiles* 4, 52.

53. Denes, op. cit., p. 60.

54. *Planned Parenthood v. Danforth,* 428 U.S 52 (1976).

55. Thomas Aquinas, *Summa Theologica,* II-II, q. 25, art. 3, reply to objection 3.

Part Eight

Abortion, Infanticide, and Euthanasia: The Deadly Trio

"The values and passions, as well as the logic of some portions of the 'abortion rights' movement, have always pointed beyond abortion," writes George F. Will. They have, in fact, led to infanticide and euthanasia. The articles here document the lethal connections among the deadly trio.

ELEVEN

The Lesson of Euthanasia

Virgil C. Blum and Charles J. Sykes

A S THE EUTHANASIA and abortion movements in the United States continue to grow in scope and intensity it becomes of the utmost importance to remind ourselves of the history of so-called "mercy-killing." We must not ignore the striking and disquieting parallels between the arguments and logic used by contemporary proponents and those used in Germany even before the Nazi period. We need not indulge in fantasizing or "divining" the future to see the ramifications of such programs. Too often predictions of the ultimate progression of abortion to euthanasia to the widespread killing of the aged and infirm are dismissed as extremist and alarmist. We must recognize, however, the progression that has *already* taken place. The relevance of the German experience, hazy and indefinite in the minds of most, is still widely misrepresented and misunderstood. But the parallels between the German experience and our own are impressive. The warnings are clear, if we will only heed them.

Virgil C. Blum, S.J., professor emeritus of political science at Marquette University, is president of the Catholic League for Religious and Civil Rights, and the author of numerous books, including *Freedom in Education*, and articles in both scholarly journals and popular magazines. Charles J. Sykes is editor of the *Northeast Post*, a suburban Milwaukee weekly, and a board member of the Catholic League. This article is reprinted from *The Human Life Review*.

Despite what some people would like to think, the mass euthanasia program cannot be written off as a Nazi aberration or as an alien element thrust upon civilization by fanaticism. The movement was not one of storm-troopers or of demented sadists, but was rather the culmination of an intellectual movement which can be traced back to 1920 with the publication of *The Release of the Destruction of Life Devoid of Value*, by the psychiatrist Alfred Hoche and the jurist Karl Binding. They developed the idea of "absolutely worthless human beings" and advocated the "killing of those who cannot be rescued and whose death is urgently necessary."[1] They stressed the economic burden of keeping these patients alive and conversely the advantages of killing them. Probably neither Hoche nor Binding had ever heard of Adolf Hitler, and it is not likely that Hitler ever read their book. But it is extremely significant that just as the Fuehrer's career was beginning, the concept of "life devoid of value" was being advanced in the intellectual community. Frederic Wertham, in his book *A Sign for Cain*, writes, "This little book influenced, or at least crystallized, the thinking of a whole generation."[2] Dr. Paul Marx in his book on mercy-killing also commenting on this book wrote that "the German atrocities began as the voluntary deeds of eminent scientists not as the reluctant response to a mad despot's commands."[3]

The German program got off to a rather modest beginning. In 1933 the Law for the Prevention of Hereditary Diseases provided for compulsory sterilization to prevent the propagation of "serious Hereditary diseases," such as hereditary imbecility, insanity, epilepsy, deafness, blindness, and alcoholism. One of the architects of the program, Dr. Arthur Guett, head of the National Hygiene Department, offered the comforting reassurance as late as 1938 that "stringent regulations have been issued to prevent any misuse."[4] But by the outbreak of the Second World War in 1939, 375,000 persons, including workers who had lost limbs in industrial accidents, had been sterilized.[5] As Wertham points out, "The compulsory sterilization law was the forerunner of the mass killing of psychiatric patients."[6]

The German professionals were heavily influenced by a utilitarian medical ethic in which the consequences alone determined whether an act was right or wrong. Michael LaChat in his article "Utilitarian Reasoning in Nazi Medical Policy," writes that such reasoning "often rests upon a rejection of any concept of a natural order imposing absolute values, an acceptance of the doctrine that the control of life is a proper function of society rightly influenced by factors such as the population explosion and an emphasis on the needs of the community."[7]

The Germans regarded national and racial purity as a biological imperative, subordinating the individual person to the eugenic ideal of the perfect Aryan man. Humanistic, Western ideals were rejected in this new biological order. Thinkers like Ernst Haeckl made repeated assaults on the traditional values of the Judeo-Christian ethic. Haeckl argued that infanticide should not be regarded as murder, but rather as "a practice of advantage both to the infants destroyed and to the community."[8] He advocated the establishment of a commission which would determine questions of life or death; careful cost-benefit analyses were made to justify such new measures.

Supporting the evolving program of mercy-killing were many of the top medical minds of Germany. Germain Grisez in his book *Abortion: the Myths, the Realities, and the Arguments* declares that "this murderous project was not initiated by Nazi officials but by the medical profession itself; in fact no law ever gave it formal sanction. . . . The vast majority of the participants in the affair were no less sane and no less upright than the members of any modern nation's medical profession."[9]

Several physicians openly refused to participate and were never punished, belying the claim that the doctors who did participate acted under compulsion.[10] Wertham writes: "From its very inception the euthanasia program was guided in all important matters, including concrete details, by psychiatrists

. . . No mental patients were ever killed without psychiatrists being involved."[11] The remarkable part of the story and the most important for the future of violence, and I believe of mankind, Wertham says, was the identity of the killers: "They were not non-entities or outsiders. Most of them had all the hallmarks of civic and scientific respectability. They were not Nazi puppets but had made their careers and reputations as psychiatrists long before Hitler came to power. . . . Most of the names read like a roster of prominent psychiatrists. . . . They are still quoted in international psychiatric literature."[12]

It was the ideas of these men, filtering down through their profession and through the public at large, that sparked the holocaust directed not at the Jews or Slavs, but at Aryan Germans who happened to be blind, or insane, or retarded.

The application of this utilitarian medical philosophy was grim. Two hundred and fifty thousand (250,000)[13] innocent men, women, and children were killed in what was described in the aseptic, conscience-dulling euphemisms of the medical community, "mercy-deaths," "mercy-killings," "help for the dying," or "destruction of life devoid of value." In 1939 Germany had 300,000 mental patients; in 1946 only 40,000 could be accounted for.[14] Children were killed in pediatric hospitals and psychiatric institutions. In the beginning only severely retarded or deformed children were killed, but later children with "badly modeled ears," "bed wetters" and those who were simply "difficult to train" were killed.[15] Many infants were killed by the injection of iodine which caused them to die in convulsions; others were simply allowed to starve to death. Many patients were killed who were merely aged and infirm. Wertham tells of psychiatrists and nurses watching as mental patients are gassed to death, gasping for breath, their faces contorted with fear.[16] Relatives were routinely informed of death by natural causes. Inexorably the list of those deemed "useless" grew.

The government had tried actively to prepare the public for the acceptance of euthanasia. Ironically, the Nazis offered the idea of sterilization and euthanasia as acts of kindness and mercy. Dr. Guett refers to a "mistaken sense of charity" which leads people to "commit acts of ruthless cruelty" against those "being racially inferior or suffering from an incurable disease" by not killing them.[17] The propaganda movie "I Accuse" coincided with the secret implementation of the mercy-killing program. It depicts a woman suffering from sclerosis who is killed by her husband who then repeats all the arguments for euthanasia at his trial. But occasionally these attempts backfired. A Nazi intelligence report notes one viewer's prophetic comments that: "In this film, the same thing happens as in the asylums where they are finishing off all the lunatics right now. What guarantee have we got that no abuses creep in?"[18]

The Bishop of Limburg wrote a moving account of the hospital at Hadamar were thousands of patients were killed. The incoming vans were well known to the inhabitants of the town, as was the smoke rising from the chimneys. In a 1941 letter the Bishop describes the scene: "You hear old folks say, 'Don't send me to a state hospital!' After the feeble-minded have been finished off, the next useless eaters whose turn will come are the old people."[19] Instinctively these people recognized the pattern of enlargement, the ever growing circle of those classified under the fatal rubric, "worthless."

Dr. Braune, a German Protestant minister, called for the immediate cessation of the program which, he said, "strikes sharply at the moral fiber of the nation as a whole. The inviolability of human life is a pillar of every social order."[20] In August, 1941, Catholic Bishop Clemens Von Galen bitterly denounced the killing of these "innocents."[21] The resulting public outcry forced the program to go underground at least for a while.

One of the great myths about the "mercy-killings" is that they were commanded by Hitler. But the only relevant Hitler document merely gave restricted authority after "a most critical diagnosis" for patients to "be accorded a mercy death."[22] This authority was far from a direct order for mass killing. The widespread nature of these killings must be attributed to the initiative of the doctors themselves.

Once the utilitarian ethic was established and the Judeo-Christian ethic of respect for the sanctity of human life was subverted, there could be no limit. As Grisez writes, "this same medical profession itself organized and pushed ahead the euthanasia program of the late 1930's which merged into the genocide program of 1941-1945."[23] Wertham writes: "Technical experience first gained with killing psychiatric murders came first."[24]

Dr. Leo Alexander, Chief Counsel at the Nuremburg trials sums up the basic course of the German experience:

> Whatever proportions these crimes finally assumed, it became evident to all who investigated them that they had started from small beginnings. The beginnings at first were merely a subtle shift in emphasis in the basic attitude of the physicians. It started with the acceptance of the attitude, basic in the euthanasia movement, that there is such a thing as life not worthy to be lived. This attitude in its early stages concerned itself merely with the severely and chronically sick. Gradually the sphere of those to be included in this category was enlarged to encompass the socially unproductive, the ideologically unwanted, the racially unwanted, and finally all non-Germans. But it is important to realize that the infinitely small wedged-in lever from which this entire trend of mind received its impetus was the attitude toward the nonrehabilitable sick.[25]

What emerges as the horrifying reality is the ready acceptance and routineness of the procedures. Our preconceptions are rudely shattered. We were prepared to encounter the iron fist of authoritarian Fascism, but not the calculating, deliberate consensus of the German medical community. Our confident assertion, "It can't happen here; after all, *we* aren't Nazis," crumbles when we see how little fanaticism there was, and how respectable, how familiar the participants and the causes were. It is always terrifying to encounter the devil and to find in his face a vague but definite resemblance to your own. Michael

LaChat has written, "No one has to believe in a Nazi racist revival or resort to mud-slinging 'ad hominem' arguments to demonstrate parallels with modern utilitarian thought."[26]

Already, thirty years after the fall of Nazi Germany, new definitions of what constitutes humanity and the right-to-life have been presented with the natural, simultaneous recurrence of the idea of lives "devoid of value." Joseph Fletcher, an Episcopalian clergyman and a leading exponent of "situation ethics," has drawn up a list of criteria by which "humanhood" ought to be judged. To be human, or rather to be regarded as such by Fletcher, one must have a "self-awareness, self-control, a sense of time, of futurity and of the past, concern for others, control of existence, curiosity, changeability, and creativity, a balance of rationality and feeling, distinctiveness. . . ." In short, Fletcher declares that "mere biological life . . . is without a personal status."[27] Even the euthanasia advocate Daniel Maguire sees the ominous implications in Fletcher's position since "it implies too strongly that fetuses and comatose persons, lacking humanhood in Fletcher's sense of the term, lack a claim to life or are reduced to merely animal or object status."[28]

This arbitrary circumscription of the human family is accompanied by an even more serious and profound development quite similar to what happened in Germany in the 1920's and 1930's. The traditional Western ethic of the sanctity and inviolability of human life is rapidly yielding before a new ethic of medicine in the areas of abortion and euthanasia. Fletcher rejects the restrictions on killing in the Hippocratic Oath saying, "There is no reason to take that unknown moralist's understanding of right and wrong, or good and evil, as permanent models of conscience for all times."[29] Fletcher's brand of situation ethics rejects the absolute prohibition against killing the innocent because "what is right or good does not transcend changing circumstances, it arises out of them."[30]

Avoiding any of the popular attempts at obfuscating the issue, *California Medicine, the Journal of the California Medical Association,*[31] clearly outlines this attack on the traditional ethic. In the September, 1970, issue it reviews the Western ethic which "has always placed great emphasis on the intrinsic and equal value of every human life regardless of its stage or condition." But noting the "human population explosion which tends to proceed uncontrolled" and the burden this puts upon our resources, *California Medicine* declares that the "quality of life" must supersede the older sanctity of life. Following the utilitarian logic of its position, the journal observes that in order to preserve this "quality of life" attainable with our new technology, "hard choices will have to be made." The journal says bluntly: "This will of necessity violate and ultimately destroy the traditional Western ethic with all that this portends." Relative values must replace absolute values "on such things as human life." It concedes that "this is quite distinctly at variance with the Judeo-Christian ethic and carries serious philosophical, social, economic, and political implications for world society." It acknowledges that already the acceptance of abortion has taken place in "defiance of the long held Western ethic."

Just how vague and ominous these relative values are, *California Medicine* makes clear: "The criteria upon which these relative values are to be based will depend upon whatever concept of the quality of life or living is developed." This argument becomes almost indistinguishable from the German argument: "This may be expected to reflect the extent that quality of life is considered to be a function of personal fulfillment; of individual responsibility for the common welfare, the preservation of the environment, the betterment of the species. . . ." Having stated this blatantly utilitarian, eugenic doctrine, it proceeds, "and whether or not, or to what extent, these responsibilities are to be exercised on a compulsory or voluntary basis." Already, in this country we have a respected medical journal writing seriously of the possibility of *compulsory* eugenic measures (including abortion and euthanasia) taken "for the betterment of the species."

Drawing the inevitable link, *California Medicine* sees the further development of birth control and birth selection to death control and death selection, "whether by the individual or by society." The article ends with an admonition to "examine this new ethic, recognizing it for what it is, and will mean for human society, and prepare to apply it in a rational development for the fulfillment and betterment of mankind in what is almost certain to be a biologically oriented world society."

The fundamental question remains what new ethic will arise out of the ruins of he destroyed ethical consensus which has held us together for centuries?

The criteria for humanity, originally propounded with regard to fetuses and comatose persons, has been logically extended to exclude newborn infants. Millard S. Everett in his book *Ideals of Life* envisions a time when "no child shall be admitted into this society who would have any social handicap, for example, any physical or mental defect that would prevent marriage or would make others tolerate his company only from a sense of mercy. . . . Only normal life shall be accepted."[32] The British jurist Glanville Williams explicitly advocates infanticide. As Grisez says, "On utilitarian grounds, he . . . proposes a tolerant and permissive view of the killing of defective infants."[33] He observes that Williams "does not see any basis for an indispensable legal principle protecting the right of life of those who cannot protect themselves—of those not useful to society."[34]

Joining with Fletcher in restricting those who qualify as human is sociologist Ashley Montagu. He denies the humanity of the unborn child, claims that the unborn "do not really become functionally humans until humanized in the human socializing process."[35] Clearly, this criterion of personality leads to infanticide as well as abortion. It further opens the door to justifying the elimination of any group not regarded by the decision makers as "functionally human." Under Montagu's criteria, according to Grisez, Helen Keller "surely ought to have been exterminated."[36]

The slogan "no unwanted child" rapidly becomes "no unwanted person." If one can commit medical homicide at the beginning of life (abortion), Fletcher suggests rhetorically, why not also at the end (euthanasia)?[37]

Employing the economic cost-benefit perspective, Fletcher

further supports killing a patient when factors such as cost "combine to outweigh the benefits of keeping him alive."[38] Echoing the German analysis, Fletcher says: "Sooner or later we shall be forced back on 'statistical morality,' " and stresses grimly the necessity of keeping hospital beds vacant and available.[39] He also proposes the establishment of "death boards" to deal with the question of life and death [40] (a proposal that prompted one physician to remark, when asked about mercy-killing, "Not unless I am on the committee").

Fletcher has nothing but contempt for fears of a "Nazi-type misuse of euthanasia" which he regards as the "reactionary fear of innovation and enhanced powers of control because they can be used for evil as well as for good."[41] He would have ridiculed the fears of the elderly Germans who watched the smoke rise from the death factory of Hadamar and, indeed, every fear of granting absolute power over life and death to an unaccountable authority. How can we help but fear when men like Fletcher dispense with the notion of intrinsic right and wrong? Where will they draw the line when they deny the existence of any firm line? It must be borne in mind, moreover, that a mistake with regard to a "mercy action" is by its very nature never reversible, never correctable.

What has already happened is frightening enough. The United States Supreme Court, in legalizing abortion in the nine months of pregnancy, adopted the "quality of life" criterion with its concept of "meaningful life." As Dr. Marx points out, the decision is of critical importance in that the court's "vague and open-ended definition" of what constitutes a person, "supplies the constitutional precedent for dehumanizing other segments of humanity by defining their lives as meaningless or incomplete."[42]

Many qualified observers see the same signposts in the United States in the 1970's as were present in Nazi Germany forty years ago. And well they might. Nobel prize winner Dr. James D. Watson has proposed that legal status be withheld from infants until three days after birth in order to allow for killing deformed or retarded children.[43] Presumably defects which take longer to diagnose would receive a further extension, some perhaps indefinitely. For Dr. Robert H. Williams this presents no problem, at least during the first year of a child's existence. He writes, "Only near the end of the first year of age does a child demonstrate intellectual development, speaking ability, and other attributes that differentiate him significantly from other species."[44]

In 1971, the nation was shocked when it became known that a mongoloid baby at Johns Hopkins Hospital was deliberately allowed to starve to death, taking fifteen days to die.[45] More recently, in Mesa, Arizona, the parents of an infant with meningitis allowed it to starve for nine days before it died.[46] No legal action was taken in either case. Such chilling events led Patrick Cardinal O'Boyle of Washington to predict: "Infanticide will be proposed for hard cases, but eventually any case will be accepted as hard enough."[47]

Even more gruesome are accounts of modern, refined techniques of experimentation on living fetuses. A new chemical, Prostin F2 Alpha, induces abortions which leave the baby alive and intact following the procedure, and thus has made experiments possible that were not even imagined by the Nazis. While the fetus's heart is still beating doctors dissect the infant, removing the brain, lungs, liver, and other organs suitable for further experimentation.[48] Babies that are still moving are packed in ice for shipment to experimental laboratories. Scientists use children destined to be killed by abortion to test the effects of potentially harmful drugs.[49]

These new scientific methods merely put a more efficient and sophisticated facade on the experimentation that took place in German psychiatric hospitals (which were, incidentally, extensively involved in experimenting on human brains extracted from their victims) and the concentration camps.[50] The Vice-President and General Manager of Upjohn Corporation, which produces such new drugs as F2 Alpha, recently said with a somewhat weak historical perspective and a somewhat startling degree of cold-bloodedness: "For the first time, the medical profession is involved in the inhibition of life, and here we look to the most effective and convenient means. . . . "[51] The wheel it seems, at least with regard to human experimentation, has come full circle.

In 1969 a bill was introduced in the Florida legislature stipulating that "life shall not be prolonged beyond the point of meaningful existence" however "meaningful existence" might be defined. Under the terms of the bill, relatives could authorize the killing of a patient, or in the case of a patient without relatives three doctors could sign the death warrant. The author of the bill, Dr. Walter Sackett, has gone so far as to propose that 90% of the patients in Florida hospitals for the mentally retarded be allowed to die. Again he uses the utilitarian economic argument that "five billion dollars could be saved in the next half century if the state's mongoloids" were permitted to die.[52]

Echoing the German eugenic position, a scientist of the eminence of Dr. Philips Handler, president of the U.S. National Academy of Science, expresses concern over "the dreadful prospect of serious damage to the human gene pool."[53] Another, like Dr. Y. Edward Hsia, a Yale geneticist, favors compulsory abortion for unborn babies ascertained to be deformed.[54] Dr. H. Tristram Engelhardt, of the University of Texas, has even developed the idea of "wrongful life" in which a person may be legally liable for committing a tort or injury against another by *not* killing them, by keeping them alive.[55] This is a concept which, if it is accepted, will exert great pressure on all of us to become "mercy-killers."

In addition, the killing of the aged could be expedited by the adoption of a proposal made in New Zealand that up to $3,750 be paid by the government to dependents of anyone who dies before the age of 65.[56]

These are the experts, the doctors. But, as Dr. Rene Dubos observed in *Reason Awake:* "A society that blindly accepts the decision of experts is a sick society on its way to death."[57]

Bernard Haring, author of the book *Medical Ethics*, asks perceptively if the "discussion on positive euthanasia unmasks the horrifying situation of a humanity that has lost its understanding of life and death?" He declares that the doctors "are unquestionably marked by that attitude which led Hitler to distinguish between 'fit' and 'unfit' life."[58]

The implication of situation ethics and utilitarianism for the sanctity of human life are of the utmost importance. Its chief proponents refuse to acknowledge the inherent danger in any system which rejects the notion of intrinsically right or wrong actions, and in which right and wrong are determined only by the situation or the consequences. In their view, temporal, material happiness constitutes the highest good; pain and suffering the worst evils, to be avoided at any cost. A principle is established in which the individual good is subordinated to the good of society. Thus, all human rights are seen to be granted not by nature but conditionally by the community, as expressed through the State, And, of course, any right which the State gives, including the right to life, it can also take away. No value, not even that of human life can be of much weight when the ultimate good is seen to be the "greatest good for the greatest number," however that might be defined in the utilitarian philosophy. What the ramifications of such a philosophy would be can only be darkly surmised. The logical progression of the present attack on the intrinsic value of human life has not yet reached its conclusion in this country. But if we will only learn from history, we have a very good idea where it will go.

It is hardly forgivable naivete to assume that we can limit the scope of the so-called "mercy-killers" by means of our normal sensibilities and instinctive humaneness when the very basis of just that morality has been shattered, when the demands of Christian mercy and the right to life are replaced by a new and, as yet, hazily defined ethic.

As Bishop Cahal Daly has said, "The end is contained in the beginning."[59] We must recognize that the first time we knowingly kill an innocent person for reasons of expediency (including that catch-all, "the public good") we are beginning a process whose pattern we have already established, but whose end we cannot control. Unless we recognize where we are going, and unless we heed the warnings of the German experience, it will be only a matter of time before the Western ethic, with its respect for the value and equality of human life, ceases to be a living reality and is consigned to the archaic curiosities of history. And then, in W.B. Yeats' words:

What rough beast, its hour come round at last,
Slouches toward Bethlehem to be born?

Notes

1. Marx, O.S.B., Rev. Paul, *Death Without Dignity: Killing For Mercy,* For Life, Inc., Minneapolis, Minn., 1975, p. 29.

2. Wertham, Frederic, *A Sign for Cain,* Warner Paperback Library, New York, N.Y., 1969, p. 159.

3. Marx, p. 29.

4. Guett, Dr. Arthur, "Population Policy," in *Germany Speaks,* ed. by Joachim von Ribbentrop, Thornton Butterworth Ltd., London, 1938, p. 53.

5. Grunberger, Richard, *The 12-Year Reich: A Social History of Nazi Germany: 1933-1945,* Holt, Rinehart and Winston, New York., N.Y., 1971, p. 225.

6. Wertham, *op. cit.,* p. 159.

7. LaChat, Michael, "Utilitarian Reasoning in NAZI Medical Policy: Some Preliminary Investigations," *Linacre Quarterly,* vol. 42, no. 1, February, 1975, p. 19.

8. LaChat, *op. cit.,* p. 18.

9. Grisez, Germain, *Abortion: the Myths, the Realities, and the Arguments,* Corpus Books, New York, N.Y., 1972, p. 203.

10. Grunberger, *op cit.*, p. 313; Wertham, *op. cit.*, p. 161.

11. Wertham, *op. cit.*, pp. 160, 163.

12. Wertham, *op. cit.*, p. 167.

13. Wertham, *op. cit.*, pp. 155, *Nuremburg Documents*, vol. I, p. 247.

14. Wertham, *Ibid.*

15. Wertham, *op. cit.*, p. 175.

16. Wertham, *op. cit.*, p. 176.

17. Guett, *op. cit.*, p. 57.

18. Grunberger, *op. cit.*, p. 385.

19. *Nuremburg Documents*, vol. V, pp. 363-64.

20. LaChat, *op. cit.*, p. 25.

21. Grunberger, *op. cit.*, p. 451.

22. *Nuremburg Documents*, vol. IV, p. 55; Wertham, *op. cit.*, p. 162.

23. Grisez, *op. cit.*, p. 203.

24. Wertham, *op. cit.*, p. 177.

25. LaChat, *op. cit.*, p. 30.

26. LaChat, *op. cit.*, p. 29.

27. Maguire, Daniel, "Death Legal and Illegal," *Atlantic*, vol. 233, February, 1974, p. 81.

28. Maguire, *Ibid.*

29. Fletcher, Joseph, "Elective Death," in *Ethical Issues in Medicine*, E. Fuller Torrey, ed., Little, Brown, and Company, Boston, 1968, p. 142.

30. Fletcher, *Ibid.*

31. *California Medicine*, vol. 113, no. 3, September, 1970, pp. 67-68. (All subsequent references to *California Medicine* are to this editorial.

32. Maguire, Daniel, "Death by Chance, Death by Choice," *Atlantic*, vol. 233, January, 1974.

33. Grisez, *op. cit.*, pp. 222-23.

34. Grisez, *op. cit.*, p. 420.

35. Grisez, *op. cit.*, p. 277.

36. Grisez, *op. cit.*, p. 278.

37. Grisez, *op. cit.*, p. 280.

38. Fletcher, *op. cit.*, p. 147.

39. Fletcher, *op. cit.*, p. 150.

40. Fletcher, *op. cit.*, p. 154.

41. Fletcher, Joseph, "Voluntary Euthanasia: The New Shape of Death," *Medical Counterpoint*, vol. 2, no. 6, June, 1970, p. 21.

42. Marx, *op. cit.*, p. 3.

43. Marx, *Ibid.*

44. Williams, Dr. Robert H., "Our Roll in the Generation, Modification, and Termination of Life," August, 1969, quoted in Marx, *op. cit.*, p. 22.

45. Maguire, *op. cit.*, p. 60.

46. Teletype AP Bulletin, Mesa, Arizona, 1975.

47. Marx, *op. cit.*, p. 13.

48. Anderson, Joan, "New Upjohn Drug Delivers Perfect Fetus for Laboratory Use," *Our Sunday Visitor*, April 13, 1975, p. 6.

49. Anderson, *Ibid.*

50. Wertham, *op. cit.*, p. 176.

51. Anderson, *Ibid.*

52. Marx, *op. cit.*, pp. 17-18.

53. Marx, *op. cit.*, p. 30.

54. Marx, *Ibid.*

55. Engelhardt, Tristram, "Euthanasia and Children, the Injury of Continued Existence," *Journal of Pediatrics*, vol. 83, July, 1973, pp. 170f.

56. Marx, *op. cit.*, p. 23.

57. Marx, *op. cit.*, p. 31-32.

58. Haring, Bernard, *Medical Ethics*, Fides, Notre Dame, Indiana, 1973, p. 150.

59. Marx, *op. cit.*, p. 28.

TWELVE

Abortion to Euthanasia: A Slippery Slope

Malcolm Muggeridge

WE HAVE NOW HAD LEGALIZED abortion in England for some three years, and it is a terrible thought that during those three years more than one million babies have been murdered. In other words, there have been more deaths, as a result of our Abortion Act, than in the First World War. I was brought up to believe that one of the great troubles of the Western World was that in the First World War we lost the flower of our population. Well, now we have destroyed an equivalent number of lives, in the name of humane principles, before they were even born. I'm not going to go over the arguments in this controversy—they have been endlessly repeated, and you all know them, at least as well as I do. I'm not going to rake over all that because I don't think it will serve any useful purpose in an assembly of this kind. But what I do want to say to you is this: that though in worldly terms the battle has been lost, and abortion is now legalized throughout Europe, and in the Western Hemisphere, it still remains the most important issue confronting us, and that nothing can take away from the importance of that issue. The fact is that government after government has surrendered on it,

Malcolm Muggeridge is an author, critic, and TV personality of international renown. This article is adapted from his address in Ottawa, Canada, and reprinted from the Fall, 1977, issue of *The Human Life Review*.

not, notice, in response to pressure from public opinion, but out of a weird kind of inertia or fatalism which seems to be inculcated by the media, as though somehow or other this is an inevitable step. Though that's happened, and though all over the Western World this dreadful slaughter of the innocents is taking place, and though, speaking for England and I imagine other countries, gynecologists cannot in fact become consultants unless they are prepared to perform abortions—despite all that, the issue remains a *live* issue, and it is of *highest* importance that gatherings like this should take place and that protests such as we propose to make *should* be made. Also, that the *contrary* proposition of the *sacredness* of the process whereby new beings come into this world should constantly and by every possible means find expression. It's interesting in this connection, and something that I find rather wonderful and hopeful, that, strangely enough in India, a country which we refer to as "underdeveloped" or "backward," and talk a lot of nonsense about a population explosion there—that in India even the ramshackle machinery of Parliamentary democracy operated in *defense* of the right of people not to be sterilized—which was happening to them, and happening, sometimes, by force. Yes, the Indian people, in our terms an illiterate people, rose up and voted, and the issue on which they voted was this very one—that God has given us the stupendous gift of *creativity*, which we must reverence and cherish. When you are as old as I am, the most beautiful thing in the world is your grandchildren. As your life comes to an end, so you see new lives beginning. And those new lives bear in their faces, in their words, in their bearing, hints of the beginning of it all, which was your marriage, your children. This is the most beautiful thing that life has; this is the most *solacing* thing that life has, when you get to the end of your days, as I'm getting to the end of my days. All the rest seems a lot of worthless rubbish. But *that* is a real thing, as these Indian women who had been *pressurized* by every sort of means, including physical force, recognized in the way they cast their votes. Why, at one point they were actually offered in return for agreeing to be sterilized—what?—a transistor set! Imagine, an allegedly advanced civilization reaches the point of sending out to an ancient one transistor sets to be the reward for giving up the most vital and beautiful creativity that's in us. That's black humor for you, and I can't help envying the future Gibbon who will have the great satisfaction of describing it. Well, I won't go on about all that. But I would say that, looking round the world today, it saddens me beyond words to note in countries like Italy, where Catholicism has been such a strong force, that now there is legalized abortion; that in France, where the medical profession, especially the Catholic doctors, put up such a magnificent fight against it—that there, too, there is legalized abortion. However, every cloud has a silver lining; I heard the other day that on the present basis of population and abortion and contraception, Sweden, in 100 years' time, will have no population. There will just be nobody there at all. That prospect at least is a tiny compensation for what we all have had to endure.

I have spoken and written about the work of Mother Teresa, which of course is something that I hold very dear, and which has, through my first accidental acquaintance with it, and with her, so enormously enriched my own life. She, as it seems to me, though a simple nun with her sisters, represents most magnificently the mighty *contrary* force to what is going on in these so-called civilized Western countries. Those of you who saw the TV program called "Something Beautiful for God"—which is Mother Teresa's description of what she is seeking to do—will remember, I'm sure, a shot of her holding a baby girl so tiny, that it seemed extraordinary that she could go on living at all. And I say to Mother Teresa in the film: "Are you *sure*, Mother, that the tremendous efforts you and the sisters make in this economically desolate country, to keep these little creatures alive are really worth while?" Some of them brought in, as this baby was, from dustbins. For answer she holds up the baby—such a tiny little creature—and says: "Look, there's *life* in her!" Now *that* to me is the picture we should all keep in our minds when we are deluged with statistics and arguments and propositions about this question—the picture of Mother Teresa holding up a tiny little creature that had been thrown away into a dustbin, and saying with such exultation: "Look, there's *life* in her!" When I contrast that with, as I gather has happened, some sort of humanist presentation to Dr. Morgentaler of an award as the humanitarian of the year, I feel delighted beyond words, unspeakably joyful and grateful to be on Mother Teresa's side.

Of course, it would be quite wrong to think that the offensive which is being mounted on our Christian way of life will stop at abortion, and already there are the rumblings of a new, strong push in the direction of euthanasia. I have absolutely no doubt that this will be the next great controversy that will arise. The fact is that because it's so costly in money and personnel to keep alive people about whom the medical opinion is that their lives are worthless, the temptation to get rid of the burden by killing them off will be even greater. And thus disposing of them will of course be dressed up in humanitarian terms as an act of humanity and compassion. Almost all the evil things that have been done in the world in the last decades have been done in the name of justice, equality, compassion, etc. There's a wonderful saying of Dr. Johnson—that wise and good man—that I like very much: "Why," he asks, "is it that we hear the loudest yelps for liberty among the drivers of slaves?" And this is of course true: it is in the name of humanitarianism that these terrible proposals are made. There would, I feel sure, have been an intensive pressure for euthanasia before now had it not been for one circumstance—that the only government so far in the history of the *world* to put a euthanasia law into effect is the government of the Nazis. *No* other government in the *whole* of recorded history has ever actually *enacted* a euthanasia law. But the Nazis did. And to a considerable extent the German medical profession cooperated with them. The law, I should add, was widely applied throughout the Reich. I happened a few years ago to be visiting a Lutheran settlement for sick and deranged people at Bethel near Bielefeld in West Germany. And there they told me all about how this monstrous piece of legislation had been enforced. They, in common with all such institutions, were asked to produce particulars of the patients that they had in their care. And they refused to do this, because they knew quite well that it would be a prelude to getting rid of a lot of them. So, in due course they were visited by an official who wanted to know why they hadn't sent the required particulars, explaining to them that the definition of a person whose life was useless was an inability to communicate. In that case, they said, there was no one in their institution who was in that category. And they proved it, demonstrating that, because their institution was run on the basis of Christian love, *all* the patients in response to love answered with love, and so were able to communicate. Anyway, the long and short of it was, that almost alone in the whole of Germany, their institution escaped the application of the Nazi euthanasia law.

But we shall not be so fortunate when the agitation for legalized euthanasia really gets going in our part of the world. In the first place, it will be argued—which is, alas, true—that in many hospitals in the Western world the lives of patients considered unfit to live are already *being* terminated by the administration of excessive sedation. So, the contention will be that there's no point in retaining a legal prohibition which is already being disregarded. Secondly, the argument will be used that the resources needed for disabled people—not just the old and the senile, but also the Mongols and others who are badly disabled and not fully conscious—can be better employed in other ways. The quality of life, it will be argued, requires that the drastically handicapped should be got rid of. We shall of course resist this, we should all—every single Christian—find such a proposal utterly abhorrent. But I feel certain—and I think everybody should get ready for it—that before long euthanasia will be legalized like abortion, like Family Planning, because all these things are closely related. They're all a slippery slope, one leading inexorably to the other.

I wanted to tell you about a little playlet that some friends of mine devised, because I think it illustrates what I'm talking about better than any kind of argument. The scene is a doctor's consulting-room in Vienna round about 1770. A peasant woman comes in and tells the doctor that she is in her second month of pregnancy; that her husband is an alcoholic and has a syphilitic infection; that one of her children is mentally incapacitated, and that there is a family history of deafness. The doctor listens, and finally agrees that there is a case for her to have her present pregnancy terminated. And so he has to fill in a form. Filling in the form he asks her name, but he can't quite hear when she tells him, so he says: "Please spell it out." And she spells out: "B-E-E-T-H-O-V-E-N." And then the Sixth Symphony strikes up. Now I think that little drama tells what we're concerned with. *How* can we ever know that such a life shouldn't be born? Or, that such a life should be terminated? On what *conceivable* basis can we in our arrogance make such decisions as that? It is out of all relation to the great Christian traditions in which our society was born, and on the basis of which it has grown up, becoming a great civilization. We have a duty in all circumstances, to say that men are not bodies; men have souls. That our narrow, self-interested human values cannot be applied to decide the fitness, or otherwise, of a God-created human being to go on living. That in the womb, when this marvellous process of gestation takes place, a life comes into existence that, like all other lives, is an infinitesimal particle of God's creation. And that that particle of creation contains within itself all the potentialities that exist in every other God-created life. If we *ever* depart from seeing it so, then it is *not just* that we've abandoned our religious faith and that we can no longer participate in the great drama of the Incarnation from which our whole way of life is derived, but we have ceased to deserve to be known as civilized men and women. That is the issue. The attack has been made in terms of this terrible legalized abortion which is upon us. It *will* be followed up, in terms of legalized euthanasia. First, of getting rid of the old and senile, and then of deciding that such and such and such persons don't rate being allowed to go on living. Out of the Christian notion of a human family has come all that is most precious to us. We have to guard it. We have to treasure it. We have to stand up for it, whatever may happen governmentally and administratively. That is our essential duty and our privilege.

I am an old man, and I shall soon be dead. Old men have a strange thing that happens to them. They often wake up in the middle of the night, at two or three o'clock, and they can see between the sheets the battered old carcass that they will soon be leaving, and it seems like a toss-up whether you go back to it to live through another day, or whether you make off. It's a moment, dear friends, of very good perceptiveness, this movement when in a weird sort of way you stand between life here and life in eternity, and you see in the distance, like you see when you're driving, the glow of a city. You see the lights of St. Augustine's City of God. And in that situation, you have some very sharp convictions. One of them is of the sheer beauty of our earth—the beauty of its shapes and its foliage and its animals and its trees and its rocks—*everything,* the incredible beauty of it. Also, of the great beauty of human relationships: between parents and children, between husband and wife, between friends, between sweethearts—all these beautiful human relationships. Of the wonder of human work and human creativity. Of all that human beings have been able to achieve. *But you also see* that all this wonder derives not from *men,* but from the participation of men in a creation which has been provided for them by a Creator. And that therefore, in existing even at the fag-end of a life, existing as this tiny, tiny part of God's creation, you are a participant in God's purposes. And that these purposes are creative, and not destructive. These purposes are loving, and not hating. These purposes are universal and not particular. *Above all*—and this relates so closely to what's drawn us here together today—*above all,* they relate to a *surrender,* an abandonment to God's purpose for men, so that on *that* relationship reposes all that is wonderful in our life. And that whenever we arrogantly, or seemingly with good intentions but still with the dreadful conceit of scientists, think to intervene *ourselves,* shape our genes, rearrange our genes as we want them, make sure that all the creatures that come into the world are beauty queens and Mensa I.Q.'s; when we seek to do all those things, to eliminate from the world whatever seems to *our* eyes imperfect or askew, that *then* we shut ourselves off from that wonderful light that awaits us. Then we shall relinquish our citizenship of the City of God, which is our precious, unique birthright. That's what I have to say to you, and God bless you all.

THIRTEEN

From Feticide to Infanticide

Joseph R. Stanton, M.D.

IN HIS INTRODUCTION to the book, *Abortion and Social Justice,* George Huntston Williams, the Hollis Professor of Divinity Emeritus at Harvard, quotes from a famous epistle from the second century written to a pagan lawyer, named Diognetus, by an unnamed Christian[1]:

> Christians cannot be distinguished from the rest of the human race by country or language or customs. They do not live in cities of their own; they do not use a peculiar form of speech; they do not follow an eccentric manner of life. Yet, although they live in Greek and barbarian cities alike, as each man's lot has been cast, and follow the customs of the country in clothing and food and other matters of daily living, at the same time they give proof of the remarkable and admittedly extraordinary constitution of their own commonwealth. They live in their own countries, but only as sojourners. They have a share in everything as citizens, and endure everything as aliens. Every foreign land is their fatherland, and yet for them every fatherland is a foreign land. They marry, like everyone else, and they beget children, but they do not cast out their offspring.

Joseph R. Stanton, M.D., a practicing physician, is an associate clinical professor of medicine at Tufts University School of Medicine. This article is adapted from an address in October, 1981, and is reprinted from the Summer, 1982, issue of *The Human Life Review.*

"Among the marks of the Christians within Roman imperial society," Williams writes, "was their abhorrence of the then common practice of casting off offspring by abortion, by exposure, or by selling them into slavery."

Today in America, we are some 120 years away from the rejection of slavery. We are also nine years into the public legalization of abortion on request.

In our nation's capital, and in New York City, more babies are aborted than are allowed to live. In the New York *Times* (October 18, 1981) it is reported that on the lower west side of Manhattan, for every 1,000 births, there were 1,772 abortions.[2] That provides a surfeit of feticide, yet even that does not satisfy the elitist abortion *apparat.* With more than ten million reported abortions now staining our national honor, a new paradox is developing. Increasingly, we can save lower and lower birth-weight *wanted* babies born prematurely, and do this with better and better results.[3] We are witnessing development of marvelous new technology by which curative or ameliorative procedures can be carried out on fetuses *in utero*—on that constitutional non-person—in order to assure that the postnatal life of that individual will be healthier. Our neonatal cape nurseries, with the regionalization of neonatal care, and increasingly sophisticated technology, daily save younger and younger premature babies. This is the positive side of medical care. The paradox to which I draw your earnest attention is that as our technology increases, a dark side of medicine—death as an "option" for afflicted newborns—arises.

Does abortion lead to infanticide? Will infanticide lead to euthanasia? Others have written of the slippery slope—the wedge argument—the camel's nose under the tent; as soon as you justify one, you justify the other. I believe the threat of infanticide, killing by neglect, is part of the evil fruit of the Supreme Court abortion decisions of January 22, 1973. It is expressed like this: "If you can kill before birth a perfectly normal healthy fetus at 20, 22 or 24 weeks by abortion because it is unwanted, why should you protect a defective child at birth?"

Joseph Fletcher[4] writes: "It is reasonable to describe infanticide as post natal abortion. . . . Furthermore, infanticide is passive. An infant cannot put an end to its own life. This makes it 'Allocide' not suicide. Its variables are only 1) with respect to the euthanasiasts' choice of direct or indirect means; and 2) whether it is done within the context of terminal illness or some other adverse state."

John Fletcher (no kin to Joseph) in the *New England Journal of Medicine* asks: "How should physicians and parents now understand their obligation to care for the *defective newborn* in the light of arguments for genetically indicated abortion after amniocentesis?"[5] This Fletcher believes you *can* tolerate the destruction of defective fetuses before birth, but hold the line and defend the right to life of defective newborns after birth.

Dr. Milton Heifetz,[6] speaking of those newborns who could not live without medical care and even with medical care would live only a "sub-human existence," writes: "We must evaluate what can really be termed the salvage value. This factor is vital in our decision making. What kind of child will result? Will life be one continuous form of agony? Will life be meaningful to any degree? What is meaningful and to whom?" Further in the same chapter, he writes: "The newborn is an organism with a potential for human qualities, qualities which are as yet non existent."

He continues: "Is life at birth more significant than at the second, fourth or sixth month of pregnancy? It is not. True, it is closer to gaining the attributes of man, but, as yet, it has only the potential for those qualities. If this difference is true for the normal newborn, how much less significant is it for the newborn who doesn't even have this potential?" You see, in Heifetz' words, the malignant dehumanization of the unwanted newborn child now spreads to the born defective child.

Significantly, in the appendix to Heifetz' book, he lists as "world supporters of euthanasia" the signers of The Humanist Manifesto II. Among the names are the following, which those of you who have followed the abortion battle closely will perhaps recognize.

—Francis Crick of Great Britain, Nobel Laureate (with Dr. James Watson) for the discovery of the structure of D.N.A. Watson wrote of Crick in the A.M.A.'s *Prism* magazine in 1973: "Perhaps, as my colleague Crick has suggested, 'the child should not be declared fully human till three days after birth,'" which would allow the dispatch of genetically flawed children by neglect and non-feeding.

—Edd Doerr, long-time spokesman of Americans United for Separation of Church and State.

—Alan Guttmacher, late President of Planned Parenthood Foundation of America.

—Lawrence Lader, pro-abortion spokesman and original Chairman of the National Association for the Repeal of the Abortion Laws (NARAL).

—Henry Morgentaler, M.D.—the notorious Canadian abortionist and past president of the Humanist Association of Canada.

—Professor B.F. Skinner of Harvard, the "Behaviorist."

—Joseph Fletcher, the "Situation Ethicist" already quoted on infanticide. Fletcher is on the Board of the Right to Die Society, and was a vice president of the foundation-funded, abortion-pushing Association for the Study of Abortion.

—Professor Sol Gordon—guru of sex education.

—Betty Friedan, the founder of the National Organization of Women.

The Humanist Manifesto II endorses 1) a non-Theistic view of man and the universe. God is irrevelant to man and his affairs. "As non-Theists, we begin with humans not God, nature not deity . . . we can discover no divine purpose or providence for the human species; 2) We affirm that moral values derive their source from human experience. Ethics is autonomous and situational needing no theological or ideological sanction." They reject the belief that God is operative in human affairs. "Thou Shalt Not Kill" is also thrown out the window: you may kill "humanely."

The absolute rights recognized in Humanist Manifesto II

include abortion, a right to "death with dignity," euthanasia, and the "right" to suicide![7]

Someone might say here: "What you say is shocking, but surely you overstate? Where is the proof?" How I wish that there were no proof.

The awful fact is that infanticide—the killing of infants—has been in and out of human experience since the dawn of recorded history. Professor Williams cited the power of the father in Roman law to murder his children under the concept *patria potestas* in Roman law. How tragic that the rights of the all-powerful *pater familias* were transferred to the mother in *Roe* and *Doe* as far as the right to life of the unborn child is concerned. In Sparta, frail or defective infants were left exposed to the elements to die. The same practice was followed by Eskimos.[8] Infanticide and child abandonment were common in the industrial revolution in England. In China, the killing of female offspring or their abandonment was widespread as late as the 1800's. The elimination of such barbaric practices has always—up to now—been regarded as evidence of civilization's "advance."

It is ironic that the liberal media today berates anyone who questions the premises of atheistic secular humanism and its handmaiden, the situation ethic, labelling such questioning as an attack on our "pluralistic society." Witness the endless and scathing denunciations of "right to lifers" and the "Moral Majority," "New Right," etc. They wrap them all together, and if you can add the Ku Klux Klan in the next sentence, so much the better. What must be pointed out, however, is that it is the secular humanist view of man, which the media does not attack, that has sustained abortion, sanctions infanticide, and provides the logic and the "ethics" of euthanasia.

It is the first rule of war to know the enemy, and what we are involved in is a war for the soul of America. There has been a profound misperception of what has been essentially an elitist attempt to change a basic view of man which, for almost 200 years, made this nation the last, best hope of peoples everywhere. In America today, the enemy of the unborn child, of the born defective child, and of the aged and impaired human is the non-Theistic secular humanist view of man. We should repeat this day in and day out, and we should recognize it whenever and wherever it appears, regardless of how it may be cloaked or covered. We should determine the attitude toward human life, born and unborn, of everyone who seeks our vote for public office. At the ballot box, in the American way and as an informed electorate, we should make our votes demand restoration and preservation of that view of man, so beautifully crystalized and captured in the basic documents associated with the nation's birth. "We hold these truths to be self-evident that all men are created equal and endowed," not by the courts or the American Medical Association, or the secular humanists, but endowed by the Creator of life (capital "C") with certain and inalienable rights, first among these life *itself*. Only this will reverse the abortion mentality; only this will end feticide and restore protection to the defective newborn now the victim of "humane" killing.

Let us look at the evidence for the reality of infanticide in modern society. You will recall the famous Kennedy Conference report in the early 1970's. It caused widespread discussion at the time. A mongoloid child was born in Johns Hopkins hospital with a duodenal atresia—that is, atrophy of a small segment of the duodenum as it leaves the stomach. No food can get out of the stomach. Untreated, the child will die. Treatment is by what the newspapers called a twenty-minute operation, to short-circuit the obstruction. In the Hopkins case, only because the child had Down's syndrome, the decision was made "not to treat." A sign was placed on the baby's crib: Do Not Feed. The baby lived fifteen long days before it died.

Of the Hopkins case, Joseph Fletcher writes:

The physicians in charge believed that direct euthanasia is wrong, that doing it indirectly, though undesirable, was morally tolerable. Hoping that the newborn would die of dehydration and starvation in three or four days, they wheeled it off into a corner where it lay dying for fifteen days, not three or four. Some form of termination would have been far more merciful as far as the infant, nurses, parents, and some of the physicians were concerned. In that case, indirect was morally worse than direct—if, as I and most of us would contend, the good and the right are determined by human well-being. Indirect euthanasia did no good at all in that case, but lots of evil.[9]

The identical defect has occurred in other Down's syndrome babies in American hospitals, and they too have been allowed to die.

In "The Way We Die,"[10] Dempsey writes as follows:

Doctors don't talk much about infanticide, and, for obvious reasons, hospitals don't specify euthanasia as the cause of death. Thus, no one knows how many deformed, brain-damaged and poor-risk "preemies" who might be coaxed into life are allowed to die, or are chloroformed outright.

When almost everyone was born at home, infanticide was rarer. But the hospital, by its very sterility, gives a curious sanction to such deaths. It speaks for society. When a parent does not want the damaged child, or when a physician decides that the world needs no more monsters, the hospital staff not infrequently omits the usual feeding orders. Starvation is seen as more merciful than outright suffocation. Yet it takes a long time for even a newborn baby to starve.

A few years ago, in a Chicago hospital, such a mongoloid was rejected by its parents; although physicians could have saved his life, parental consent would have been necessary for the operation that would make it possible for him to ingest milk. Instead, the baby was placed in a side room where its cries would not offend others. Nurses, torn by this decision, went in from time to time to hold and rock the infant as they might any normal baby. They did this for the eleven days it took the child to die.

Newborn Siamese twins were recently transferred by court order from Lakeview Hospital in Danville, Illinois, to the Children's Memorial Hospital in Chicago. At birth, the doctor instructed the nurses not to resuscitate them. The babies surprised everyone with the vigor of their fight for life. In the chart was entered the note: "Do not feed in accordance with the parents' wishes."[11] Reporting on a case from England last August, the Chicago *Tribune* headlined an article "Court condemns baby girl to live." Overruling the decision of parents to allow their Down's syndrome daughter to starve to death, Lord Justice Tempelman said: "We are asked to condemn her to life because we cannot be certain we should condemn her to death."[12]

Dr. Anthony Shaw probably fired the opening gun for American acceptance of infanticide-by-neglect in the non-treatment of defective newborns in an article, "Doctor, Do We Have a Choice?" in the New York *Times* Sunday Magazine in 1972.[13] Then, Dr. Shaw and Doctors Duff and Campbell in companion pieces in the *New England Journal of Medicine*[14] (in 1973) put the issue out in the open. *Death,* as an option in the treatment of the newborn. In the New Haven Hospital, of 299 consecutive deaths in the special care nursery, 14%—*forty-three*—were due to withholding or stopping treatment.

Infanticide, the killing of born infants by direct and indirect acts, is presently forbidden by the laws of every one of the fifty states. Wrote Duff and Campbell: "If working out these dilemmas (in defective newborns) such as these we suggest is in violation of the law, we believe the law should be changed."

These are but a few citations from an increasing body of medical reports, books, and symposia in which calls are made to withhold life-saving treatment because a "quality of life" judgment or a social judgment of the worth of a newborn should be the determinant factor.

Listen now to Professor Victor Rosenblum of Northwestern University Law School. Incidentally, Professor Rosenblum has a son Josh, who is retarded. Rosenblum writes:

Modern advocacy of infanticide betrays an hostility toward and fear of the disabled. When the defective newborn is left to die, something vital dies within us all, our sense of justice, our self respect, our mission as human beings. When that child is left to die, we become idolators of the plastic, the cosmetic, the illusory and the elitist. When, on the other hand, we help that child to live we affirm our capacity to love, our respect for human differences, our dedication to the democratic values of heterogeneity as instruments of creative achievement.[15]

In response to the question "How shall we respond to malformed babies?" Jean Rostand, the French biologist, rather prophetically wrote[16]:

Above all, I believe a terrible precedent would be established if we agree that life could be allowed to end because it was not worth preserving, since the notion of biological unworthiness, even if carefully circumscribed at first, would soon become broader and less precise. After first eliminating what was no longer human, the next step would be to eliminate what was not significantly human, and, finally, nothing would be spared except what fitted a certain level of humanity. . . . I would almost measure a society's degree of civilization by the amount of effort and vigilance it imposes on itself out of pure respect for life.

In considering extensions of the mentality that would tolerate infanticide, Rostand writes further:

If eliminating "monsters" became common practice, lesser defects would come to be considered monstrous. There is only one step from suppression of the horrible to suppression of the undesirable. If it became customary to thin out the ranks of people over ninety, those in their eighties would begin to seem very decrepit, and then those in their seventies.

Little by little the collective mentality, the social outlook, would be altered. Any physical or mental impairment would diminish the right to live. Each passing year, each stress, each illness would be felt as an exclusion; the sadness of aging and deteriorating would be combined with a kind of shame at still being there.

Such may become the pressures on the aged and infirm if our toleration of infanticide is not reversed.

Well, the mongoloid or exceptional children are one group of the impaired. What about others without mental impairment? In the United States and in England, as the technology of helping, through reparative surgery, children born with myelomenigocele improves, there is a move to withhold surgery from some of these children in the name of the quality of their lives.

The *Lancet* is the leading British medical journal. An editorial (November 24, 1979) written by "a pediatric surgeon" was titled "Non-Treatment of Defective Newborns."[17]

Early in the editorial, the writer proclaims: "Even with the splendid words of Pope John Paul II, in his sermon in Phoenix Park on the sacredness of human life ringing in our ears, God (I am a Christian) asks us to be merciful. This does not include forcing a half man to eke out a miserable existence when it is in our power to end it." Incredibly, the "half man" he talks about is a newborn paralyzed from the waist down. He then details how a colleague "let slip the information that it takes as least 30 cc. of intravenous air to produce fatal embolus." He calls the newborn only "potential," and states that potential is fulfilled "by the capital of love that parents invest in him after birth."

Who does he propose for subjects of treatment by non-treatment? "Among treatable infants are those with severe spina bifida and hydrocephalus, babies with more severe chromosome disorders, and even straight-forward Down's Syndrome, and babies with rubella syndrome."

What is this new treatment? "I offer the baby careful and loving nursing, water sufficient to satisfy thirst, and increasing doses of sedative." The sedative is chloral hydrate. What happens with this treatment? Babies starve to death, or become so weak and sedated they die of dehydration.

At a well-publicized pediatric and ethical conference in 1974 at Sonoma Valley in California, 17 of the 20 participants felt there were circumstances that would validate direct intervention to kill a dying infant.[18]

Now listen to Dr. Jerome Lejeune, the discoverer of the genetic defect Trisomy 21, or Down's syndrome, responding[19] to the *Lancet* proposal for destroying the defective:

In your introduction to an unsigned paper on Non-treatment of Defective Newborn Babies (Nov. 24, p. 1123) you state that "the editorial view was that the balance of benefit lay in anonymity." Balance of benefit to whom? To the anonymous children's physician nursing to death babies with Trisomy 21 and mourning them so tactfully thereafter? Or to a hospital in which such a mortuary facility is replacing a treatment ward? Or to you, Sir, indulging yourself in an anti-medicine scoop without revealing its source? Or to all three, because infanticide is still a criminal offence in civilized countries?

The whole history of medicine is at hand to answer any unknown death-doctor. Those who delivered humanity from plague and rabies were not those who burned the plague-stricken alive in their houses or suffocated rabid patients between two mattresses. Health by death is a desperate mockery of medicine.

Victory against Down's syndrome—i.e., curing children of the ill-effect of their genic overdose—may not be too far off, if only the disease is attacked, not the babies. The length of the road to be covered before such an achievement cannot be predicted, but at least wounded parents have the right to know that life-doctors still exist and that we will never give up.

The propaganda for infanticide is coming under the aegis of "quality of life" and cost control. We should not really be surprised. Eleven years ago, a frank editorial in a major American medical journal said we would reach this point. The only real surprise is that we have reached it so quickly. The editorial was titled "A New Ethic for Medicine and Society." It speaks of medicine's changing role in society "as the problems of birth control and birth selection are extended inevitably to death selections and death control whether by the individual or by society."[20]

Feticide and infanticide, and the poison of the situation ethic, have already badly corrupted the professions of law and medicine both here and in England. It is very doubtful that corrective actions will come from the elites of either profession, that is, from the *official* organizations of law or medicine.

The protection of the unborn child and the born defective child lies then in the hearts, the consciences, and the dedication and action of "ordinary" people like us. We must sound the call to action, to perseverance—a call for rededication to those noble impulses of the human spirit that initially impelled us to join the fight against abortion. John Donne (in 1631) wrote these famous lines:

No man is an island, entire of itself; every man is a piece of the continent, a part of the main; if a clod be washed away by the sea, Europe is the less, as well as if a promontory were, as well as if a manor of thy friends or thy own were. Every man's death diminishes me, because I am involved in mankind; and therefore never send to know for whom the bell tolls; it tolls for thee.

Whenever an innocent human life ends, whether it be in the suction trap of an abortion clinic owned and operated by Planned Parenthood, or in a pediatric ward of a university hospital, where a decision is made "not to treat"—to sedate and starve to death a defenseless, defective newborn—each time and every time the bell tolls.

May we never grow insensitive to its pealing, and may the

Author of life strengthen the efforts to bear witness to an unchanging value, to defend, to serve, and to love these, the least of our brethren.

Notes

1. Hilgers and Horan, *Abortion and Social Justice* (Sheed & Ward, 1973).

2. The New York *Times* Sunday Magazine, October 18, 1981, p. 62.

3. "The Smallest Patients," *Medical World News,* September 14, 1981, pp. 28-36.

4. Joseph Fletcher, "Infanticide and the Ethics of Loving Concern," in *Infanticide and the Value of Life,* ed. Kohl (Prometheus Books, 1978).

5. John Fletcher, Ph.D., "Abortion, Euthanasia and Care of Defective Newborns," *New England Journal of Medicine,* Vol. 292, 1975, pp. 75-78.

6. Milton D. Heifetz, M.D., and Charles Mangel, *The Right to Die* (New York: G.P. Putnam's Sons, 1975).

7. Humanist Manifesto I and II (Prometheus Books, 1973), pp. 16-17, 18-19.

8. P.J. Resnick, "Murder of the Newborn: A Psychiatric Review of Neonaticide," *American Journal of Psychiatry,* April 1970, pp. 58-64.

9. Joseph Fletcher, *Humanhood: Essays in Biomedical Ethics* (Prometheus Books, 1979), p. 142.

10. David Dempsey, *The Way We Die* (Macmillan, 1975), pp. 102-103.

11. A.M.A. *News,* October 9, 1981.

12. The Chicago *Tribune,* August 8, 1981, Section 3, p. 17.

13. Anthony Shaw, M.D., "Doctor, Do We Have a Choice?", the New York *Times,* January 30, 1972.

14. (a) Anthony Shaw, M.D., "Dilemmas of Informed Consent in Children," *New England Journal of Medicine,* Vol. 289, 1973, pp. 885-890. (b) Raymond S. Duff, M.D., and A.G.M. Campbell, M.D., "Moral and Ethical Dilemmas in the Special Care Nursery," *New England Journal of Medicine,* Vol. 289, 1973, pp. 890-894.

15. Victor Rosenblum, *Infanticide and the Handicapped Person* (Brigham Young University Press, In Press).

16. J. Rostand, *Humanly Possible* (Saturday Review Press, 1973), pp. 89-92.

17. *Lancet,* November 24, 1979, pp. 1123-1124.

18. A.R. Jonsen et al., "Critical Issues in Newborn Intensive Care," *Pediatrics* 55, 1975, p. 756.

19. Jerome Lejeune, Letter to Editor, *Lancet,* January 5, 1980, p. 49.

20. "A New Ethic for Medicine and Society," *California Medicine,* Vol. 113, No. 3, September 1970, pp. 67-68.

FOURTEEN

The Murder Case of Dr. Waddill

Michael Novak

IT IS NO HELP to live on illusions. Which is why the small minority of Americans in favor of unrestricted abortion is in deep political and moral trouble. Public revulsion is growing— and the murder trial of Dr. William B. Waddill in Orange County, California, shows why.

On March 2, 1977, it is alleged, Dr. Waddill tried to abort the infant of an eighteen-year-old girl. His saline solution failed to cause the internal destruction and skin damage it was supposed to, and the infant survived. A nurse found the two-and-one-half pound infant breathing, moving, and making weak cries, and took it to the nursery stubbornly alive.

When Dr. Waddill was so informed, he is reported to have told the hospital staff "not to do a goddam thing. Just leave the baby the hell alone." When he arrived at the hospital, according to testimony, Dr. Waddill asked to be alone with the baby. However, a pediatrician, Dr. Ronald J. Cornelsen, came to the nursery where, he later testified, he saw Dr. Waddill make four separate attempts to strangle the baby. Dr. Waddill complained aloud: "I can't find the goddam trachea [windpipe]," and

---

Michael Novak is a nationally syndicated columnist and the author of many books. This column originally appeared on April 1, 1978.

according to testimony pressed so hard that the baby's head snapped up into a "v" position.

Still failing at his task, Dr. Waddill, according to testimony, spoke of injecting potassium chloride, or filling a bucket with water to drown the tiny girl. Dr. Cornelsen persuaded him that an autopsy would find him out. Only after days of anguish did Dr. Cornelsen report his colleague.

The Supreme Court decision of 1973 permits abortion on demand. This child was between 29 and 31 weeks along in gestation—a good seven months. At the murder trial, Dr. Waddill's lawyers have complained that what was legal in the womb is, oddly, being charged as murder outside the womb. This doesn't, they say, make sense.

In addition to the murder charge, Dr. Waddill is being sued by the dead infant's mother for $17 million because she had no opportunity, she claims, for informed consent. She had not been told, she says, that she could give birth to a live baby.

Informed consent is the pillar of free choice. Surely, those who are "pro-choice" are in favor of informed consent. The requirement of informed consent is at the heart of the ordinance recently passed in Akron, Ohio.

More and more feminists are becoming appalled at the realities of abortion. Like the U.S. military describing air raids on Vietnam, pro-abortionists have tried to use a sanitized, euphemistic language to hide what actually happens in abortion. Like the few early protesters against that war, "Feminists for Life" and other activists are beginning to make the realities known. They are awakening the nation's conscience.

"Women Exploited" is one such feminist group. Leader Sandra Haun testified before the Pennsylvania legislature: "The members of our organization have all had an abortion and have come to realize, too late, that our decision was wrong. We were encouraged and pushed into a hasty decision that now we find impossible to live with. We were lied to and deliberately misinformed."

The campaign for abortion has up until now depended on ignorance and euphemism—and also on the passion to do away cheaply with the poor before they become expensive. Like the hawks on Vietnam, this well-financed and lavish campaign benefited by having the establishment behind it. Gradually, from the grass roots, the citizenry is being aroused; the establishment is wavering. When the reality finally gets pictured on television—as the war was—the tide will shift with even more force than it already has.

It is an illusion to believe that resistance to abortion is based on religion. It is, in fact, based upon biology, nature, and common sense. All one has to do is look with one's eyes upon what is being aborted. It is not a "mass of cells." It is a living organism, with every appearance of a child. It resists its own death. It struggles. Granted its own fundamental rights, it will live, grow, and be born—not by faith but by nature itself.

This issue will not die. Not all the taxpayers' millions of Planned Parenthood can long cover up reality. Take this issue to the people. Let the people choose, ye advocates of pro-choice.

FIFTEEN

The Killing Will Not Stop

George F. Will

THE BABY WAS BORN in Bloomington, Ind., the sort of academic community where medical facilities are more apt to be excellent than moral judgments are. Like one of every 700 or so babies, this one had Down's syndrome, a genetic defect involving varying degrees of retardation and, sometimes, serious physical defects.

The baby needed serious but feasible surgery to enable food to reach its stomach. The parents refused the surgery, and presumably refused to yield custody to any of the couples eager to become the baby's guardians. The parents chose to starve their baby to death.

Their lawyer concocted an Orwellian euphemism for this refusal of potentially lifesaving treatment—"Treatment to do nothing." It is an old story: language must be mutilated when a perfumed rationalization of an act is incompatible with a straightforward description of the act.

Indiana courts, accommodating the law to the *Zeitgeist,* refused to order surgery, and thus sanctioned the homicide. Common sense and common usage require use of the word "homicide." The law usually encompasses homicides by negligence. The Indiana killing was worse. It was the result of

George F. Will is a nationally syndicated columnist. This *Washington Post* syndicated column originally appeared on April 22, 1982.

premeditated, aggressive, tenacious action, in the hospital and in courts.

Such homicides can no longer be considered aberrations, or culturally incongruous. They are part of a social program to serve the convenience of adults by authorizing adults to destroy inconvenient young life. The parents' legal arguments, conducted in private, reportedly emphasized—what else?—"freedom of choice." The freedom to choose to kill inconvenient life is being extended, precisely as predicted, beyond fetal life to categories of inconvenient infants, such as Down's syndrome babies. There is no reason—none—to doubt that if the baby had not had Down's syndrome the operation would have been ordered without hesitation, almost certainly, by the parents, if not by them, by the courts. Therefore the baby was killed because it was retarded. I defy the parents and their medical and legal accomplices to explain why, by the principles affirmed in this case, parents do not have a right to kill by calculated neglect any Down's syndrome child—regardless of any medical need—or any other baby that parents decide would be inconvenient.

Indeed, the parents' lawyer implied as much when, justifying the starvation, he emphasized that even if successful the surgery would not have corrected the retardation. That is, the Down's syndrome was sufficient reason for starving the baby. But the broader message of this case is that being an unwanted baby is a capital offense.

In 1973 the Supreme Court created a virtually unrestrictable right to kill fetuses. Critics of the ruling were alarmed because the court failed to dispatch the burden of saying why the fetus, which unquestionably is alive, is not protectable life. Critics were alarmed also because the court, having incoherently emphasized "viability," offered no intelligible, let alone serious, reason why birth should be the point at which discretionary killing stops. Critics feared what the Indiana homicide demonstrates: the killing will not stop.

The values and passions, as well as the logic of some portions of the "abortion rights" movement, have always pointed beyond abortion, toward something like the Indiana outcome, which affirms a broader right to kill. Some people have used the silly argument that it is impossible to know when life begins. (The serious argument is about when a "person" protectable by law should be said to exist.) So what could be done about the awkward fact that a newborn, even a retarded newborn, is so incontestably alive?

The trick is to argue that the lives of certain kinds of newborns, like the lives of fetuses, are not sufficiently "meaningful"—a word that figured in the 1973 ruling—to merit any protection that inconveniences an adult's freedom of choice.

The Indiana parents consulted with doctors about the "treatment" they chose. But this was not at any point, in any sense, a medical decision. Such homicides in hospitals are common and will become more so now that a state's courts have given them an imprimatur. There should be interesting litigation now that Indiana courts—whether they understand this or not—are going to decide which categories of newborns (besides Down's syndrome children) can be killed by mandatory neglect.

Hours after the baby died, the parents' lawyer was on the "CBS Morning News" praising his clients' "courage." He said, "The easiest thing would have been to defer, let somebody else make that decision." Oh? Someone had to deliberate about whether or not to starve the baby? When did it become natural, even necessary, in Indiana for parents to sit around debating whether to love or starve their newborns?

The lawyer said it was a "no-win situation" because "there would have been horrific trauma—trauma to the child who would never have enjoyed a—a quality of life of—of any sort, trauma to the family, trauma to society." In this "no-win" situation, the parents won: the county was prevented from ordering surgery; prospective adopters were frustrated; the baby is dead. Furthermore, how is society traumatized whenever a Down's syndrome baby is not killed? It was, I believe,

George Orwell who warned that insincerity is the enemy of sensible language.

Someone should counsel the counselor to stop babbling about Down's syndrome children not having "any sort" of quality of life. The task of convincing communities to provide services and human sympathy for the retarded is difficult enough without incoherent lawyers laying down the law about whose life does and whose does not have "meaning."

The *Washington Post* headlined its report: "The Demise of 'Infant Doe'" (the name used in court). "Demise," indeed. That suggests an event unplanned, even perhaps unexplained. ("The Demise of Abraham Lincoln"?) The Post's story began: "An Indiana couple, backed by the state's highest court and the family doctor, allowed their severely retarded newborn baby to die last Thursday night. . . ."

But "severely retarded" is a misjudgment (also appearing in *The New York Times*) that is both a cause and an effect of cases like the one in Indiana. There is no way of knowing, and no reason to believe, that the baby would have been "severely retarded." A small fraction of Down's syndrome children are severely retarded. The degree of retardation cannot be known at birth. Furthermore, such children are dramatically responsive to infant stimulation and other early interventions. But, like other children, they need to eat.

When a commentator has a direct personal interest in an issue, it behooves him to say so. Some of my best friends are Down's syndrome citizens. (Citizens is what Down's syndrome children are if they avoid being homicide victims in hospitals.)

Jonathan Will, 10, fourth-grader and Orioles fan (and the best Wiffle-ball hitter in southern Maryland), has Down's syndrome. He does not "suffer from" (as newspapers are wont to say) Down's syndrome. He suffers from nothing, except anxiety about the Orioles' lousy start.

He is doing nicely, thank you. But he is bound to have quite enough problems dealing with society—receiving rights, let alone empathy. He can do without people like Infant Doe's parents, and courts like Indiana's asserting by their actions the principle that people like him are less than fully human. On the evidence, Down's syndrome citizens have little to learn about being human from the people responsible for the death of Infant Doe.

Part Nine

The Testimony of Personal Experience

It is not easy to describe the feelings that accompany abortion. In this section, a mother, a father, a nurse, and one who might have been aborted speak out.

SIXTEEN

"There Just Wasn't Room in Our Lives Now for Another Baby"

Jane Doe

WE WERE SITTING IN A BAR on Lexington Avenue when I told my husband I was pregnant. It is not a memory I like to dwell on. Instead of champagne and hope which had heralded the impending births of our first, second and third child, the news of this one was greeted with shocked silence and Scotch. "Jesus," my husband kept saying to himself, stirring the ice cubes around and around. "Oh, Jesus."

Oh, how we tried to rationalize it that night as the starting time for the movie came and went. My husband talked about his plans for a career change in the next year, to stem the staleness that fourteen years with the same investment-banking firm had brought him. A new baby would preclude that option.

The timing wasn't right for me either. Having juggled pregnancies and child-care with what freelance jobs I could fit in between feedings, I had just taken on a full-time job. A new baby would put me right back in the nursery just when our youngest child was finally school age. It was time for *us*, we tried

Jane Doe is the pseudonym of the author, who "works in publishing," according to *The New York Times,* in which this article first appeared. Copyright © 1976 by The New York Times Company.

to rationalize. There just wasn't room in our lives now for another baby. We both agreed. And agreed. And agreed.

How very considerate they are at the Women's Services, known formally as the Center for Reproductive and Sexual Health. Yes, indeed, I could have an abortion that very Saturday morning and be out in time to drive to the country that afternoon. Bring a first morning urine specimen, a sanitary belt and napkins, a money order or $125 cash—and a friend.

My friend turned out to be my husband, standing awkwardly and ill at ease as men always do in places that are exclusively for women, as I checked in at 9 A.M. Other men hovered around just as anxiously, knowing they had to be there, wishing they weren't. No one spoke to each other. When I would be cycled out of there four hours later, the same men would be slumped in their same seats, locked downcast in their cells of embarrassment.

The Saturday morning women's group was more dispirited than the men in the waiting room. There were around 15 of us, a mixture of races, ages and backgrounds. Three didn't speak English at all and a fourth, a pregnant Puerto Rican girl around 18, translated for them.

There were six black women, and a hodgepodge of whites, among them a tee-shirted teenager who kept leaving the room to throw up and a puzzled middle-aged woman from Queens with three grown children.

"What form of birth control were you using?" the volunteer asked each one of us. The answer was inevitably "none." She then went on to describe the various forms of birth control available at the clinic, and offered them to each of us.

The youngest Puerto Rican girl was asked through the interpreter which she'd like to use: the loop, diaphragm or pill. She shook her head "no" three times. "You don't want to come back here again, do you?" the volunteer pressed. The girl's head was so low her chin rested on her breastbone, "Si," she whispered.

We had been there two hours by that time, filling out endless forms, giving blood and urine, receiving lectures. But unlike any other group of women I've been in, we didn't talk. Our common denominator, the one which usually floods across language and economic barriers into familiarity, today was one of shame. We were losing life that day, not giving it.

The group kept getting cut back to smaller, more workable units, and finally I was put in a small waiting room with just two other women. We changed into paper bathrobes and paper slippers and we rustled whenever we moved. One of the women in my room was shivering and an aide brought her a blanket.

"What's the matter?" the aide asked her. "I'm scared," the woman said. "How much will it hurt?" The aide smiled. "Oh, nothing worse than a couple of bad cramps," she said. "This afternoon you'll be dancing a jig."

I began to panic. Suddenly the rhetoric, the abortion marches I'd walked in, the telegrams sent to Albany to counteract the Friends of the Fetus, the Zero Population Growth buttons I'd worn, peeled away, and I was all alone with my microscopic baby. There were just the two of us there and soon, because it was more convenient for me and my husband, there would be one again.

How could it be that I, who am so neurotic about life that I step over bugs rather than on them, who spends hours planting flowers and vegetables in the spring even though we rent out the house and never see them, who makes sure the children are vaccinated and inoculated and filled with Vitamin C, could so arbitrarily decide that this life shouldn't be?

"It's not a life," my husband had argued, more to convince himself than me. "It's a bunch of cells smaller than my fingernail."

But any woman who has had children knows that certain feeling in her taut, swollen breasts, and the slight but constant ache in her uterus that signals the arrival of a life. Though I would march myself into blisters for a woman's right to exercise the option of motherhood, I discovered there in the waiting room that I was not the modern woman I thought I was.

When my name was called, my body felt so heavy the nurse had to help me into the examining room. I waited for my husband to burst through the door and yell "stop," but of course he didn't. I concentrated on three black spots in the acoustic ceiling until they grew in size to the shape of saucers, while the doctor swabbed my insides with antiseptic.

"You're going to feel a burning sensation now," he said, injecting Novocain into the neck of the womb. The pain was swift and severe and I twisted to get away from him. He was hurting my baby, I reasoned, and the black saucers quivered in the air. "Stop," I cried. "Please stop." He shook his head, busy with his equipment. "It's too late to stop now," he said. "It'll just take a few more seconds."

What good sports we women are. And how obedient. Physically the pain passed even before the hum of the machine signaled that the vacuuming of my uterus was completed, my baby sucked up like ashes after a cocktail party. Ten minutes start to finish. And I was back on the arm of the nurse.

There were twelve beds in the recovery room. Each one had a gaily flowered draw sheet and a soft green or blue thermal blanket. It was all very feminine. Lying on these beds for an hour or more were the shocked victims of their sex life, their full wombs now stripped clean, their futures less encumbered.

It was very quiet in that room. The only voice was that of the nurse, locating the new women who had just come in so she could monitor their blood pressure, and checking out the recovered women who were free to leave.

Juice was being passed about and I found myself sipping a Dixie cup of Hawaiian Punch. An older woman with tightly curled bleached hair was getting up from the next bed. "That was no goddamn snap," she said, resting before putting on her miniskirt and high white boots. Other women came and went, some walking out as dazed as they had entered, others with a bounce that signaled they were going right back to Bloomingdale's.

Finally then, it was time for me to leave. I checked out, making an appointment to return in two weeks for an IUD insertion. My husband was slumped in the waiting room, clutching a single yellow rose wrapped in a wet paper towel and stuffed into a baggie.

We didn't talk the whole way home, but just held hands very tightly. At home there were more yellow roses and a tray in bed for me and the children's curiosity to divert.

It had certainly been a successful operation. I didn't bleed at all for two days just as they had predicted, and then I bled only moderately for another four days. Within a week my breasts had subsided and the tenderness vanished, and my body felt mine again instead of the eggshell it becomes when it's protecting someone else.

My husband and I are back to planning our summer vacation and his career switch.

And it certainly does make more sense not to be having a baby right now—we say that to each other all the time. But I have this ghost now. A very little ghost that only appears when I'm seeing something beautiful, like the full moon on the ocean last weekend. And the baby waves at me. And I wave at the baby. "Of course, we have room," I cry to the ghost. "Of course, we do."

SEVENTEEN

He (or She) Would Be 23 . . .

Bill Stout

DOCTORS AND THEOLOGIANS are usually the only men who argue the abortion issue. Mostly, it's a women's debate. On one side: "We have the right to control our own bodies," and on the other: "It's a human life and killing it is wrong." That sort of thing.

But I had a jolt recently that set me thinking seriously, *personally,* about abortion for the first time in more than 20 years. I suspect it was a shock that has hit a great many men, although few ever talk about it.

It came late on a Friday afternoon, at the start of a long holiday weekend. The freeways were jammed, of course, and when I started out for a business meeting on the far side of Los Angeles, the radio was full of "sigalerts." Since there was plenty of time, it seemed logical to skip the freeway mess and loaf across the city on the side streets. Easy enough, until even that oozing pace of traffic squeezed to a dead stop because of an accident at the corner of Beverly and Vermont. There my eye caught the window of a second floor office, and it hit me like a knee in the groin.

Bill Stout was for many years a nationally known CBS network correspondent. He currently does TV commentary for station KNXT in Los Angeles. A somewhat shortened (and revised) version of this article appeared in the *Los Angeles Times* on February 16, 1976. This article is reprinted from the Summer, 1976, issue of *The Human Life Review*.

That office, in a building I hadn't even noticed in many years, was where I had taken my new bride for an abortion one blistering summer day in 1952. Suddenly I remembered . . . and I relived every detail.

We had been married two years and did not consider ourselves poor, but we were close. We had an old car, a few dollars in the bank, and I had a temporary job writing news stories for radio announcers. And she was pregnant.

We had argued for more than a week after her first cautious announcement. I had adopted her young son by a previous marriage, but this would be our first baby together, and I was delighted. Minutes later I was appalled, then infuriated, by her insistence she would not go through with it. Even more hurtful, I suppose, in the callowness of that encounter so long ago, was that she had talked with several women friends before telling me anything. She already had the name of the doctor and was ready to make an appointment when I would be off from work to drive her to and from.

There was a lot of shouting and pleading that week and a good deal of pumping up (by me) of my prospects at the radio station. She pointed out that those were prospects only. She noted the sickly condition of our bankbook, plus the fact that we had 12 payments to go on our first television set. She also made the point hammered home today by the women's pro-abortion groups: it was, after all, *her* body, and the *decision* should be hers and hers alone.

That was the most painful week of our marriage, until the final anguish (of divorce) many years later. Of course, she got her way. I dropped her at the curb outside the doctor's office, then pulled around the corner to park and wait. It would be forty-five minutes, she said, no more than an hour at most. She had $200 in cash in her bag. No checks were accepted.

I spent the time multiplying and dividing. How much did this doctor *make* per hour? Per minute? How many of these jobs could he do in a day? Or in a year? Did he take just a two-week vacation so he could hurry back to the women with so many different reasons for ending pregnancies?

I remember his name. I can see the sign in his office window as clearly as if it were there now, just a few feet away. Seven letters, four in the first name; below them, centered on a separate line, "M.D." I never saw the man but I hated him then, and do to this moment, even though he died long ago.

When I saw her come out of his office, pale and wincing with each step, I leaped out of the car and ran to her. A couple of days later she was moving around with her usual energy and she made it clear that it was all over, with nothing to talk about. A year and a half later, with everything going fine for me in my work, she gave birth to our first baby, a normal healthy boy, and not long after that there came a daughter.

Yet, again and again, I have found myself wondering what that first one would have been like. A boy or a girl? Blonde or brunette? A problem or a delight? Whatever kind of person the lost one might have been, I feel even now that we had no right to take its life. Religion has nothing to do with that feeling. It was a "gut" response that overwhelmed me while stalled in the traffic that afternoon at Beverly and Vermont.

Now we were moving again. A few minutes later I was at my meeting in the Civic Center, in the office of an old friend, luckily, because by then I was in tears and they wouldn't stop. It wasn't easy but I finally told him how that glance at an office window had simply been too much for me, sweeping away a dam that had held for more than 20 years.

If I am still wondering about that first one that never was, what about other men? How many of them share my haunted feelings about children who might have been? Why are we, the fathers who never were, so reluctant to talk about such feelings? And if it can be so painful for the men, how much worse must it be for the women who nurture and then give up the very fact of life itself?

Clearly, as the saying goes about wars and generals, abortion is far too important to be left to a woman and her doctor.

EIGHTEEN

Abortion: A Nurse's View

Mary Roe

I WAS FOR ABORTION. I thought it was a woman's right to
terminate a pregnancy she did not want. Now I'm not so
sure. I am a student nurse nearing the end of my OB-GYN
rotation at a major metropolitan hospital and teaching center. It
wasn't until I saw what abortion involves that I changed my
mind. After the first week in the abortion clinic several people in
my clinical group were shaky about their previously positive
feelings about abortion. This new attitude resulted from our
actually seeing a Prostaglandins abortion, one similar in nature
to the widely used Saline abortion.

What the medical professionals proudly feel is an advancement in gynecological medicine—the Prostaglandins-induced
abortion—is actually, I now believe, a biochemical murder. It is
a natural body substance being used to produce what is an
unnatural body action: an abortion. Prostaglandins is a fatty
acid present in many body tissues and affects the contractability
of smooth muscles, especially useful in stimulating the muscles
of the uterus. It is now being used in some medical centers to
bring on labor post 16 weeks of conception and up to 20 weeks.
These second-trimester abortions are induced by Prostaglandins by I.V., vaginal suppositories or most often by intra-

Mary Roe is the pseudonym of a young student nurse in a large
metropolitan hospital. This article was sent originally as a letter to the
editor of *The Human Life Review*, and originally appeared in the Summer,
1976, issue of that journal.

amniotic deliverance of Prostaglandins. Actual labor is induced and the average abortion time is anywhere from 6 to 20 hours but can be longer. The pains are strong rhythmic contractions (just like the labor pains a woman has prior to the birth of a child). The fundus, the firm height of the uterus during pregnancy, moves under the nurse's hand. The fetus is moving too.

The placenta, the biological separation between maternal and fetal systems, is jarred by the passage of pain medications. The strong analgesics quickly pass through the maternal blood stream and into the fetal system to be absorbed there at a many-times-greater potency. Further assault. Ironically, it is an obstetrician who carefully advises against the use of even aspirin during pregnancy, for the child's sake, but who now orders the dose of Demerol or Valium for the woman in the pains of abortion.

The fetus continues to move, harshly pushed down the birth canal by the strong muscle contractions of the uterine myometrium caused by Prostaglandins. The woman remains in bed, unattended much of the time. It is a long wait. Hours pass. Vital signs and the progress of labor are checked by the nurse at intervals. This nurse is one who is generally used to dealing with the advent of life, not death. She has at one time reassured a tired woman in labor that the tedious process will bring on the birth of a child, not a "termination of unwanted pregnancy"; an unnamed fetus.

Finally the violent contractions and the Prostaglandins have done their job. The fetus is expelled wet, reddened, mucous covered and warm. Limbs are flexed. The head and chin are bent into the chest. The slit-like eyes are closed innocently. It is a miniature human being, being awakened from a sleep too soon by a woman who was given the choice to interrupt her pregnancy.

The umbilical cord is cut. The fetus is taken away and the woman waits to expel the placenta. In an hour or two the entire process is over. She sleeps and then is discharged if there are no complications. She goes home. But I wonder if she realizes just how much she has left behind.

By that time in gestation chromosomes are laid out—distinctive markers of heredity. Crossing over of the genes assures that this fetus would have been unlike any other human being: alone, special, and unique. Had it lived.

Although still in the experimental stage, this method is being used for termination of pregnancies of 16 weeks and over. I used to find rationales. The fetus isn't real. Abdomens aren't really very swollen. It isn't "alive." No more excuses. By 16 weeks the fetus is well formed. By 20 weeks the face, eyelids, nose and mouth are formed. Organs are well defined. The heart and circulatory system has been laid down and I have heard a fetal heart beat at 20 weeks (a pregnant friend tells me she heard her baby's heartbeat at 10 weeks) with the Doppler Machine—fast and bounding. Hair begins to appear on the head. The arms and limbs are formed. Sex of the fetus is evident. This is what is expelled from the uterus into a hospital bed or bedpan to be wrapped up quickly and carried to pathology and disposed of.

I am a member of the health profession and members of my class are now ambivalent about abortion. Whereas before I was firm on my stand for abortion, I now know a great deal more about what is involved in this issue. Women should perceive fully what abortion is; how destructive an act it is both to themselves and to the unborn child. Whatever psychological coping mechanisms are employed during the process, the sight of a fetus in a hospital pan remains the final statement.

I've lost the steadiness in my voice when I discuss abortion. I find it difficult to say the word. That firm conviction, "a woman's right," is gone. There is a time to live and a time to die but I feel that there is a far greater authority to decide that time than a woman or her doctor.

NINETEEN

On Being Alive

Sondra Diamond

I HAVE BEEN PHYSICALLY DISABLED since birth as a result of brain damage. My disability is called Cerebral Palsy. Many people believe that Cerebral Palsy is synonymous with mental retardation. However, this is not true. When I was born my parents were told that I would never be able to speak, hear, or do anything that other children could do. It was suggested that I be put away in an institution. My parents, however, felt that I had as much potential as their two older children.

In the November 12th, 1973, issue of *Newsweek* magazine in the Medicine section, there appeared an article titled "Shall This Child Die?" It was about the work of Doctors Raymond S. Duff and A.G.M. Campbell at the Yale-New Haven Hospital of Yale University. The article reported that these doctors were permitting babies born with birth defects to die by deliberately withholding vital medical treatments. The doctors were convincing the parents of these children that they would be a financial burden; that they had "Little or no hope of achieving meaningful 'humanhood.'" The doctors recognized that they were breaking the law by doing away with these "vegetables," as they choose to call these children, but they felt that the

Sondra Diamond is a professional counselor now in private practice; she has written and lectured widely on the problems of the disabled. This article originally appeared in the Fall, 1977, issue of *The Human Life Review*.

law should be changed to make it legal to let these children die.

I was incensed by this article in *Newsweek*, although I was glad that the subject finally was coming above ground. For I had been aware of this practice for many years.

Feeling that I had to do something about this article, I wrote a Letter to the Editor of *Newsweek* magazine. It was published in the December 3rd, 1973, issue, as follows:

> I'll wager my entire root system and as much fertilizer as it would take to fill Yale University that you have never received a letter from a vegetable before this one, but, much as I resent the term, I must confess that I fit the description of a "vegetable" as defined in the article "Shall This Child Die?" (MEDICINE, Nov. 12).
>
> Due to severe brain damage incurred at birth, I am unable to dress myself, toilet myself, or write; my secretary is typing this letter. Many thousands of dollars had to be spent on my rehabilitation and education in order for me to reach my present professional status as a Counseling Psychologist. My parents were also told, 35 years ago, that there was "little or no hope of achieving meaningful 'humanhood'" for their daughter. Have I reached "humanhood"? Compared with Doctors Duff and Campbell I believe I have surpassed it!
>
> Instead of changing the law to make it legal to weed out us "vegetables," let us change the laws so that we may receive quality medical care, education, and freedom to live as full and productive lives as our potentials allow.

The physically disabled in our society have historically been second class citizens. And, as such, they have been subject to the same indignities that other minority groups have had to endure. Some 10% of the population of the United States is physically disabled. And that figure is merely an estimate, for these are the people who are on record in hospitals, agencies, and the like.

For most able-bodied people, willingness to contemplate the problems of the physically disabled is tempered by the fact that they have a set of notions and feelings about people different from themselves, whether they be a different race, nationality, sex—or the physically disabled. I am, of course, especially interested in the feelings about the physically disabled. These feelings can not be ignored; they must be faced head-on. One tends to examine his feelings about the disabled in terms of his own fears, self-doubts, and his own self-concepts about his own body image. It is too easy to project how you think *you* might feel if you were physically disabled. Being disabled is not the same as thinking about what it would be like if you were disabled. Being disabled is not intrinsically a burden. It only becomes so when society makes it difficult to function as a normal person. Technology allows the disabled to move about and function freely. It is only when society says *stop* that a physical disability becomes a handicap. In view of the fact that society sees a physical disability as a burden, it is, for many, a natural assumption that the physically disabled would be better off dead. I cannot agree with such a solution.

Perhaps we should take a closer look at how I feel about being disabled. What *is* it like to be disabled? It's happy, it's sad, it's exciting, it's frustrating, it's probably just like being non-disabled. You worry what will become of you when your parents are no longer around to help you with your special needs. You want to go places and do things just like everyone else. You have the same sexual drives, the same hopes and dreams for marriage and a family, the same aspirations for a successful life.

Being disabled is also a puzzling experience because people don't react to you the way *you* feel inside. People look at you and assume that you are retarded or incompetent or a pitiful sight. But you don't feel retarded, incompetent, or pitiful.

The right to life issue affects the disabled in three principal ways: first, there is negative euthanasia which is practiced on newborn infants who are born with physical disabilities and abnormalities. When a child is born with a disability, many members of the medical profession do not administer the necessary supportive medical services. It is argued that the child will be physically disabled the rest of its life anyway. If this were to be done to a child who would not grow up to be disabled, the courts would intervene. There have been many cases where the parents, for reasons such as religion, have not wanted their newborn infant to receive medical care. Court orders have been obtained by the physicians so that they could perform the necessary procedures.

Second, euthanasia affects the physically disabled when we are hospitalized for medical problems other than other disabilities. To give you a personal example: in 1962 I was severely burned over 60% of my body by 3rd-degree burns. When I was taken to the hospital the doctors felt that there was no point in treating me because I was disabled anyway and could not lead a normal life. They wanted to let me die. My parents, after a great deal of arguing, convinced the doctors that I was a junior in college and had been leading a normal life. However, they had to bring in pictures of me swimming and playing the piano. The Doctors were not totally convinced that this was the best procedure—grafting skin and giving me medication as they would with other patients—but my parents insisted that I be ministered to. Mine was not an unusual case. To take the time and effort to expend medical expertise on a person who is physically disabled seems futile to many members of the medical profession. Their handiwork will come to nought, they think.

The third way euthanasia affects the physically disabled is when a person in adulthood becomes disabled. There are two parts to this problem. First, should that person be treated and rehabilitated if he is not going to lead a normal life? Second, what if that person asks to die? If you have never been disabled you are not aware of the many options in life. Therapeutic rehabilitation techniques, self-help devices, and prosthetic and assistive equipment make the lives of the disabled very functional. It takes a great deal of time to discover these things. First the medical problem must be overcome and this is up to the medical profession. It is only after the critical period of illness that a rehabilitation team can take over. If a person who knows that he will be disabled for the rest of his life asks to die, it sounds like an attractive option to his family: Why should he have to suffer? Intensive psychological counseling is needed to show the individual who will be physically disabled (and his family) that life holds a great deal of potential. We cannot deny that there will be problems, but one can enjoy a full and happy life even though physically disabled. I would not give up one moment of life in which I could have another cup of coffee, another cigarette, or another interaction with someone I love.

Many people ask me about the person who is so severely disabled that he or she can only lie in bed. Shouldn't he be allowed to die? they ask me. We cannot know what is going on in that person's head—especially if he cannot communicate with us through speech. Perhaps he is enjoying the sensual experience of lying on cool sheets, or the pleasure of good food, or being held by another human being.

A friend of mine is unable to move as a result of severe arthritis which struck him in adulthood. He cannot see. He can only speak. He is the Editor of a newspaper for disabled people and conducts a very busy telephone life by means of special equipment. Believe me, he inspires many people. My friend is leading a full life and is one of the happiest people I know. Should we put him to death because he can't move the way other people do?

We have posed the problem of euthanasia and its effects on the physically disabled. What can be done to alleviate this problem?

First of all, as I said, you must face your feelings about the physically disabled—the negative ones as well as the positive ones. For you are human beings and must not think "I shouldn't feel this way." In the abstract it is easier to fight against abortion, infanticide, and euthanasia if we know that these children will grow up to be whole human beings. Physical attractiveness has become very important in our society. What I am asking you to do is fight abortion, infanticide, and euthanasia on behalf of people who will be, or are, physically disabled. You can not begin to do this until you throw away your prejudices and preconceived notions about the life of a physically disabled person.

I have concentrated here on the obvious ways euthanasia threatens the disabled, because those dangers are of course most obvious to me. I know that, for most people, the right to life issue means primarily saving the lives of the unborn from abortion. But there is a least common denominator: life itself. It is the right of the disabled to appreciate the gift of life, to celebrate it *for* itself. Thus I think we can help you. I know we *want* to help you, every bit as much as we want you to help us.

Part Ten

On a Human Life Amendment

Almost everyone in the prolife movement
agrees that a constitutional amendment is
necessary to grant full legal protection to the
unborn. It will take time and a considerable
degree of political organization to secure an
amendment. A constitutional amendment
must be passed by a two-thirds majority of
the Congress and approved by three-quarters
of the state legislatures.

In 1981, the National Right to Life
Committee drafted a proposed Human Life
Amendment. Nearly every prolife organization in the country agrees that an amendment of this type is necessary. The Human
Life Amendment, also known as "the unity
amendment," will not be adopted soon.
Most prolife activists believe that other legislation must precede it. The language of this
amendment may well change as prolife legislative activity continues. Nevertheless, the
Human Life Amendment represents the best
current thinking about what it will take to
give permanent legal protection to all human

including their unborn offspring at every stage of their biological development including fertilization.

Section 3. No unborn person shall be deprived of life by any person: Provided, however, that nothing in this article shall prohibit a law allowing justification to be shown for only those medical procedures required to prevent the death of either the pregnant woman or her unborn offspring as long as such law requires every reasonable effort be made to preserve the life of each.

Section 4. Congress and the several States shall have power to enforce the article by appropriate legislation.

Adopted by the Board, without dissent, this is the first Human Life Amendment unanimously endorsed by NRLC.

I. History of the Human Life Amendment

In January 1974, NRLC endorsed a version of the Human Life Amendment. This amendment was recommended by its Legal Advisory Committee after a year studying and discussing various amendment proposals. Late in 1973 a special drafting sub-committee of legal scholars, under the chairmanship of Martin McKernan, Jr., Esq., of New Jersey, began working on the problem of drafting such an amendment, shortly after the Supreme Court decisions in *Roe v. Wade*, 410 US 113 (1973), and *Doe v. Bolton*, 410 US 179 (1973). In June of 1973, a Legal Advisory Committee was formed by the National Right to Life Committee under the chairmanship of Dennis J. Horan, Esq., of Chicago. This Committee was charged with developing a strong Human Life Amendment which the National Right to Life Committee could propose to Congress and work towards adoption. This Legal Advisory Committee had the assistance and advice of several outstanding legal scholars and lawyers, including Prof. Robert M. Byrn of Fordham University, Prof. David W. Louisell of the University of California at Berkeley, Prof. Victor R. Rosenblum of Northwestern University, Prof. Charles E. Rice of Notre Dame University, Prof. Walter J. Trinkaus of Loyola University at Los Angeles, Robert Green,

Esq., of Kentucky, and Prof. Joseph Witherspoon of the University of Texas, the latter two having been consultants to the Committee. In their work, the Committee carefully studied the leading proposals for a Human Life Amendment then pending in Congress. Eventually the Committee recommended its own version to the National Right to Life Committee Board of Directors. This version, adopted by the National Right to Life Committee in 1974, reads as follows:

NRLC Amendment

Section 1: With respect to the right to life, the word "person," as used in this article and in the fifth and fourteenth articles of amendment to the Constitution of the United States, applies to all human beings, irrespective of age, health, function, or condition of dependency, including their unborn offspring at every stage of their biological development.

Section 2: No unborn person shall be deprived of life by any person: Provided, however, that nothing in this article shall prohibit a law permitting only those medical procedures required to prevent the death of the mother.

Section 3: Congress and the several States shall have the power to enforce this article by appropriate legislation within their respective jurisdictions.

This Amendment has been submitted to the 97th Congress as S. J. RES. 22 by Senator Jake Garn of Utah and as H. J. RES. 139 by Congressman James Oberstar of Minnesota. It has 30 co-sponsors in the Senate and 55 in the House.

In June of 1980, Dr. J.C. Willke of Ohio, newly elected President of the National Right to Life Committee, appointed a committee of lawyers and doctors to reexamine the National Right to Life Committee's recommended version of a Human Life Amendment. Since 1974, several new versions of amendments have been introduced in Congress and considerable scholarly consideration has been given to NRLC's amendment. Dr. Willke felt the time had come for NRLC to reexamine its amendment to insure that it remained the best vehicle to accomplish NRLC's fundamental purpose: to reverse the U.S. Supreme Court decisions in *Roe v. Wade* and *Doe v. Bolton,* their antecedents and progeny, and to restore to unborn children full legal protection to the right to life.

The Committee appointed by Dr. Willke included James Bopp, Jr., Esq., General Counsel for the National Right to Life Committee, as Chairman; Prof. Joseph Witherspoon, University of Texas Law School; Prof. Robert Byrn, University of Fordham Law School; Prof. Charles Rice, University of Notre Dame Law School; and Dr. Matthew Bulfin, President of the American Association of Pro-Life Obstetricians and Gynecologists. The Committee was asked to examine carefully NRLC's prevailing version of the HLA and determine whether or not modifications were required to maximize the legal protection of the unborn.

To assist them in their work, the Committee solicited comments from more than seventy prolife groups and dozens of individual legal and medical scholars. In addition, the Committee invited oral testimony from Nellie Gray, Esq., President of March for Life; Carl Anderson, Legislative Aide for Senator Jesse Helms; Dennis Horan, Esq., Chairman of the American Bar Association's Right-to-Live/Right-to-Die Committee; and Dr. John Masterson, Professor of Obstetrics and Gynecology at Loyola University of Chicago. In addition, many individuals and groups responded to the request of the Committee for comments.

The Committee also sought to form a consensus within the right-to-life movement around one version of a Human Life Amendment. The Committee attempted to narrow the disagreements within the movement and to define those disagreements as clearly as possible.

Specifically, the Committee made several substantial changes in NRLC's version, the most important of which is to provide that the right to life is superior to all the rights granted under the Constitution. The Committee unanimously agreed on Sections 1, 2, and 4 of the Amendment.

Sections 1, 2, and 4 were as follows:

Human Life Amendment

Section 1. The right to life is the paramount and most fundamental right of a person.

Section 2. With respect to the right to life guaranteed to persons by the fifth and fourteenth articles of amendment to the Constitution, the word "person" applies to all human beings, irrespective of age, health, function, or condition of dependency, including their unborn offspring at every stage of their biological development including fertilization.

Section 4. Congress and the several States shall have power to enforce this article by appropriate legislation.

The Committee members, however, were not able to agree on the proper formulation of Section 3. This section was intended to provide two essential elements in the formulation of the Human Life Amendment: the prohibition against private taking of the lives of the unborn and the creation of a basis for a private cause of action to protect unborn children when the State and Federal governments refuse to do so. Section 3, therefore, would reverse the second essential holding of *Roe v. Wade,* that a woman has the right to take the life of her unborn child. The majority of the Committee, consisting of members Bopp, Witherspoon, Byrn, and Bulfin, supported the following Section 3:

Section 3. No unborn person shall be deprived of life by any person: Provided, however, that nothing in this article shall prohibit a law permitting only those medical procedures required to prevent the death of a pregnant woman; but this law must require every reasonable effort be made to preserve the life and health of the unborn person.

A minority of the Committee, consisting of Prof. Rice, supported the following language:

Section 3: The right to life of an unborn person is protected by the Constitution against infringement by any person.

During subsequent months, considerable comment was received by NRLC on the HLA Committee's work. In addition, many state and local right-to-life groups conducted in-depth studies of the recommendations. On September 11 and 12, the National Right to Life Educational Trust Fund conducted a major seminar, cosponsored by St. Louis University, to professionally examine proposals for a human life amendment. Finally, on Oct. 4, the Board of Directors formally considered the Committee's recommendation. The Board of Directors appointed a committee to determine if the difference of opinion on Section 3 could be resolved. As a result of their work, the committee recommended a revised version of Section 3 which was unanimously adopted by the Board. The language of this revised Section 3 can be found at the beginning of this article.

II. The Holdings of Roe v. Wade

In *Roe v. Wade,* the Supreme Court first declared that one of the "liberties" constitutionally protected against state infringement by the Fourteenth Amendment is the right of privacy which "encompasses a woman's decision whether or not to terminate her pregnancy." Finding this to be a "fundamental" constitutional right, the Court declared that state laws infringing upon this right cannot be sustained unless they are necessary to effectuate a compelling state interest.

Having clarified the standard of judicial review, the Court then proceeded to determine whether the states had a "compelling" state interest to support abortion restrictions. The first possible compelling state interest it considered was that the unborn were "persons" and that states had a compelling interest in protecting their lives. The Court rejected that argument, concluding that the unborn are not "persons." In reaching this conclusion, Justice Blackman, who wrote the opinion for the Court, (1) analyzed the text of the Constitution and the usage of the word "person" therein, (2) referred to the history of less restrictive abortion practices throughout the major portion of the nineteenth century (when the Fourteenth Amendment was enacted), and (3) noted that the Court's conclusion that the unborn are not constitutional "persons" was in accord with the results reached by state courts and lower federal courts that had addressed the issue.

The Court went on to consider whether there were any other potentially "compelling" state interests that would justify criminal abortion prohibitions. The Court examined two primary arguments: (1) that the state's interest in protecting maternal health is a compelling justification for abortion restrictions, and (2) that, even if the unborn are not persons, they are at least human beings and the state interest in protecting the life of human beings is compelling. The Court concluded that the interest in human life was not compelling throughout pregnancy, only after "viability."

There are, therefore, two distinct holdings in the Court's 1973 decisions: (1) a woman's right to privacy included her decision on whether or not to terminate her pregnancy, and (2) the state's interest in unborn life is not sufficiently compelling to permit regulation of abortion before viability (or afterwards if needed for maternal "health"). The holding, which resulted in abortion on demand, found a constitutional right of privacy for the woman under which was protected the right to abort. Without it, states could still protect unborn life since it is a legitimate state interest even under *Roe v. Wade,* albeit not a compelling one.

III. Objectives of NRLC's Human Life Amendment

The goal of the amendment is to restore full legal protection to the unborn. However, there are limitations to the protection even under a constitutional amendment. Subsequent state and federal laws will be necessary to fashion remedies and criminal and civil actions against abortion. Nonetheless, much can be done by a constitutional amendment. The following objectives guided NRLC's work:

1. To restore to unborn children of human parents the constitutional status and protection of persons, with respect to

their right to life, under the Fifth and Fourteenth Amendments, which right was specifically destroyed by the Supreme Court decisions in *Roe v. Wade* and *Doe v. Bolton*;

2. Specifically, to protect for all persons the fundamental right to life;

3. To insure to all human beings, irrespective of their age, health, function, or condition of dependency, the constitutional status and protection of persons, with respect to their right to life under the Fifth and Fourteenth Amendments, which right was seriously jeopardized for at least some of these human beings by the principles enunciated by the Supreme Court on January 22, 1973;

4. To insure that the lives of unborn children be protected at every stage of their biological development, from the first stage of fertilization of the female ovum by the male sperm through all subsequent stages;

5. To protect the lives of unborn children not only against action of the state and federal governments but also against the action of private individuals, such as pregnant women and physicians, upon whom the Supreme Court conferred the constitutional right to obtain and perform abortions on demand, respectively;

6. To establish that the right to life of persons is the paramount and most fundamental right protected by the Constitution, superior to all other constitutional rights such as the right to privacy;

7. To provide the basis for a private cause of action to protect the lives of unborn children in those states and localities where federal, state, or local governments will not act to insure their protection;

8. To permit the medical procedures necessary to treat a cancerous uterus, ectopic pregnancy, and severely traumatized uterus in a pregnant woman when the treatment is necessary to prevent the death of the woman even if the treatment results in the termination of the pregnancy, these operations not being abortions in the legal sense;

9. To preserve and protect to the same extent the life of each

human being regardless of state of health or condition of dependency;

10. To ensure when two or more human beings are in the situation in which their lives are mutually endangered during a pregnancy that all ordinary means and reasonable efforts are used to preserve and protect the life of each and every human being so endangered; and

11. To give to both the Congress and the several States the power to enforce the Amendment by appropriate legislation.

All of these objectives for a constitutional amendment are met by NRLC's recommended version. Thus, full legal protection would be restored to the unborn under the United States Constitution upon the Amendment's adoption.

IV. Discussion of the Human Life Amendment

Section 1. The right to life is the paramount and most fundamental right of a person.

This section accomplishes objective 6 by specifically establishing that the right to life is superior to any other right guaranteed by the Constitution. This section is inspired by the Paramount Human Life Amendment, introduced in Congress by Senator Helms as S. J. RES. 19. Helm's HLA had as its principal thrust the concept that the right to life must be superior to any other right guaranteed by the Constitution—such as the right to privacy—to insure that the courts will give priority to the right to life of the unborn when they seek to balance it against the right to privacy of the woman. With the right to life superior to any other right, this meant that the Court, in employing its traditional balancing test, would balance this constitutional right only against the right to life of another person.

Section 2. With respect to the right to life guaranteed to persons by the fifth and fourteenth articles of amendment to the Constitution, the word "person" applies to all human beings, irrespective of age, health, function, or condition of dependency, including their unborn offspring at every stage of their biological development including fertilization.

The Supreme Court in *Roe v. Wade* and *Doe v. Bolton* also separated the traditional concept of human being from the concept of persons. Thus, although a being might be a human being, that fact alone did not entitle that being to the constitutional protection of human persons. The Court had destroyed the traditional common sense and scientific view equating the concept of human being and the concept of human personhood.

In addition, this separation of the two concepts destroyed the very work of the framers of the Fourteenth Amendment. Those framers were very aware that these two concepts had been separated in the actual administration of the Constitution of the United States by the Supreme Court in *Dred Scott v. Sandford*, 60 US 393 (1856). It was their clear, demonstrable purpose to prevent for all time thereafter any separation of the two concepts.

The basic error of the Supreme Court in *Roe v. Wade* is thus corrected. By combining this provison of Section 2 with its recognition that the Fifth and Fourteenth Amendments guarantee a right to life in all persons, the Amendment strikes at the very roots of the Supreme Court's tragic error in *Roe v. Wade.*

This Amendment is also more precise and full in its protection of human beings as persons. It provides that illness, age, or incapacity are not relevant criteria to determine whether or not human beings are persons. Thus the Amendment is explicit in providing that biological existence of a human being is sufficient to affirm personhood and thus the constitutionally protected right to life.

Section 2 would declare, therefore, the unborn to be a person entitled to the right to life as guaranteed in the United States Constitution. The right to life is guaranteed against actions of the federal government by the Fifth Amendment which provides that "(n)o person shall . . . be deprived of life, liberty, or property, without due process of law." Similarly, the Fourteenth Amendment provides that "(n)o state shall . . . deprive any person of life, liberty, or property, without due process of law; nor deny to any person within its jurisdiction the equal protection of the laws." Therefore, the Fifth and Fourteenth Amendments are the provisions of the Constitution guaranteeing the right to life dealt with in this Amendment.

As a result of the adoption of this Amendment, states and the federal government would be prohibited from taking the lives of unborn children "without due process of law." The courts would determine what the requirements of "due process of law" would be under future court decisions. The states and the federal government are, however, not taking the lives of unborn children. Except to the extent that some abortions are performed in government facilities or paid at government expense, most abortions are private ones with no state involvement whatsoever. For those abortions performed in government facilities or funded by government, the courts would determine what are the guidelines of "due process of law." This may only entail committee approval for an abortion or it may result in more extensive protection such as prohibiting abortion to be performed in government facilities or denying government funding except to prevent the death of the mother.

In addition, by application of the equal protection clause of the Fourteenth Amendment, a state would be required to provide some degree of effective protection to the unborn if the killing of born persons is illegal. Under this standard, a legislature could recognize degrees of evil and is not required to treat things which are different in fact or opinion as though they were the same. Thus, a state need not provide abstract symmetry, and may recognize degrees of evil. A class of offenders or a family of offenses, therefore, may receive special treatment. All illegal abortions would not be murder in the first degree but could be punished as a felony or even a misdemeanor. Before 1965, when the trend toward permissive abortion laws began, fifty of the fifty-one jurisdictions in the United States made the procurement of non-lifesaving abortions a felony. New Jersey, the lone exception, made it a high misdemeanor. Abortion, in some states, was murder when the woman died as a result of the abortion. In that instance, twenty-two states increased the punishment by characterizing the death as either murder, manslaughter, or assault with intent to murder. States, therefore, would be forced to extend some degree of criminal protection to the unborn against illegal abortions. While the states would have some discretion, the penalty would have to be of sufficient severity to effectively protect the lives of the unborn.

Section 3. No unborn person shall be deprived of life by any person: Provided, however, that nothing in this article shall prohibit a law allowing justification to be shown for only those medical procedures required to prevent the death of either the pregnant woman or her unborn offspring as long as such law requires every reasonable effort be made to preserve the life of each.

This section reverses the second holding of *Roe v. Wade*—that a woman has a constitutionally protected right of privacy to decide whether or not to terminate her pregnancy—by directly protecting every unborn person from being deprived of its life by another person. In this respect, the proposal is modeled upon the Thirteenth Amendment, which provides direct protection to a human being from being subject to slavery or involuntary servitude by any other person or by any government. By so doing, this section enables the federal government, as well as the states, to enforce its terms against the action of private parties, by appropriate legislation under Section 4.

This Amendment also avoids the possibility of the Court acting to engraft exceptions upon the Amendment's anti-abortion policy. It is left to each state or to Congress to decide whether to create an exception to the policy of this Amendment. In the event a state or Congress does act to create an exception, it is limited to an exception permitting only those medical procedures required to prevent the death of the mother. This language precludes either a state or Congress from engrafting any exception upon the basic policy of the Amendment, except one narrowly restricted to preventing the death of the mother or her child.

The phrase "required to prevent the death of the pregnant woman or her unborn offspring" is more specific and definitive and less subject to court misconstruction. The Amendment's language avoids the word "life" which has been previously been expanded to include health. This section prevents the state from permitting health abortions since the states may "only" authorize, if they wish, abortions "required to prevent the death of the pregnant woman." Moreover, in creating this exception, the states or Congress may only permit it to be raised as a defense. In any criminal or civil action for violation of this provision, the defendant would only be allowed to assert that the abortion was justified if it was necessary under the terms of the exception.

Moreover, the state must also require that all reasonable efforts be expended to preserve the life of the other. If an abortion is necessary to prevent the death of the mother, the physician must act in all reasonable ways to preserve the life of the unborn child. This Amendment makes clear the medical procedures necessary to prevent the death of the unborn child are also allowable, as long as every reasonable effort is made to preserve the life of the pregnant woman. Thus, each life involved in a pregnancy, mother and child, is given equal consideration and treatment.

Section 3, therefore, accomplishes many of the objectives of full restoration of legal protection to the unborn. It protects the lives of unborn children against both state and private action, objective 5; provides the basis for a private cause of action to protect unborn lives, objective 7; permits maternal lifesaving procedures, objective 8; protects all human beings equally, objective 9; and ensures that, when one life is endangered in a pregnancy, reasonable efforts are used to protect all others, Objective 10.

Section 4. Congress and the several States shall have power to enforce this article by appropriate legislation.

This section gives both Congress and the several States the power to enforce this Amendment. This section closely resembles the enforcement clause in the Eighteenth Amendment which was the only Amendment which gave concurrent enforcement power to both the state and federal governments. This section is intended to accomplish objective 11 by giving back to Congress and to the several States the power to enforce the Amendment.

Conclusion

NRLC's version of a life-protective type human life amendment offers full legal protection to the lives of the unborn. Under its provisions, the holdings of *Roe v. Wade* are fully reversed. The unborn child's right to life, and the state's compelling interest in protecting it, could not be balanced against a woman's right to privacy to decide whether or not to have an abortion since this right to privacy would be abrogated. In addition, the circumstance where abortion would be permitted would be restricted to those necessary to prevent the death of the mother or her child. A state, therefore, would not permit health abortions which are equivalent to abortion on demand. This Amendment meets all the objectives to restoration of full legal protection to the lives of the unborn.

Part Eleven

The Testimony of Religion: Protestant, Catholic, and Jewish Viewpoints

The articles in this section present the Christian and Jewish positions on abortion and other life issues. The authors speak authoritatively for their traditions; they are the Roman Catholic Pontiff, a leading Protestant theologian, and the Chief Rabbi of the British Commonwealth.

TWENTY-ONE

Protestants and the Abortion Issue

Harold O.J. Brown

THE OPINION THAT OPPOSITION to abortion stems chiefly from Roman Catholic sources remains widely held, although it is contrary to fact. The overwhelming consensus of the spiritual leaders of Protestantism, from the Reformation to the present, is clearly anti-abortion. There is very little doubt among biblically oriented Protestants that abortion is an attack on the image of God in the developing child and is a great evil. Where differences of opinion arise is in two areas: (1) what society may be expected to legislate in the area; and (2) the extent to which Christians should actively seek to influence legislation. It is at this point that a traditional concern of American Protestants, dedication to the separation of church and state, cuts across the consensus that destruction of developing life is an evil, and leads to the disarray with which Protestants confront the challenge posed by America's abortion legislation, or lack of it. The most recent pro-abortion decision of the United States Supreme Court, *Planned Parenthood of*

Harold O.J. Brown is Professor of Theology at Trinity Evangelical Divinity School in Deerfield, Illinois, and the author of *Death Before Life*. He has been an associate editor of the *Human Life Review* and *Christianity Today*, a leading Protestant journal of opinion. This article is reprinted from the Fall, 1976, issue of *The Human Life Review*.

Missouri V. Danforth, is certain to turn many politically quietist Protestants more strongly against American abortion practices, inasmuch as it represents a clear repudiation of principles of paternal and parental authority and responsibility that are fundamental to Christianity.

The Protestant Consensus

We have stated that the overwhelming consensus of Protestant spiritual leaders is against abortion. This is almost self-evident in the case of evangelicals and fundamentalists[1] with their strong concern to preserve the spiritual heritage of early Christianity and of the Protestant Reformation. Inasmuch as both the early Church and the Reformation unambiguously condemned deliberate abortion, often describing it as worse than murder, it is not surprising that the heirs of the Reformation take a similar if sometimes less massive position.

The churches with the clearest direct ties to the Reformation, the Lutheran and Reformed (Calvinist) churches of the Continent, are explicitly anti-abortion and make common cause with the Roman Catholics on this issue, despite the fact that they may have liberalized their theology and social ethics. All the great Continental theologians of our century who discuss abortion strongly oppose it. Karl Barth, the most productive Protestant theologian since the Reformation,[2] Emil Brunner, his slightly less didactic contemporary,[3] Dietrich Bonhoeffer, the Lutheran pastor and teacher of ethics who died for his role in the German opposition to Hitler,[4] Helmut Thielicke, the youngest of the giants of mid-century European theology and the only one still active,[5] and Francis Schaeffer, American-born but resident in Switzerland for twenty years and one of the foremost Reformed thinkers of our age.[6] According to Lutheran Bishop Per Lonning of Borg, Norway, only *one* of Norway's thousand Lutheran pastors was willing to endorse the Norwegian government's pro-abortion initiative.

The situation in the United States seems different, for a number of the most prestigious churches have taken a pro-abortion or pro-Supreme Court stand, e.g. The United Presbyterian Church in the United States of America ("northern Presbyterian") as well as the recently split Presbyterian Church in the United States ("southern Presbyterian"). Most extreme is the position of the large United Methodist Church. The actions of church governing boards in endorsing some form of permissive abortion are often typified by the most recent United Methodist action at the church's quadrennial General Conference meeting in Portland, Oregon (May, 1976). On the one hand, a Methodist-commissioned poll had revealed, immediately prior to the General Conference, that a majority of Methodists oppose abortion on demand, and on the other, the foremost spiritual leaders of Methodism in the United States, theologians Paul Ramsey, Albert Outler and J. Robert Nelson, are strongly opposed to abortion, and in fact lead the fight of intellectual Protestants against it. Nevertheless the General Conference not merely failed to condemn *Roe v. Wade* but actually approved it.

This action simply does not represent what church members in their majority think, even in the so-called liberal bodies such as the United Methodist Church, and it certainly does not represent the views of the numerous smaller, more evangelical bodies, nor of the great number of independent, unaffiliated Protestants. The National Association of Evangelicals, representing perhaps forty million theologically conservative Protestants, has repeatedly condemned abortion on demand, including a specific condemnation of *Roe v. Wade*. The most vigorous of the Lutheran bodies in America, the Lutheran Church-Missouri Synod, is resolutely committed to a constitutional amendment overturning *Roe v. Wade*. Billy Graham, Bruce Waltke, and Francis Schaeffer, to name the outstanding evangelical figures in biblical studies and theology, are strongly opposed to abortion, as is George H. Williams, who as Hollis Professor of Divinity at Harvard occupies the most distinguished chair of Protestant theology in America. By contrast, there is no Protestant of remotely similar distinction who *endorses* abortion. Figures such as J. Philip Wogaman of

American University, who do support *Roe v. Wade,* do so in such ambivalent terms that their arguments could be used with better logic to plead for its overthrow. Inasmuch as it is undeniable that the Protestant biblical and ethical tradition, taken as a whole, strongly condemns abortion, why is it that so few Protestants actively oppose the Supreme Court decision to the extent of calling for a constitutional amendment to overthrow it? The attitude of Democratic presidential candidate Jimmy Carter, whose "personal Christian testimony" has become a household word, is rather inconsistent and therefore typical of most Protestants. He considers abortion wrong but is, for the moment at least, unwilling to do anything against it. A somewhat similar stand was taken by his denomination, the sprawling Southern Baptist Convention, meeting in Norfolk, Virginia, virtually on the eve of Carter's nomination. The net effect of such moral disapproval followed by a commitment to total inaction is, of course, in effect approval, or at least toleration, of the status quo. It reinforces the widespread erroneous opinion that Protestantism as a whole approves of abortion. What then is the source of this evident inconsistency between Protestant principle and Protestant policies?

Piety and Power

Any scruples that one might have had about the propriety of introducing the particular religious beliefs of a specific candidate into a general discussion such as this may well have been banished by Governor Carter's refreshing candor in presenting them himself. By himself bringing them into the glare of media attention, he has relieved us of this suspicion of prying and has made it possible for us to raise, with his aid as a concrete example, the significant principal question of the relationship between personal piety and political power.

This question was raised before, during the 1960 presidential campaign. The interest and controversy at that time centered not on Catholic piety but on Catholic power. The fear—fanciful though it was—was that the election of a Roman Catholic as president would "put the Pope in the White House," i.e., give American political power and influence to a foreign religious potentate. There is no similar apprehension concerning Governor Carter. He is a Southern Baptist. His denomination is *congregational* in polity and has no hierarchy: hence, no "pope" to put into the White House. In addition, the Southern Baptists are among the strongest supporters of a total "separation of church and state." It may well be true that Baptist opposition to state support of religion was motivated in part by the fear that such support would go primarily to a rival denomination, the Roman Catholics, but it is also true that Baptists have been remarkably consistent in applying the same standards of non-entanglement to themselves that they demanded for others. The apprehension with respect to Carter concerns not power but piety. This apprehension has led him, the most outspokenly evangelical candidate since William Jennings Bryan, to take considerable pains to separate his admitted personal piety from this stated public policy.

The line that Carter has rather clearly taken is that his piety will not influence his policy. This is exactly the principle stated by Kennedy. But there is one significant distinction: John F. Kennedy gained support among Catholics (and lost it among some non-Catholics) not for the sincerity of his Catholicism, but for the mere *fact* of it. Baptists are not numerous enough, nor clannish enough, for Carter to secure much support from the mere fact of being one of them. The point at which his evangelical profession gains support and sympathy for him among a broad electorate is the point at which it is perceived as *genuine.* Thus where Kennedy was stating that his *membership,* specifically his formal loyalty to a "foreign chief of state," namely the Pope, would not influence his official conduct, Carter seems to be in the position of having to promise that his *beliefs* will not influence his conduct. And this is indeed a perplexing situation for one whose appeal is clearly based on his evident sincerity, on the correspondence, until now, between principle and policy. It is no doubt correct to predict that if Carter continues to garner wide support among his fellow-evangelicals, it will be precisely because they think that he will in fact be influenced by his beliefs, despite any demurrals he may make to the contrary.

Surely it is *not* an ethically defensible principle to state that one's character and deepest personal convictions ought not, in high office, to influence one's decisions. Yet that is the effect of assurance such as Governor Carter is now giving, and Kennedy and Nixon gave before him. How is it possible to accept them without discrediting the integrity or consistency of character of those making them? Evidently, another principle must intervene to allow this separation between personal principle and public policy. This intervening principle, which apparently frees national candidates from the need to practice what they preach, is nothing other than a misunderstanding of the constitutional doctrine of the separation of church and state. This separation is perceived at two levels: morality is not to influence law, and the church is not to attempt in any way whatsoever to influence the government. Each of these is in itself an unworkable principle, one that results in absurdities if carried to a logical conclusion. In addition, neither is a legitimate application of the First Amendment prohibition of an establishment of religion.

The purpose of the First Amendment—adopted at a time when two states, Massachusetts and Connecticut—still had established churches, was to guarantee that the State (at the time, the federal government; since the Fourteenth Amendment, the states as well) could not dictate to the conscience of the citizens. But it was never intended to mean that the conscience of citizens—which at that time and ever since has been largely formed by *religious* traditions—could not speak to the State. Since, in a nation peopled by a majority of Christians, the common moral sense will in large measure be a Christian moral sense, to say that Christian morality may in no sense be reflected in law would be to say that morality as such may not be reflected in law. This would be an absurdity. Clearly much of the criminal code is derived from and consistent with principles of biblical, Jewish, Christian, and other religious morality.

Those principles could not be purged from the law without creating chaos; indeed, in large measure they remain fundamental to the law codes even of anti-religious states such as the Soviet Union and Communist China. The traditional theological explanation for this is the idea that the Law of God is written in the heart of man. Whatever the reason, it is evident that it would be an absurd undertaking to attempt to purge all principles of religious origin from the civil law.

The slogan, "one cannot legislate morality," was rejected when used in defense of traditional segregationist practices. Integration is surely a *moral* issue, yet few Americans felt or feel that for that reason it is not a proper concern of law. This slogan is taken seriously only at the point when the morality in question is *sexual* morality. Even then it is questionable whether it would be generally accepted. Certainly it is doubtful that most Christians would ever accept the contention that no principles of sexual morality at all should be reflected in public law. But even when limited to sexual morality, the slogan does not justify disinterest in legislative action on abortion, for the primary concern of the anti-abortionists is respect for *life,* not for sexual morality. This is recognized by the eminent jurist and critic of the Supreme Court, Archibald Cox, who charges the Court with failing, in this issue to consider the essence of the matter at stake.[8]

The second aspect of the extremist view of the First Amendment, that churches should make no attempt whatsoever to influence law is clearly a kind of Red Queen rule, made to suit the occasion and to apply only to one specific class of offender. Churches, whatever else they are, are associations—the Greek word *ekklesia* means *assembly*—of people, constituting what can be called interest groups. American democracy is based on the interplay of divergent interest groups, and it is impossible to find a valid principle whereby one substantial class of interest groups—those held together by a common religious orientation—should be denied the right to speak their concerns to the State.

In other words, the suggestion that piety may not influence

policy, applied to an individual, implies either that faith should not influence character, or that character should not influence conduct. Neither would be accepted either as a general principle of education or as a principle of Christian practice. Applied to law, the idea that morality may not influence law would logically mean that laws may be based on nothing more ultimate than statistics. It is true that Francis Schaeffer has already charged twentieth-century civilization with reducing ethics to statistics, and that both Associate Justice Blackmun in *Roe v. Wade* and several pro-abortion witnesses in Senate and House hearings leaned heavily on statistical arguments in favor of abortion-on-demand. However, though the practice of substituting statistics for ethics is creeping in, surely the majority of Americans would not yet be willing to accept this as a principle, least of all those of evangelical Protestant convictions. Applied to institutions, it means that churches alone among voluntary associations must be muzzled in political debate.

Protestant Quietism

Earlier allusion was made to "evangelicals or fundamentalists." Although evangelical and fundamentalist are not mutually exclusive terms, the evangelical is less inclined to separatism, which is a characteristic feature of fundamentalism. The fundamentalist has traditionally withdrawn from various aspects of the general culture: the avoidance of movies, dancing, alcoholic beverages and sometimes even of television is indicative of the importance most fundamentalists attach to the biblical injunction, "Come out from among them and be separate" (2 Corinthians 6:17). Accompanying such separatism is the feeling that the world and its structures are primarily under the domination of evil, and can be but slightly influenced, if at all, by Christians. In addition, most fundamentalists look forward to an early return of Christ, and many draw from this the unwarranted conclusion that in the present age, prior to his return, there is little use in attempting to ameliorate society and

its structures. This leads to the traditional attitude of fundamentalist political quietism, expressed in a quasi-religious
endorsement of the social and political *status quo* and a general
reluctance to work for any changes. This is sometimes seen as
conservatism, but it is not principled conservatism, as fundamentalists of the quietist type are no more willing to work to
prevent the establishment of liberal structures than to defend
existing conservative ones.

Evidently the emerging Protestant political leaders, although
professedly fundamentalists in faith, are not of the quietist
variety, as they involve rather than separate themselves. The
salient question is: although not or no longer quietists, will
they be only *personal* pietists? That is, will they seek to
maintain a strict separation between the piety they practice at
home and the policies they enact and enforce in public? This
is certainly possible, and some of the assertions made by
Governor Carter, among others, suggest a trend in the direction of subordinating piety to policy. However, such subordi-
nation surely is not what the growing number of politically
interested evangelical Protestants expect from "Christian"
candidates.

Significance of the Abortion Issue

The answer to the question of the degree to which Protestant
principle may influence public policy when that policy is guided
by a pious Protestant will be indicated by the direction in which
national political leaders of acknowledged piety move on the
abortion issue. The reaction to abortion is clearly a significant
indicator of Protestant integrity and commitment in two ways.
First, there is no other issue on the horizon in which the Law of
God, as understood from the Bible, and the laws of man in
America are so clearly in conflict. As though to make *Roe v.
Wade* a perfect challenge to those who believe in biblical
principles, Associate Justice Harry A. Blackmun explicitly
appealed to "ancient religion," i.e., Roman paganism, in
seeking precedents for his decision.[9] On the level of principle,

if evangelicals do not react in overwhelming number to this challenge, it is difficult to imagine another to which they might rise.

Second, from the nature of the forces already committed on this issue, it is evident that evangelical Protestants hold the key to success or failure of anti-abortion efforts. The second-largest religious group, the Roman Catholics, is already strongly committed to a pro-amendment effort. It is seconded by other groups, some, like the Lutheran Church-Missouri Synod, having much in common with the other evangelicals but not usually aligned with them organizationally, and others, such as the Mormons, who have a significantly different religious orientation but coincide with Catholics and Missouri Synod in their views on abortion. The largest religious group, that of conservative Protestants, is generally anti-abortion but passive. *If* it reacts in significant strength, it is hard to see how an anti-abortion amendment could be resisted, particularly if an evangelical is Chief of State. If it fails to do so, since the other groups of pro-life conviction are, in Patrick Henry's words, "already in the field," the failure of an amendment will be the direct responsibility of evangelical Protestantism's failure to match practice to preaching.

Principles vs. Personalities

The question, ultimately, will turn on whether Protestants in large numbers think in terms of the general principles involved, and act on them, or are content to vote for personalities. How the issue is resolved, both in terms of voter interest and choice and in terms of the way in which elected evangelical Protestants apply professed principles to policies, will determine not only the concrete question of restriction or total permissiveness of abortion, but also the long-term issue of whether the principle of the seperation of church and state in America will come to mean the total separation of morality and law and the reduction of justice to regulations, of ethics to statistics.

Notes

1. A clarification may be helpful to the reader who is not conversant with this terminology. Evangelicals and fundamentalists, with minor fluctuations, hold the same doctrinal position, emphasizing the divinity and the absolute trustworthiness of Scripture, but fundamentalists insist on a much greater degree of separation from non-evangelical elements in the churches and from secular society in general.

2. The general Christian attitude in its radical break with pre-Christian paganism is well summarized by William E.H. Lecky in *History of European Morals* (New York: Braziller, 1955), Vol. II, pp. 20-24. For Barth, "The unborn child is from the very first a child. It is still developing and has no independent life. But it is a man and not a thing, nor a mere part of the mother's body . . . He who destroys germinating life kills a man . . . The fact that a definite No must be the presupposition of all further discussion cannot be contested, least of all today." Karl Barth, *Church Dogmatics*, English translation edited by G.W. Bromiley and T.F. Torrance (Edinburgh, T. & T. Clark, 1961), Vol III, *The Doctrine of Creation*, Part IV, pp. 415ff.

3. Emil Brunner, *The Divine Imperative*, translated by Olive Wyon (Philadelphia: Westminster, 1947), pp. 367ff.

4. Dietrich Bonhoeffer, *Ethics*, translated by Neville Horton Smith (New York: Macmillan, 1955), pp. 130-131: "The simple fact is that God intended to create a human being and that this human being has been deliberately deprived of his life. And that is nothing but murder" (p. 131).

5. Helmut Thielecke, *The Ethics of Sex*, (New York: Harper, 1964), pp. 227-228.

6. Personal conversation with the author. Dr. Schaeffer's forthcoming volume will include a detailed treatment of the ethics of abortion, he advised this writer in Washington in February, 1976.

7. J. Philip Wogaman, "Abortion: A Protestant Debate," *Human Life Review*, Vol. 1, No. 2.

8. Archibald Cox, *The Role of the Supreme Court in American Government* (New York: Oxford, 1976), pp. 113-114.

9. *Roe V. Wade,* VI,. No. 8.

TWENTY-TWO

"Stand Up for Life"

Pope John Paul II

Dear brothers and sisters in Jesus Christ,

1. In his dialogue with his listeners, Jesus was faced one day with an attempt by some Pharisees to get him to endorse their current views regarding the nature of marriage.

Jesus answered by reaffirming the teaching of scripture: "At the beginning of creation God made them male and female; for this reason a man shall leave his father and mother and the two shall become one. They are no longer two but one in flesh. Therefore let no man separate what God has joined" (Mk 10:6-9).

The Gospel according to Mark immediately adds the description of a scene with which we are all familiar. This scene shows Jesus becoming indignant when he noticed how his own disciples tried to prevent the people from bringing their children closer to him. And so he said: "Let the children come to me and do not hinder them. It is to just such as these that the kingdom of God belongs. . . . Then he embraced them and blessed them, placing his hands on them" (Mk 10:14-16).

In proposing these readings, today's liturgy invites all of us to reflect on the nature of marriage, on the family and on the value of life—three themes that are so closely interconnected.

This is the text of a homily given by Pope John Paul II at the Capitol Mall in Washington, D.C., October 7, 1979.

2. I shall all the more gladly lead you in reflecting on the word of God as proposed by the church today, because all over the world the bishops are discussing marriage and family life as they are lived in all dioceses and nations. The bishops are doing this in preparation for the next world Synod of Bishops, which has as its theme: "The Role of the Christian Family in the Contemporary World."

Your own bishops have designated next year as a year of study, planning and pastoral renewal with regard to the family. For a variety of reasons there is a renewed interest throughout the world in marriage, in family life and in the value of all human life.

This very Sunday marks the beginning of the annual Respect Life program, through which the church in the United States intends to reiterate its conviction regarding the inviolability of human life in all stages. Let us then, all together, renew our esteem for the value of human life, remembering also that, through Christ, all human life has been redeemed.

3. I do not hesitate to proclaim before you and before the world that all human life—from the moment of conception and through all subsequent stages—is sacred, because human life is created in the image and likeness of God.

Nothing surpasses the greatness or dignity of a human person. Human life is not just an idea or an abstraction. Human life is the concrete reality of a being that lives, that acts, that grows and develops. Human life is the concrete reality of a being that is capable of love and of service to humanity.

Let me repeat what I told the people during my recent pilgrimage to my homeland: "If a person's right to life is violated at the moment in which he is first conceived in his mother's womb, an indirect blow is struck also at the whole of the moral order which serves to ensure the inviolable goods of man. Among those goods, life occupies the first place.

The church defends the right to life, not only in regard to the majesty of the creator, who is the first giver of this life, but also in respect of the essential good of the human person" (June 8, 1979).

4. Human life is precious because it is the gift of a God whose love is infinite; and when God gives life, it is forever. Life is also precious because it is the expression and the fruit of love. This is why life should spring up within the setting of marriage, and why marriage and the partners' love for one another should be marked by generosity in self-giving.

The great danger for family life in the midst of any society whose idols are pleasure, comfort and independence lies in the fact that people close their hearts and become selfish. The fear of making permanent commitments can change the mutual love of husband and wife into two loves of self—two loves existing side by side, until they end in separation.

In the sacrament of marriage, a man and a woman—who at baptism became members of Christ and hence have the duty of manifesting Christ's attitudes in their lives—are assured of the help they need to develop their love in a faithful and indissoluble union and to respond with generosity to the gift of parenthood. As the Second Vatican Council declared: Through this sacrament, Christ himself becomes present in the life of the married couple and accompanies them, so that they may love each other and their children, just as Christ loved his church by giving himself up for her (cf. *Gaudium et Spes,* 48; cf. Eph 5:25).

5. In order that Christian marriage may favor the total good and development of the married couple, it must be inspired by the Gospel, and thus be open to new life—new life to be given and accepted generously. The couple is also called to create a family atmosphere in which children can be happy and lead full and worthy human and Christian lives.

To maintain a joyful family requires much from both the parents and the children. Each member of the family has to become, in a special way, the servant of the others and share their burdens (cf. Gal 6:2; Phil 2:2). Each one must show concern, not only for his or her own life, but also for the lives of the other members of the family: their needs, their hopes, their ideals.

Decisions about the number of children and the sacrifices to be made for them must not be taken only with a view to adding to comfort and preserving a peaceful existence. Reflecting upon this matter before God, with the graces drawn from the sacrament and guided by the teaching of the church, parents will remind themselves that it is certainly less serious to deny their children certain comforts or material advantages than to deprive them of the presence of brothers and sisters who could help them to grow in humanity and to realize the beauty of life at all its ages and in all its variety.

If parents fully realized the demands and the opportunities that this great sacrament brings, they could not fail to join in Mary's hymn to the author of life—to God—who has made them his chosen fellow workers.

All human beings ought to value every person for his or her uniqueness as a creature of God, called to be a brother or sister of Christ by reason of the incarnation and the universal redemption. For us, the sacredness of human life is based on these premises. And it is on these same premises that there is based our celebration of life—all human life. This explains our efforts to defend human life against every influence or action that threatens or weakens it, as well as our endeavors to make every life more human in all its aspects.

And so, we will stand up every time that human life is threatened.

—When the sacredness of life before birth is attacked, we will stand up and proclaim that no one ever has the authority to destroy unborn life.

—When a child is described as a burden or looked upon only as a means to satisfy an emotional need, we will stand up and insist that every child is a unique and unrepeatable gift of God, with the right to a loving and united family.

—When the institution of marriage is abandoned to human selfishness or reduced to a temporary, conditional arrangement that can easily be terminated, we will stand up and affirm the indissolubility of the marriage bond.

—When the value of the family is threatened because of social and economic pressures, we will stand up and reaffirm that the family is "necessary not only for the private good of every person, but also for the common good of every society, nation and state" (General Audience, Jan. 3, 1979).

—When freedom is used to dominate the weak, to squander natural resources and energy, and to deny basic necessities to people, we will stand up and reaffirm the demands of justice and social love.

—When the sick, the aged or the dying are abandoned in loneliness, we will stand up and proclaim that they are worthy of love, care and respect.

I make my own the words which Paul VI spoke last year to the American bishops:

"We are convinced, moreover, that all efforts made to safeguard human rights actually benefit life itself. Everything aimed at banishing discrimination—in law or in fact—which is based on race, origin, color, culture, sex or religion (cf. *Octogesima Adveniens,* 16) is a service to life. When the rights of minorities are fostered, when the mentally or physically handicapped are assisted, when those on the margin of society are given a voice—in all these instances the dignity of life, and the sacredness of human life are furthered. . . . In particular, every contribution made to better the moral climate of society, to oppose permissiveness and hedonism, and all assistance to the family, which is the source of new life, effectively uphold the values of life" (May 26, 1978).

Much remains to be done to support those whose lives are wounded and to restore hope to those who are afraid of life. Courage is needed to resist pressures and false slogans, to proclaim the supreme dignity of all life, and to demand that society itself give it its protection.

A distinguished American, Thomas Jefferson, once stated: "The care of human life and happiness and not their destruction is the just and only legitimate object of good government" (March 31, 1809). I wish therefore to praise all members of the Catholic Church and other Christian churches, all men and women of the Judeo-Christian heritage, as well as all people of good will who unite in common dedication for the defense of life in its fullness and for the promotion of all human rights.

Our celebration of life forms part of the celebration of the eucharist. Our Lord and savior, through his death and resurrection, has become for us "the bread of life" and the pledge of eternal life. In him we find the courage, perseverance and inventiveness which we need to promote and defend life within our families and throughout the world.

Dear brothers and sisters: We are confident that Mary, the mother of God and the mother of life, will give us her help so that our way of living will always reflect our admiration and gratitude for God's gift of love that is life. We know that she will help us to use every day that is given to us as an opportunity to defend the life of the unborn and to render more human the lives of all our fellow human beings, wherever they may be.

And through the intercession of Our Lady of the Rosary, whose feast we celebrate today, may we come one day to the fullness of eternal life in Christ Jesus our Lord. *Amen.*

TWENTY-THREE

Jewish Views on Abortion

Rabbi Dr. Immanuel Jakobovits

IN RECENT YEARS, no medico-moral subject has undergone a more revolutionary change of public attitudes than abortion. What was previously either a therapeutic measure for the safety of the mother or else an actionable criminal offense is now widely and legally performed not only as a means to prevent the birth of possibly defective children or to curb the sordid indignities and hazards endured by women resorting to clandestine operators, but simply for convenience to augment other birth-control devices. Under the mounting pressure of this shift in public opinion, generated by intense agitation and skillful propaganda campaigns, the abortion laws have been liberalized in many countries, starting with the British Abortion Act of 1967 and culminating in the decisions of the United States Supreme Court of January 22, 1973. In effect, abortion is now—or, pending anticipated changes in existing laws, will soon be—available in most parts of the Western world virtually on request, or at least at the discretion of doctors within some general guide-lines.

Many physicians have, of course, always claimed that the

Dr. Immanuel Jakobovits is the Chief Rabbi of the British Commonwealth of Nations, and the author of *Jewish Medical Ethics* and other books. This article, reprinted from the Winter, 1975, issue of *The Human Life Review,* is based on an earlier work published in *Abortion, Society & the Law* (edited by D.F. Walbert and J.D. Butler, Case Western Reserve University Press, Cleveland and London, 1973).

decision whether or not to terminate a pregnancy should be left to their judgment—a claim already for some time asserted on a wide scale through the establishment at many hospitals of "abortion boards," composed solely of physicians, charged with the responsibility of sanctioning all such operations.

In the Jewish view, this line of argument cannot be upheld.

The judgment that is here required, while it may be based on medical evidence, is clearly of a moral nature. The decision whether, and under what circumstances, it is right to destroy a germinating human life, depends on the assessment and weighing of *values*, on determining the title to life in any given case. Such value judgments are entirely outside the province of medical science. No amount of training or experience in medicine can help in ascertaining the criteria necessary for reaching such capital verdicts, for making such life-and-death decisions. Such judgments pose essentially a moral, not a medical problem. Hence they call for the judgment of moral, not medical specialists.

Physicians, by demanding that as the practitioners in this field they should have the right to determine or adjudicate the laws governing their practice, are making an altogether unprecedented claim not advanced by any other profession. Lawyers do not argue that, because law is their specialty, the decision on what is legal should be left to their conscience. And teachers do not claim that, as the profession competent in education, the laws governing their work, such as on prayers at public schools, should be administered or defined at their discretion. Such claims are patently absurd, for they would demand jurisdiction on matters completely beyond their professional competence.

There is no more justice or logic in advancing similar claims for the medical profession. A physician, in performing an abortion or any other procedure involving moral considerations, such as artificial insemination or euthanasia, is merely a technical expert; but he is no more qualified than any other layman to pronounce on the rights or legality of such acts, let alone to determine what these rights should be, relying merely on the whims or dictates of his conscience. The decision on whether a human life, once conceived, is to be or not to be, therefore, properly belongs to moral experts, or to legislatures guided by such experts.

The Claims of Judaism

Every monotheistic religion embodies within its philosophy and legislation a system of ethics—a definition of moral values. None does so with greater precision and comprehensiveness than Judaism. It emphatically insists that the norms of moral conduct can be governed neither by the accepted notions of public opinion nor by the individual conscience. In the Jewish view, the human conscience is meant to enforce laws, not to make them. Right and wrong, good and evil, are absolute values which transcend the capricious variations of time, place, and environment, just as they defy definition by relation to human intuition or expediency. These values, Judaism teaches, derive their validity from the Divine revelation at Mount Sinai, as expounded and developed by sages faithful to, and authorized by, its writ.

The Sources of Jewish Law

For a definition of these values, one must look to the vast and complex corpus of Jewish law, the authentic expression of all Jewish religious and moral thought. The literary depositories of Jewish law extend over nearly four thousand years, from the Bible and the Talmud, serving as the immutable basis of the main principles, to the great medieval codes and the voluminous rabbinical *responsa* writings recording practical verdicts founded on these principles, right up to the present day.

These sources spell out a very distinct attitude on all aspects of the abortion problem. They clearly indicate that Judaism, while it does not share the rigid stand of the Roman Catholic Church which unconditionally proscribes any direct destruction of the fetus from the moment of conception, refuses to endorse the far more permissive views of many

Protestant denominations. The traditional Jewish position is somewhere between these two extremes.

The Rulings of Jewish Law

While the destruction of an unborn child is never regarded as a capital act of murder (unless and until the head or the greater part of the child has emerged from the birth canal), it does constitute a heinous offense except when indicated by the most urgent medical considerations. The foremost concern is the safety of the mother. Hence, in Jewish law an abortion is mandatory whenever there is a genuine fear that a continued pregnancy might involve a grave hazard to the life of the mother, whether physical or psychiatric (such as the risk of suicide, following previous experiences of mental breakdown).

More difficult to determine—and still widely debated in recent rabbinic writings—is the judgment on abortions in cases of risks to the mother's health rather than to her life; of rape or incest; and of fears of physical or mental defects in children born to mothers who had German measles (rubella) or took certain teratogenic drugs (e.g. thalidomide) during the first months of pregnancy. Quite recently, several leading authorities have reaffirmed the Jewish opposition to abortion even in these cases, branding it as an "appurtenance of murder." But some others have lately given more lenient rulings in these circumstances, provided the operation is carried out within the first forty days following conception, or at least within the first three months. However, whatever the verdict in these particular cases, they are of course exceptional, and Jewish law would never countenance abortions for purely social or economic reasons.

Moral and Social Considerations

These conclusions, though deduced from ancient principles and precedents by legal reasoning, must be viewed in the context of Judaism's moral philosophy and against the background of contemporary social conditions. In Jewish thought the law, while legalistically constructed, is always but the concrete expression of abstract ideas, the vehicle to convey, as well as to implement, moral and religious concepts. Judaism uses the medium of law much as an artist presents the genius of his inspiration in colours on canvas, in sounds of music or in the building-blocks of sculptured and architectural designs. Accordingly, neither the rationale nor the significance of the Jewish rules on abortion—as indeed on any other subject with social ramifications—can be properly understood except by enucleating the spirit, the moral ethos, from the somatic letter of the law.

The moral thinking set out in the rest of this article, especially insofar as it concerns abnormal births and the products of rape or incest, reflects in particular the majority view of the stricter school of thought which sanctions abortions only for the safety of the mother.

The "Cruelty" of the Abortion Laws. At the outset, it is essential, in order to arrive at an objective judgment, to disabuse one's mind of the often one-sided, if not grossly partisan, arguments in the popular (and sometimes medical) presentations of the issues involved. A hue and cry is raised about the "cruelty" of restrictive abortion laws. Harrowing scenes are depicted, in the most lurid colors, of girls and married women selling their honor and their fortunes, exposing themselves to mayhem and death at the hands of some greedy and ill-qualified abortionist in a dark, unhygienic back-alley, and facing the prospect of being hunted and haunted like criminals for the rest of their lives—all because safe, honorable, and reasonably priced methods to achieve the same ends are, or were, barred from hospitals and licensed physicians' offices by "barbaric" statutes. Equally distressing are the accounts and pictures of pitifully deformed children born because "antiquated" abortion laws did not permit us to forestall their and their parents' misfortune. And then there are, of course, always heart-strings of sympathy to be pulled by the sight of "unwanted" children taxing the patience and resources of parents already "burdened" with too large a brood, not to mention the embarrassing encumbrance of children "accidentally" born to unwed girls.

There is, inevitably, some element of cruelty in most laws. For a person who has spent his last cent before the tax-bill arrives, the income tax laws are unquestionably "cruel"; and to a man passionately in love with a married woman the adultery laws must appear "barbaric." Even more universally "harsh" are the military draft regulations which expose young men to acute danger and their families to great anguish and hardship.

Moral Standards in Society. All these resultant "cruelties" are surely no valid reason for changing those laws. No civilized society could survive without laws which occasionally spell some suffering for individuals. Nor can any public moral standards be maintained without strictly enforced regulations calling for extreme restraints and sacrifices in some cases. If the criterion for the legitimacy of laws were to be the complete absence of "cruel" effects, we should abolish or drastically liberalize not only our abortion laws, but our statutes on marriage, narcotics, homosexuality, suicide, euthanasia, and numerous other laws which inevitably result in personal anguish from time to time.

So far our reasoning, which could be supported by any number of references to Jewish tradition, has merely sought to demolish the "cruelty" factor as a valid argument *per se* by which to judge the justice or injustice of any law. It still has to be demonstrated that restrictions on abortion are morally sound enough and sufficiently important to the public welfare to outweigh the consequential hardships in individual cases.

The Hidden Side of the Problem. What the fuming editorials and harrowing documentaries on the abortion problem do not show are pictures of radiant mothers fondling perfectly healthy children who would never have been alive if their parents had been permitted to resort to abortion in moments of despair. There are no statistics on the contributions to society of outstanding men and women who would never have been born had the abortion laws been more liberal. Nor is it known how many "unwanted" children eventually turn out to be the sunshine of their families.

A Jewish moralistic work of the twelfth century relates the following deeply significant story:

> A person constantly said that, having already a son and a daughter, he was anxious lest his wife become pregnant again. For he was not rich and asked how would he find sufficient sustenance. Said a sage to him: "When a child is born, the Holy One, blessed be He, provides the milk beforehand in the mother's breast; therefore, do not worry." But he did not accept the wise man's words, and he continued to fret. Then a son was born to him. After a while, the child became ill, and the father turned to the sage: "Pray for my son that he shall live." Exclaimed the sage: "To you applies the biblical verse: 'Suffer not thy mouth to bring thy flesh into guilt.' "

Some children may be born unwanted, but there are scarcely unwanted children aged five or ten years.

Abortion Statistics. There are, then—even from the purely utilitarian viewpoint of "cruelty" *versus* "happiness" or "usefulness"—two sides to this problem, and not just one as pretended by the pro-abortion lobby. There are the admittedly tragic cases of maternal indignities and deaths as well as of congenital deformities resulting from restrictive abortion laws. But, on the other hand, there are the countless happy children and useful citizens whose births equally result from these laws. What is the ratio between these two categories?

Clearly, any relaxation of the abortion laws is bound greatly to increase the rate of abortions, which was already high even under rigid laws. In England, for example, the figure shot up from a rate of 25,000 *per annum* in 1967 to 90,000 by 1971. On the apparently realistic assumption that the demand for abortions, in the absence of restrictive legislation, might be 500 or more per thousand live-births, it is estimated that the figure will approach three million in the United States by 1980.

Out of this staggering number of annual abortions only a minute proportion would be fully justified for the principal reasons advanced by the advocates of liberalization. Based on the approximate rate of 30,000 abnormal births annually (as reliably estimated), and making allowance for the number of women whose hazards would be reduced if they did not resort to clandestine operations, well over 95% of all abortions would eliminate normal children of healthy mothers.

In fact, as for the mothers, the increased recourse to abortion (even if performed by qualified physicians), far from reducing hazards, would increase them, since such operations leave at least five per cent of the women sterile, not to mention the rise in the resultant mortality rate. One can certainly ask if the extremely limited reduction in the number of malformed children and maternal mortality risks really justifies the annual wholesale destruction of three million germinating, healthy lives, most of them potentially happy and useful citizens, especially in a country as under-populated as America (compared to Europe, for instance, which commands far fewer natural resources).

The Individual's Claim to Life. These numerical facts alone make nonsense of the argument for more and easier abortions. But moral norms cannot be determined by numbers. In the Jewish view, "he who saves one life is as if he saved an entire world"; one human life is as precious as a million lives, for each is infinite in value. Hence, even if the ratio were reversed, and there was only a one per cent chance that the child to be aborted would be normal—in fact the chances invariably exceed 50% in any given case—the consideration for that one child in favor of life would outweigh any counter-indication for the other 99 per cent.

But, in truth, such a counter-indication, too, is founded on fallacious premises. Assuming one were 100 per cent certain (perhaps by radiological evidence or by amniotic fluid tests) that a child would be born deformed, could this affect its claim to life? Any line to be drawn between normal and abnormal beings determining their right to live would have to be altogether arbitrary. Would a grave defect in one limb or in two limbs, or an anticipated sub-normal intelligence quotient of seventy-five or fifty make the capital difference between one who is entitled to live and one who is not? And if the absence of two limbs deprives a person of his claim to life, what about one who loses two limbs in an accident? By what moral reasoning can such a defect be a lesser cause for denying the right to live than a similar congenital abnormality? Surely life-and-death verdicts cannot be based on such tenuous distinctions. The only cases possibly excluded by this argument might be to prevent the birth of children who would in any event not be viable, such as Tay-Sachs babies, if their foetal affliction is definitely established by amniocentesis.

The Obligations of Society. The birth of a physically or mentally maldeveloped child may be an immense tragedy in a family, just as a crippling accident or a lingering illness striking a family later in life may be. But one cannot purchase the relief from such misfortunes at the cost of life itself. Once any innocent person can be sacrificed because he has lost his absolute value, the work of every human life would become relative—to his state of health, his usefulness to society or any other arbitrary criterion—and no two human beings would have an equal claim to life, thus destroying the only foundation of the moral order. So long as the sanctity of life is recognized as inviolable, the cure to suffering cannot be abortion before birth, any more than murder (whether in the form of infanticide, euthanasia or suicide) after birth. The only legitimate relief in such cases is for society to assume the burdens which the individual family can no longer bear. Since society is the main beneficiary of restrictive public laws on abortion (or homicide), it must in turn also pay the price sometimes exacted by these laws in the isolated cases demanding such a price.

Just as the state holds itself responsible for the support of families bereaved by the death of soldiers fallen in the defense of their country, it ought to provide for incapacitated people born and kept alive in the defense of public moral standards. The community is morally bound to relieve affected families of any financial or emotional stress they cannot reasonably bear, either by accepting the complete care of defective children in public institutions, or by supplying medical and educational subsidies to ensure that such families do not suffer any unfair economic disadvantages from their misfortune.

Illegitimate Children. Similar considerations may apply to children conceived by rape. The circumstances of such a conception hardly have bearing on the child's title to life, and in the absence of any well-grounded challenge to this title there cannot be any moral justification for an abortion. Once again, the burden rests with society to relieve an innocent mother (if she so desires) from the consequences of an unprovoked assault upon her virtue if the assailant cannot be found and forced to discharge this responsibility to his child.

In the case of pregnancies resulting from incestuous, adulterous, or otherwise illegitimate relations (which the mother did not resist), there are additional considerations militating against any sanction of abortion. Jewish law not only puts an extreme penalty on incest and adultery, but also imposes fearful disabilities on the products of such unions. It treats relations as capital crimes, and it debars children born under these conditions from marriage with anyone except their like (*Deut.* 23:3).

(1) *The Deterrent Effect.*

Why exact such a price from innocent children for the sins of their parents? The answer is simple: to serve as a powerful deterrent to such hideous crimes. The would-be partners to any such illicit sexual relations are to be taught that their momentary pleasure would be fraught with the most disastrous consequences for any children they might conceive.

Through this knowledge they are to recoil from the very thought of incest or adultery with the same horror as they would from contemplating murder as a means to enjoyment or personal benefit. Murder is comparatively rare in civilized society for the very reason that the dreadful consequences have evoked this horror of the crime in the public conscience. Incest and adultery, in the Jewish view, are no lesser crimes; hence the juxtaposition of murder and adultery in the Ten Commandments, for it makes little difference whether one kills a person or a marriage. Both crimes therefore require the same horror as an effective deterrent.

(2) *Parental Responsibility*

Why create this deterrent by visiting the sins of the parents on their innocent children? First, because there is no other way to expose an offense committed in private and usually beyond the chance of detection. But, above all, this responsibility of parents for the fate of their children is an inexorable necessity in the generation of human life; it is dictated by the law of nature no less than by the moral law. If a careless mother drops her baby and thereby causes a permanent brain injury to the child, or if a syphilitic father irresponsibly transmits his disease to his offspring before birth, or if parents are negligent in the education of their children, all these children may innocently suffer and for the rest of their lives expiate the sins of their parents. This is what must be if parental responsibility is to be taken seriously. The fear that such catastrophic consequences ensue from a surrender to temptation or from carelessness will help prevent the conception of grossly disadvantaged children or their physical or mental mutilation after birth.

Public Standard v. Individual Aberration. In line with this reasoning, Jewish law never condones the relaxation of public moral standards for the sake of saving recalcitrant individuals from even moral offenses. A celebrated Jewish sage and philosopher of the fifteenth century, in connection with a question submitted to his judgment, averred that it was always wrong for a community to acquiesce in the slightest evil, however much it was hoped thereby to prevent far worse excesses by individuals. The problem he faced arose out of a suggestion that brothels for single people be tolerated as long as such publicly controlled institutions would reduce or eliminate the capital crime of marital faithlessness then rampant. His unequivocal answer was, "It is surely far better that individuals should commit the worst offenses and expose themselves to the gravest penalties than publicly to promote the slightest compromise with the moral law."

Rigid abortion laws, ruling out the *post facto* "correction" of rash acts, compel people to think twice *before* they recklessly embark on illicit or irresponsible adventures liable to inflict lifelong suffering or infamy on their progeny. To eliminate the scourge of illegitimate children more self-discipline to prevent their conception is required, not more freedom to destroy them in the womb. For each illegitimate child born because the abortion laws are strict, there may be ten or more such children *not* conceived because these laws are strict.

The exercise of man's procreative faculties, making him (in the phrase of the Talmud) "a partner with God in creation," is man's greatest privilege and gravest responsibility. The rights and obligations implicit in the generation of human life must be evenly balanced if man is not to degenerate into an addict of lust and a moral parasite infesting the moral organism of society. Liberal abortion laws would upset that balance by facilitating sexual indulgences without insisting on corresponding responsibilities.

Therapeutic Abortions. This leaves primarily the concern for the mother's safety as a valid argument in favor of abortions. In the view of Judaism, all human rights, and their priorities, derive solely from their conferment upon man by his Creator. By this criterion, as defined in the Bible, the rights of the mother and her unborn child are distinctly unequal, since the capital guilt of murder takes effect only if the victim was a born and viable person. "He that smites a *man*, so that he dies, shall surely be put to death" (*Exodus* 21:12); this excludes a foetus, according to the Jewish interpretation. This recognition does not imply that the destruction of a foetus is not a very grave offense against the sanctity of human life, but only that it is not technically murder. Jewish law makes a similar distinction in regard to the killing of inviable adults. While the killing of a person who already suffered from a fatal injury (from other than natural causes) is not actionable as murder, the killer is nevertheless morally guilty of a moral offense.

This inequality, then, is weighty enough only to warrant the sacrifice of the unborn child if the pregnancy otherwise poses a threat to the mother's life. Indeed, the Jewish concern for the mother is so great that a gravid woman sentenced to death must not be subjected to the ordeal of suspense to await the delivery of her child. (Jewish sources brand any delay in the execution, once it is finally decreed, as "the perversion of justice" *par excellence*, since the criminal is sentenced to die, not to suffer. It should be added, however, that in practice Jewish law abolished the death penalty to all intent and purposes thousands of years ago, by insisting on virtually impossible conditions, such as the presence of and prior warning by two eye-witnesses.)

Such a threat to the mother need not be either immediate or absolutely certain. Even a remote risk of life invokes all the life-saving concessions of Jewish law, provided the fear of such a risk is genuine and confirmed by the most competent medical opinions. Hence, Jewish law would regard it as an indefensible desecration of human life to allow a mother to perish in order to save her unborn child.

This review may be fittingly concluded with a reference to the very first Jewish statement on *deliberate* abortion. Commenting on the *Septuagint* version (itself a misrepresentation) of the only Biblical reference, or at least allusion, to abortion in *Exodus* 21:22-23, the Alexandrian-Jewish philosopher, Philo, at the beginning of the Current Era declared that the attacker of a pregnant woman must die if the fruit he caused to be lost was already "shaped and all the limbs had their proper qualities, for that which answers to this description is a human being . . . like a statue lying in a studio requiring nothing more than to be conveyed outside." The legal conclusion of this statement, reflecting Hellenistic rather than Jewish influence, may vary from the letter of Jewish law; but its reasoning certainly echoes the spirit of Jewish law. The analogy may be more meaningful than Philo could have intended or foreseen. A classic statue by a supreme master is no less priceless for being made defective, even with an arm or a leg missing. The destruction of such a treasure *in utero* can be warranted only by the superior worth of preserving a living human being.

Part Twelve

Inspiration and Action

The prolife struggle, writes Richard John Neuhaus, is "a contest over the meaning of America. . . . By this issue we define the America that we will pass on to our children and to all children who claim a place in the community that is rightfully theirs." Rev. Neuhaus' article appears here, along with two other articles, to encourage those who wage the fight for life.

TWENTY-FOUR

A New Birth of Freedom

Richard John Neuhaus

A NEW BIRTH OF FREEDOM. The theme you have chosen for your convention contains the key terms of conflict now testing our nation. On the one hand is "birth," which speaks of the right to life; on the other is "freedom," which speaks of the right to choose. Thus the forces arrayed in political and moral conflict are called pro-life and pro-choice. Some say that we have here a case of rights in conflict and that the conflict is irresolvable. We cannot and we do not accept that. Life and liberty are not enemies.

The idea of pitting liberty against life is alien to those who believe that every person has an inalienable right to life, liberty, and the pursuit of happiness. Today that belief is as radical, and at least as imperiled, as it was two centuries ago. As it was almost exactly one century ago when at Gettysburg Abraham Lincoln expressed the resolve "that these dead shall not have died in vain; that this nation, under God, shall have a new birth of freedom; and that government of the people, by the people, for the people, shall not perish from the earth." Then too it was

Rev. Richard John Neuhaus, a minister of the Evangelical Lutheran Church, is editor of *Forum Letter* and is a senior fellow of *Worldview* magazine. His books include *In Defense of People, Movement and Revolution,* and *To Empower People,* coauthored with Peter Berger. This essay is adaped from Rev. Neuhaus' address on July 15, 1982, at the National Right to Life Convention, Cherry Hill, New Jersey.

claimed that the liberty of some justified the denial of liberty to others. The story of America is the story of constant challenge to that claim.

1982 is not 1882 or 1782. Yet the proposition that all are created equal is as new and controversial today as it was then. Once again the nation dedicated to that proposition is engaged in a great testing whether it or any nation so conceived and so dedicated can long endure. If it is to endure, we must reclaim liberty for the defense, not the denial, of life. Unless there is life there can be no experience of liberty. Unless liberty is devoted to the defense of life, neither life nor liberty can survive.

Six months after Gettysburg, Lincoln talked about liberty in Baltimore. He said, "The shepherd drives the wolf from the sheep's throat, for which the sheep thanks the shepherd as his liberator, while the wolf denounces him for the same act. . . . Plainly the sheep and the wolf are not agreed upon a definition of liberty." And so with respect to the poorest and most vulnerable today, there is no agreement upon a definition of liberty.

From liberty comes the word liberal. Scholars have remarked that all politics in America, even what is called conservative politics, is essentially liberal. That is to say, the American experiment is premised upon the promise of freedom. Everyone possesses the right to pursue that promise. Contrary to the logic of *Roe v. Wade,* the existence of that right does not depend upon the power to exercise that right. It is the business of just government to see that the liberty of the strong is checked by the rights of the weak. Ours is not a movement against government but a movement demanding that government attend to its proper business. The first and most urgent business of government is the protection of human life.

I have a confession to make. I am a liberal. More than that, I am a democrat, both upper and lower case. I know that among some pro-life advocates liberalism is almost a dirty word. I know it and I regret it. I know that among others there has been a determined effort to portray the pro-life movement as anti-liberal and, indeed, as reactionary. I know it and I regret it.

There is liberalism and then there is liberalism. As Lincoln suggested, the sheep and the wolf do not agree on what it means to be liberal.

We are today engaged in a great contest over the meaning of liberalism, over the meaning of liberal democracy, indeed over the meaning of America. In that contest, abortion is not just one issue among many. Upon this issue depend millions of lives yearning for the freedom to be. By this issue we define the America that we will pass on to our children and to all children who claim a place in the community that is rightfully theirs.

Will it be an America that is inclusive, embracing the stranger and giving refuge to the homeless? Or will it be an exclusive America in which we grasp what we have for ourselves and beat off those who call us to share? Will it be a caring America, nurturing the helpless and protecting the vulnerable? Or will it be a cruel America, discarding the undeveloped, destroying the uninvited, and disguising its cruelty of life as concern for quality of life? Will it be a hopeful America, open to a future of high peril and yet higher promise, welcoming every would-be pilgrim to our company of faith? Or will it be a fearful America, hunkered down, guarding against intruders the cave in which we seek security but find only a prison? Will it be a democratic America, trusting once again the competence of ordinary people to order our public life in harmony with their dreams, their values and, yes, their religious beliefs? Or will it be a controlled America, handed over to experts in courts and classrooms who too often show contempt for the convictions of those whom they are to serve?

This, then, is the choice: An America inclusive or exclusive, caring or cruel, hopeful or despairing, democratic or controlled by those who would relieve us of the burden of our freedom. I know the decision that is mandated by my understanding of liberalism. But it really matters little whether we call ourselves liberal or conservative, Democrat or Republican. What matters is that we are radical. The pro-life position is radical, not in the sense of extremism, whether it be extremism of the left or of the right. This movement is radical not by virtue of how far out it is but by virtue of how deep and central is the question it raises. That question, which is the beginning of all moral judgment and all just law, is simply this: Who, then, is my neighbor?

The mark of a humane and progressive society is an ever more expansive definition of the community for which we accept responsibility. The American people do not subscribe to the narrow and constrictive logic of *Roe v. Wade* that would exclude from the community those who fail to meet the criteria for "meaningful human life." Meaningful human life. Meaningful to whom? Meaningful to the justices of the Supreme Court? Meaningful to those who participated in that life's creation? Meaningful to the one living the life in question? Meaningful to God?

If we say a life is without meaning, we are not saying something about that life; we are saying something about ourselves. Meaning is not ours to give or withhold; meaning is there for us to acknowledge and revere. Likewise, if we say a child is unloved, we are not saying something about the child; we are saying something about our failure to love. Every child a wanted child? Oh yes, please God. And toward that end, the pro-life movement must continue to join its concern for the unborn with concern for those who give birth. The child and the mother must be elevated and protected together—both in life and in law. Ours must be seen more clearly as a women's movement, protecting especially the poor and young against the cruel pressures to abort their children. Some say that since only women can have children, only women should speak to the issue of abortion. Consistency would suggest that only women of child-bearing age should have a voice, or, more consistent yet, only pregnant women. That might not be a bad idea, since we know that women, and especially mothers, are even more pro-life than the general population. But, in truth, just as we cannot accept racial segregation, so we cannot accept such a segregation of moral concern. We are all in this together and we must all speak up for one another. Most particularly must we speak up for those who cannot speak for themselves. Every sister and brother is bound to us in the sacred communion of humanity.

No court has the competence—it has not the authority and it has not the power—to break that bond and excommunicate those whom we find bothersome. The bothersome too are our brothers, and the tiresome are our sisters. The humanity of a nation is measured not by the respect it shows the strong and successful but by the care it demonstrates toward the weak and the failing. It is not along the strength lines but along the fault lines that a society is judged.

Some years ago the Urban League distributed lapel buttons that read, "Give a Damn." Give a damn—about our cities, about racial justice, about the poor in our midst. But *why* give a damn? By what rational calculus of utility or self-interest should we be concerned about a starving twelve-year-old girl in Somalia; why should we care about senile remnants of lives that have long since outlived their usefulness; why should we be bothered by a black teenager awaiting trial on Rikers Island; why should we sustain the so-called vegetables who are consuming space and money in institutions across the country? Why, in short, should we give a damn? It is much easier to make the argument that our society and our world would be well rid of parasites beyond numbering who demand much and contribute nothing. After all, is it not the law of life that "The race is to the swift/The battle to the strong"?

Yes, that is one law; but there is a higher law, a law that joins reason to love. The words of John Donne are not mere sentimentality, not mere poetry. It is not wafting idealism but the weightiest of truths that no man—no woman, no old person, no child—is an island. We are each part of the main, and the unheeded death of one diminishes us all. For the sake of the vulnerable, but also for the sake of our own humanity, we must stand guard at the entrance gates and the exit gates of life, and all along life's way. How fragile and fleeting is the moment in which we imagine ourselves to be the swift and the strong. In our beginnings and in our endings, and with every breath between, we cannot live in the absence of love.

But isn't this soft and unrealistic? What does love have to do with public policy? When it comes to public policy, we speak not about love but about justice. Our response must be that justice and love are intertwined in a relationship of mutual support. Justice needs love for its motivation and love may require justice for its exercise. Some years ago many people opposed civil rights legislation, saying, "You cannot legislate morality." Dr. Martin Luther King responded, "It is true, the law cannot make a white man love me, but it can discourage him from lynching me." The point is that the chances of learning to love someone are greatly enhanced if you haven't lynched him first.

As love and justice are intertwined, so law and morality need one another. It is said that our goal is to impose our morality upon others. It is more accurate to say that our goal is to restore the legitimacy of law by bringing law back into democratic conversation with the values and beliefs of the American people. *Roe v. Wade* broke off that conversation. Among the victims of that broken conversation is the legitimacy of law itself. When law is supported neither by conviction nor by consensus, it must rely upon coercion. The proper word for law that is not democratically accountable to the people is tyranny. It might be argued that laws against racial discrimination were sometimes imposed from the top down, and that is correct. Once established, however, those laws were overwhelmingly ratified by the conviction and consensus of the American people. The last nine years bear witness to an equally over-whelming repudiation of *Roe v. Wade.* The pro-life movement is one with the movement for the emancipation of slaves. This is the continuation of the civil rights movement, for you are the champions of the most elementary civil, indeed human right— simply the right to be.

An honest reading of the evidence makes clear that a great majority of Americans believe that our sisters and brothers who are yearning to be born should be provided the protection of law. In other sessions and workshops of this convention you will be dealing with the strategies whereby that consensus can at last find political expression. Here I would only underscore that the progressive impulse of the American people is toward an open, caring, and democratic society. Here I would only ask: Why do our opponents so distrust the judgment of the people? Why are they so afraid of the democratic process? Are their numbers so few, are their arguments so weak, that they dare not expose their case to the light of public debate in the legislatures of this land?

They accuse pro-life advocates of being inconsistent, and we would not claim to be perfect. But where is the consistency of those who demanded and received additional years to prolong the defeat of an amendment they favored but now oppose even the initial consideration of an amendment they do not like? Why are they now so afraid of the democratic process?

We do not believe that right and wrong can be determined by majority vote. If the majority were against us, we believe that majority would be wrong and we would persist in trying to persuade them of the rightness of this cause. All we are asking is that the question be put and the majority be given a chance to be right.

I believe that in this great testing of the American experiment the will of the people will prevail; it will prevail sooner rather than later; and it will prevail on the side of life. And yet, if that hope is deferred for a time, we must not be discouraged. We are recruited for the duration; we must be long distance radicals; we must never give up. Let it be clear that we have not chosen this battle. It has been imposed upon us. We are not always agreed on how this cause is to be advanced, but by this cause we have been brought together and we will remain together until this cause is vindicated. We will not be divided.

We must persist because we acknowledge a judgment greater even than the judgment of the democratic process. An open society cannot survive unless it is open to realities greater than itself. In the pledge of allegiance we declare this to be "one nation under God." Similarly, at Gettysburg Lincoln expressed the hope "that this nation, under God, shall have a new birth of freedom." To be under God means, first and most importantly, to be under judgment. We as a people can defy but we cannot escape the judgment of God.

Recently there has been a Broadway play and then a movie

called "Whose Life Is It Anyway?" Precisely, whose life is it? The message of that drama is that when a person is dependent, no longer productive, no longer capable of sexual satisfaction, then that person should be free to terminate a life that in fact has already ended. But whose life is it anyway? The logic of the drama is consistent: if life is no more than property, then we are free to dispose of it as we will. Against that lethal logic, the pro-life movement declares that people are not property.

Every life is a miracle, every person a mystery. In the words of Rabbi Abraham Heschel, "Just to be is a blessing; just to live is holy." We live in a world within worlds. Francis Thompson wrote, "Thou canst not stir a flower/Without troubling a star." If nature is possessed of such mystery, how much greater is the mystery of human life. All civilization begins with the capacity for astonishment. The astonishment that there is something rather than nothing; the astonishment that there are others who need our care and whose care we need. And that we are here for one another to care. And astonishment leads to tenderness as we shelter one another against the heartless dark. All of civilization—of religion, of ethics, of law, of beauty—is the long brave march of humanity waving our little banners of hope in the face of death. To be civilized is to be pro-life.

Ah yes, they say, life, but what quality of life? I lived and worked as a pastor for seventeen years in the poorest black and hispanic section of New York City. We were sometimes visited there by white, upper middle class people of obvious good will. They were appalled by what they saw and frequently they said that life in conditions such as these would not be worth living. I remember reading a "quality of life index" devised by a famous social scientist at Princeton. No child should be brought into the world, he said, unless it is guaranteed a long list of basic securities—physical, psychological, educational, financial. And I looked into the faces of the hundreds and hundreds of my people, of God's people, in Brooklyn, and they are to be told that not one of them should ever have been born, for none could begin to qualify by the professor's index of a quality life.

But I tell you that they are quality people: great in their quality of love when it would be so easy to hate; great in their quality of endurance when it would be so easy to despair; great in their striving to succeed when they have every excuse to fail; great in the laughter and grief that is our common lot; and especially great in welcoming into lives already heavily burdened the gift of new life.

We must not only care about the poor, we must learn from the poor. Ask the poor about what constitutes a life worth living. Many who presume to speak for the poor are not on speaking terms with poor people. Alleged friends of the poor write editorials in our most distinguished newspapers calculating the costs of welfare and concluding that abortion is a bargain. The war against poverty has been replaced by the war against the poor. From time immemorial the way to reduce poverty is to reduce the number of poor people.

We do not kill off full-grown poor people. How much easier it is to destroy early; so that we do not have to look upon it and see how very much like it is unto ourselves. We will pay others to do the ghastly work, to retrieve the pieces and dispose of the evidence. And they will do it. In necessity and sorrow, some of them say. Others say it's a job and, after all, if they didn't do it someone else would. Yet others express no qualms. Readily, and for money, for much money, they surrender their vocation to healing and become servants of the industry of death.

Thus these threatening newcomers are stopped; they are stopped before they enter our line of moral vision. They are stopped early, still in the darkness of the womb, before they can force us to recognize them as ourselves, before their all too person-like presence can lay a claim upon our comfort and maybe upon our conscience.

And some who approve and promote this industry of death are not content to talk about necessary evil. Because they call themselves liberal what they do must be deemed a positive good. Therefore they say they have rendered a service to these little ones; they have spared them a wrongful life. And so far has the corruption spread that even the courts use the phrase "a wrongful life." The words of the rabbi have been reversed: Just to live is a horror; just to be is a curse.

There is another and authentically liberal vision of an America that is hospitable to the stranger, holding out arms of welcome to those who would share the freedom and opportunity we cherish. "Give me your tired, your poor,/Your huddled masses yearning to breathe free,/The wretched refuse of your teeming shore,/Send these, the homeless, tempest-tossed, to me,/I lift my lamp beside the golden door." Let us proclaim that we are not prepared to erase that inscription from the Statue of Liberty nor that sentiment from the soul of America. The unborn child is the ultimate immigrant. Elsewhere the immigrant was viewed as wretched refuse. Here, when we were true to our better selves, they were welcomed as participants in the great adventure that is America.

In 1973 the court invoked the darker side of our national character. We were given license, indeed encouragement, to close our hearts to the stranger, to patrol the borders of our lives with lethal weaponry, in order not only to exclude but to destroy those who do not suit our convenience. Last year, and the year before, and the year before that more than one and a half million of these strangers were destroyed; strangers who, like immigrants past, brought nothing with them but their need for our acceptance and the plea that they be given a chance.

The analogy between the unborn and the immigrant may seem strained. I fear, however, that it is painfully to the point. The logic of abortion insinuates itself into every dimension of our common life. That logic teaches that there is no goal higher than self-satisfaction; that logic teaches, like the logic of the Dred Scott decision a century earlier, that others possess no rights, no claims, which we are bound to respect. Behind the culture of narcissism is the logic of narcissism articulated by the highest court of the land.

Thus we say *No* to the stranger. There is no place for you at life's banquet table, your presence would disrupt our party planning, our resources are already stretched, the promise exhausted, the invitation withdrawn. The year 1973 is remembered as the year of the energy crisis, and so it should be: the year of a moral energy crisis which has almost extinguished the lamp beside the golden door. You who are gathered here tonight are the keepers of the flame, for you know that upon that light depend the lives of millions yearning to breathe free; that upon that light depends our own life as a humane and caring people.

You are light keepers in a time of darkness. Nobody knows how long this already too long night will last, but I do believe we can see the dawning of the day. You are not the defenders of an old order but the forerunners of a world yet to be. What we would retrieve from the past is the promise of the future. Another word for promise is potentiality.

"It is only potential human life," our opponents say. Yes, we respond, and the only alternative to potential human life is dead human life. Potentiality *is* life, and life is potentiality. We are all potential human beings in the process of becoming what we are called to be. Nothing that is not human life has the potential of becoming human life, and nothing that has the potential of becoming human life is not human life. Only what is human can become human, if we will simply let it be. All is promise, all is potentiality.

If this movement is to be worthy of the name pro-life, everything we do must be informed and inflamed by that vision. Those who dream the better dream for America will finally prevail with the American people. From the Mayflower Compact of the 17th century, through Abraham Lincoln at Gettysburg, to Martin Luther King at the March on Washington in August, 1963—those visions have prevailed in America that have lifted up the promise.

I do not know if there will again be a new birth of freedom—for the poor, the aged, the crippled, the unborn. But we commend this cause to the One who is the maker and the sure keeper of promises, to the Lord of life. In that commendation is our confidence: confidence that the long night of *Roe v. Wade* will soon be over; confidence that the courts will yet be made responsive to the convictions of a democratic people; confidence, ultimately, in the dawning of a new and glorious day in which law and morality will be reconciled and liberty will no longer wage war against life.

Let this be, then, a convention of confidence; not because we trust in our own strength but because, under God, that last word belongs not to death but to love and life—because, even now, our eyes have seen the glory of the coming of the Lord.

TWENTY-FIVE

Grace, Prophecy, and Saving Babies

Jeff Hensley

LINDA WAS TWENTY-FIVE. With three small kids and a fourth on the way, she worked evenings in a small cocktail lounge three states away from the husband she had recently divorced. Because she was a large woman, she was unaware of child number four until she'd been away from her former husband for a few weeks.

Under the pressure of her new job, lots of new responsibilities, and little income, she set up an appointment at a local abortion clinic.

As she lay on the cold surgical table waiting her turn to be freed of the child she had helped create, Linda expected never to awaken again. She was sure her three children would be raised by their grandparents or her alcoholic ex-husband. She was penitent, scared, and ready to meet her fate at the hand of a harsh and vengeful God.

As she recovered the next day, she began instead to experience the healing touch of a God who forgives. Not having received the punishment she felt she had earned, Linda went forward from that day with a tangible knowledge of the grace and love—the forgiving nature—of God.

Jeff Hensley is the editor of this book. He lives in Fort Worth, Texas.

There's more to the story. Forgiven herself, Linda went back to her husband. Gradually, over a period of years, she and her husband became loving Christians, full of the Spirit of God, actively extending that love to others. Their home became a place of joy.

Here's another woman's story. This one took place quite a few years further back. Let's call the woman Rebecca. She was doing something she knew was wrong, too—she was in the arms of someone else's husband, committing adultery. And worse than in Linda's case, she was caught at it by some of the prominent religious citizens of her town. Having caught her in the very act, they dragged her before Jesus. Bodily twirling her into the dust before Him, they made their charge. Rebecca's face must have looked much like Linda's as she lay on the surgical cart about to enter the abortion chamber. Disheveled and huddled in the dust just where they had left her, she must have cried as she waited, fearfully expecting what she too felt was her earned punishment.

Like Linda though, what she experienced instead was the loving grace of a forgiving God. Jesus dismissed her accusers with a few words by skillfully turning their condemnation back on them. He and Rebecca were left alone in the temple courtyard. Knowing her heart and thereby knowing her repentance, He refused to condemn her. As He sent her away, He expected that she had been changed by her brief contact with Him. "Go and sin no more," He admonished, confidently sending her off.

Millions of women who have made the horrible, fear-motivated decision to abort their own babies know the need for forgiveness that the woman spun down to the dust knew. And millions face each day with corroding doubt, fear, and self-condemnation about what might have been had they borne their children. And they know no way to kill the pain of these self-recriminations.

But these two, separated by centuries, found life. And they found forgiveness and grace.

Many of us have experienced the forgiving, making-whole love of Jesus in our own lives. Because we have experienced His forgiveness we can speak of it to the women and girls who have had abortions. Because we have been touched by Jesus' love ourselves, we know there is power and grace and love enough in the heart of Jesus to draw even the most fearful father and mother out of the self-centeredness that allows them to destroy their own offspring.

But how much better to tell them of the reality of what they're considering before another child's body has been suctioned out or cut out or pumped with killing, saline solution.

For the same Jesus who forgave sin also taught the people so they wouldn't have to experience the grief and guilt and heartache of sin in the first place. And He expected their lives to change when He taught them just as when He forgave them. He knew the power and truth of the words He spoke would give life to those who would respond.

We who know the reality of the unborn child's life in the womb can speak with power and expectation of change too. We can expect our words to bring life to those who hear them.

But if we fail to speak when the opportunity arises or when we feel called upon to do so, we may carry the burden of guilt for a lost life along with the non-parents. In Ezekiel 3, the prophet Ezekiel learns from God the responsibility the prophet bears: If he fails to speak up to turn the sinful man from his destructive path, then he must share the burden of his guilt. May God keep any of us from carrying that burden because we have failed to let the abortion-headed know they are planning on killing a child, not having a ball of tissue cut out of the mother.

One 72-year-old woman in Houston, Agnes Sanborn, has responded to this call more radically than most of us would. Rising at 4:00 A.M. each Saturday, this slight but strong-willed woman reaches the Cullen Women's Center, an abortion clinic, at 5:30 A.M. to plead for the lives of unborn children.

Demonstrating the same variety of gentleness and love that Jesus bestowed on the woman caught in adultery, Agnes seeks to counsel each woman who enters the Cullen Center parking lot. She has precious few seconds to influence the woman scheduled for abortion, a woman often under great pressure from family or boyfriend to go through with the killing act.

"I always ask the woman how many months along she is," Agnes said. "Then I open the brochure and show her the stage of fetal development of the baby. 'See,' I say, 'this is a real baby. That's *your* baby.'" It's a hard reality to face at that late moment, but some of the mothers-to-be have the courage to allow their hearts to be touched by Agnes.

One Saturday, she made her appeal to a young, newly married couple. Wrapped up in their love for each other, they were just not ready to allow a new life into that love—until Agnes spoke to them. It was an approach she had never thought of before, but sensing it might work, she offered it, "Just remember that when you come out of that clinic, you will leave part of both of you there that you'll never have again." They drove past her to park. There they sat, talking for a long time. Then the engine came to life. As they drove past Agnes, heading out of the parking lot this time, she watched them. "I looked at her face," she said. "I've never seen such a radiantly happy girl." Agnes was almost afraid to look at the young man's face because she wasn't sure two people could share such great happiness. "But his face was the same," she said.[1]

All of us can't do what Agnes does. It takes a particular brand of courage tempered by a special kind of love to stand in the gap in just that way. But each of us can do something. Each of us can take some action to help spread the truth about the life carried in the womb. And we can do it much earlier than the last minute before the woman enters the abortion chamber.

One of the simplest and most effective ways is by breaking the conspiracy of silence that keeps the topic of the unborn child's right to life out of most conversation. If most people knew the facts, facts like the lack of argument in the field of biology as to when human life begins (it begins at conception), facts like those revealed by one look at a picture of a 10-week-old fetus (the toes, ears, and fingers are easily distinguishable), they would know that they stand on the side of the unborn child's *very real* right to life rather than for the abstraction of "a mother's right to choose." So arm yourself with the facts—and the pictures—so you can be prepared to use them.

A neighbor of mine learned that a friend of his secretary's was planning an abortion. He learned from the secretary that this friend had not even considered bearing the child and putting it up for adoption. By telling his secretary to tell her friend about some of the other options, a life was saved.

Not everyone can persuade others by their speech, but everyone can do something that employs skills they do have. Carpenters can erect signs at right-to-life rallies; electricians can set up sound systems for them. Families can take unwed mothers into their homes, or they can adopt children of unwed mothers and make them "wanted" children. PTA members can work for the adoption of pro-life educational materials in the schools. Some will be able to work in the campaigns of pro-life candidates for public office. We all can write letters to our Congressmen, Senators, and city council members urging the adoption of measures designed to safeguard the sanctity of human life. And we can all pray.

If you can't think of any particular way you can help, or if you want to join your efforts effectively with others, join a local pro-life group. There are plenty of jobs not being done for lack of man or woman power. Just give them a call. They'll have something you can do.

Or, as Dr. Mildred Jefferson, former president of the National Right to Life Committee has said jokingly, those who, "Don't want to do anything public at all can, in the privacy of their rooms, write checks, lots and lots of checks, because we need lots and lots of checks."

Whatever we do to help, let's do it soon, and do it to the best of our abilities. Recently I received an appeal for funds for the Houston-based Foundation for Life. One of their programs sends speakers to high schools to show the reality of life in the womb. One high school girl returned to class after watching the presentation saying, "I didn't know, I just didn't know. They didn't tell me it was a baby." Questioned about her meaning, she replied, "I had an abortion, but I didn't know it was a baby."

Notes

1. Material adapted from "At Death's Door . . ." by Phyllis McAndrew (Copyright © 1978, Phyllis McAndrew). First published in the June 1978 issue of *Life Advocate,* official publication of Foundation for Life, 4901 Richmond, Suite 101, Houston, Texas 77027.

TWENTY-SIX

Handling Tough Questions

James Manney

M OST AMERICANS DO NOT LIKE to discuss abortion, including those who hate it. The immense fact of more than a million abortion deaths each year in this country is too awesome. The circumstances that lead many women to abortionists are undeniably painful. The social pressures to be silent on the issue—to say, "I am personally opposed, but . . ."—are intense.

Yet abortion must be discussed. You should discuss it. When you bring the subject up, you should be prepared to face some hostility. You should also be prepared to encounter specific objections and questions with calm objectivity and factual knowledge. The following questions and answers are offered as an aid to help you do that.

People who want to prohibit abortion are trying to impose their morality on others.

The desire to protect the unborn is not a sectarian belief. It is based on the most fundamental of human rights—the right to live. Like all civil rights, the right to life needs legal protection. Our society should forbid abortion for the same reason that it forbids a crime like rape. Both abortion and rape are crimes against basic human rights, and we rightly impose sanctions against them.

James Manney is a writer and editor in Ann Arbor, Michigan.

301

The decision to give birth should be a private matter between the woman and her doctor.

We cannot sacrifice the civil rights of a minority group—unborn children—to the preferences of others. We fought a Civil War, endured social upheaval, and waged political battles to establish this principle firmly. We cannot say, for example, that the decision to segregate a school system is a private matter between the school board and voters, or that the decision to abuse a child is a private matter between parents. Neither can a pregnant woman and her doctor decide whether an unborn child shall live.

But the Supreme Court couldn't decide when life begins. How can we?

One of the many errors in the Court's *Roe v. Wade* decision was its evasion of the fact that human life begins at the moment of conception. When human sperm fertilizes the egg, a new creature is formed, completely distinct in genetic character from either of its parents. The fetus is not part of the mother's body; he or she is a human being. No scientist—even those favoring abortion—denies this. The Court evaded this evidence and declared that unborn humans are not "persons"—that is, human beings who possess constitutional rights. The Court was wrong. Its decision does not make unborn humans any less alive or any less human.

People will get abortions anyway. At least legal abortions are safer than the "back alley" illegal abortions.

Abortions, legal and otherwise, are not safe; they are much more dangerous than normal childbirth. Legal abortions cause a variety of complications, including 27 documented deaths in 1975. One study found that 87 percent of a group of 486 obstetricians and gynecologists have had to hospitalize patients for complications following legal abortions. Abortions often cause serious problems with subsequent pregnancies. They usually lead to psychological and emotional trauma. The devastating medical facts about abortion show that stopping abortion is a genuine "women's issue."

Many Americans do not understand that the 1973 Supreme Court abortion decision did nothing to make abortions safer. By virtually eliminating state regulation of abortions, the Court simply allowed illegal "back room" abortionists to go legal, with their procedures unchanged.

A law against abortion would discriminate against the poor. Rich people will always be able to get abortions, even if they are illegal, and the rich are better able to care for unplanned children.

The superior ability of one class of people to break a law cannot determine whether we should have such a law. Professional accountants are more likely to get away with tax evasion. We do not conclude from this that tax laws should be repealed because they discriminate against non-accountants. Neither can we refuse to protect the unborn because some wealthy people may get abortions anyway.

"Social justice" arguments in favor of abortion often contain more than a hint of contempt for the poor, combined with elements of racism. The implicit point is that poor people should have abortions because they are not capable of making sacrifices and maintaining strong families. Some note with satisfaction that abortions on poor women will reduce welfare costs. Racists are pleased that they eliminate many blacks, Hispanics, and members of other minority groups. Abortion advocates like these are no friends of the poor.

Surely abortion is justified in cases of rape and incest.

Why? The remedy for these crimes is not to kill the innocent victim—the unborn child. Abortion will not relieve the emotional pain of rape and incest; abortion carries severe emotional trauma of its own and is more likely to add to the victim's distress. As public policy, a rape and incest exception would be most unwise because claims of rape and incest by women who want abortions would be virtually impossible to prove or disprove. The predictible rise in false claims of rape and incest would cause people to take these crimes less seriously and make it more difficult to convict those guilty of them. In any case, this objection gets far more attention than it deserves. For a variety of physiological and psychological reasons, the incidence of pregnancy resulting from rape and incest is extremely low.

Abortion should be available to save the life of the mother.

The issue of the "therapeutic abortion" is a genuine moral dilemma. The moral principle of "unintended secondary effect" and the legal principle of self-defense can help guide those faced with such a decision. However, the goal is to save both lives, and the principle that unborn life should be preserved can only reinforce this goal. In any case, such a dilemma almost never arises. Many physicians argue that advancements in obstetrical care in recent years have eliminated it.

Every child should be wanted. Look at the shocking amount of child abuse in this country.

What does "wanted" mean? Studies show that many pregnant women go through periods when they wish they weren't pregnant—even when they planned it. Studies have also found that most women with unplanned pregnancies come to desire the pregnancy by the time they give birth. On the other hand, there is no correlation between unplanned pregnancies and subsequent abuse of the children. One study of 500 battered children in California found that 91% of the children were planned. Child abuse has continued to rise in the United States in the decade since abortion was legalized. There is good reason to think that legalized abortion contributes to the atmosphere of disregard for life and resentment of children that leads to child abuse. The answer for children who are truly unwanted is adoption by loving parents.

The real answer to abortion is better contraception. Meanwhile, abortion should be available as a backup when other means of contraception fail.

Abortion is not a method of contraception; it is the destruction of human life after conception has occurred. In reality, legalized abortion seems to contribute to inefficient contraception. Every nation that has legalized abortion, including the United States, has found that the number of abortions go up over time, not down.

It seems to me that abortion is a "Catholic" issue. The prolife movement violates the principle of separation of church and state.

Catholics are active in the prolife movement, but so are large numbers of Protestants, Jews, and nonbelievers. Fundamentally, protecting innocent human life is a universal moral imperative, cutting across religious lines and including those with no religious identification. The issue of separation of church and state is a complicated legal and constitutional question. However, no one believes that the Constitution bans political activity by members of churches, or that no view can be pressed in the political arena if a church somewhere in the United States supports it.

Prolife people want everyone to become single-issue voters.

Consider the prolife position as a "crucial issue" instead of a "single issue." Politicians must take positions on many issues if they are to be elected, and voters should consider all these positions before they cast ballots. But some issues are more important than others. Almost all groups—from the United Auto Workers to the National Rifle Association—identify the issues that are most important to their members and urge their members to vote largely on the basis of those crucial issues. This is how issues get addressed in a democratic political system. The prolife movement shouldn't be derided as a "single-issue" movement for operating within the political system to make sure abortion gets the attention it deserves.

I don't like abortion, but the prolife people turn me off. Why don't they talk about nuclear war, capital punishment, poverty, and other life issues?

Many do, but the prolife movement brings together people with many different views. If you want to protect the unborn, then join with the people who agree with you on at least that issue. Abortion is a compelling issue, serious enough so that differences on other issues shouldn't deter you.

I have no taste for lost causes. Stopping abortion looks like one of them.

The prolife movement has strong support in the U.S. A bill that might have overturned the *Roe v. Wade* decision failed by only one vote in the Senate in 1982. There is much work to be done in thousands of local communities to educate the public, counsel and assist pregnant women, and develop alternatives to abortion. Let's not fail to protect life because the struggle is difficult.

Index

Abortion Law Reform
  Association, 17
abortion techniques, 53-54,
  102-3, 150-51, 221-23
adoption, 67, 79, 88-90, 304
Ainsworth, Mary, 129
Alexander, Leo, 6, 164
American Civil Liberties
  Union, 11
American College of Obstetrics
  and Gynecology, 64
American Law Institute, 16
American Medical Association,
  20, 62, 71
amniocentesis, 9, 127
Anderson, Carl, 236
Aquinas, Thomas, 145
Avery, Mary Ellen, 63

Badgley Report, 85
Barth, Karl, 250
Beethoven, Ludwig van, 182
Binding, Karl, 160
birth defects, 9, 46-47, 168, 170,
  185-98, 225-30, 270, 275-76
Blackmun, Harry A., 15-26,
  56- 57, 238, 256, 257
Blum, Virgil C., 159-75
Bopp, James R., 233-46
Brown, Harold O.J., 249-60
Brunner, Emil, 250
Bulfin, Matthew J., 97-105, 236
Burger, Warren, 18, 57
Byrn, Robert M., 234, 236

Calderone, Mary, 8
California Medicine, 27, 59,
165-67, 196
Campbell, A.G.M., 192, 225
Canada, abortion in, 85
capital punishment, 53
Carter, Jimmy, 252-54
Cavenar, J.D., 125
Center for Disease Control, 91,
  97, 103
child abuse, 128-29, 304
Christian Action Council, 43
Clark, Colin, 35, 36
Coale, Ansley J., 33, 37
Commoner, Barry, 37
contraception, 85-88, 305
Cornelsen, Ronald J., 199
Cox, Archibald, 255
Crick, Francis, 188
Czechoslovakia, abortion in,
  60, 111

Daly, Cahal, 171
Declaration of Human Rights,
  54
Denes, Magda, 8, 91, 152
Diognetus, Epistle to, 185
Doe v. Bolton, 15-26, 54-58,
  234-46
Doerr, Edd, 188
Down's snydrome, 10, 190-92,
  195, 203-7
Doxiadis, Constantin, 36
Dred Scott, 25, 69, 242, 292
Dubos, Rene, 170
Duff, Raymond S., 192, 225

Eighteenth Amendment, 245
Eissler, K.R., 125

Engelhardt, H. Tristram, 170
euthanasia, 68, 70, 72, 159-75,
    177-84, 187, 189, 227-30, 272
Everett, Millard S., 167

feminism, 67, 77-95
fertility, 110
fetal development, 78, 51-52,
    147-49, 169, 223
Fifth Amendment, 240
First Amendment, 254-56
Fletcher, John, 187
Fletcher, Joseph, 23, 165,
    167- 68, 187, 188, 190-91
food production, 34-36
Ford Foundation, 72
Foundation for Life, 299
Fourteenth Amendment, 15, 17,
    20, 21, 24-25, 238, 240
France, abortion in, 179
Freud, Anna, 125
Freund Committee, 25
Friedan, Betty, 188

Gallup Poll, 62
Garn, Jake, 235
Germany, abortion in, 72
Gordon, Sol, 188
Graham, Billy, 251
Gray, Nellie, 236
Green, Robert, 234
Greer, Germaine, 87
Grisez, Germain, 161, 164, 167
Guett, Dr. Arthur, 160
Guttmacher, Alan, 63, 188

Haeckl, Ernst, 161
handicapped children, 6, 11, 61,
    162
Handler, Philips, 170
Haring, Bernard, 170
Haun, Sandra, 200

Haynsworth, Clement, 141
hedonism, 83, 85
Heifetz, Milton, 187
Hellegers, Andre, 23
Helms, Jesse, 236, 241
Hensley, Jeff, 295-300
Hern, Warren, 8
Heschel, Abraham, 290
Hippocratic oath, 6, 56
Hoche, Alfred, 160
homosexuality, 70, 272
Horan, Dennis J., 234, 236
Hsia, Y. Edward, 170
Human Life Amendment, 26,
    231-46
Humanist Manifesto II, 188-89

illegitimacy, 276-78
incest, 113-14, 117, 270, 276-77,
    303
India, sterilization in, 178
infanticide, 48, 70-71, 185-98,
    199-201, 225-30
intrauterine device, 64
Italy, abortion in, 179

Jakobovits, Immanuel, 267-80
Japan, abortion in, 59, 98
Jefferson, Mildred, 299
Jefferson, Thomas, 47, 265
Jekel, T.F., 124
John Paul II, 194, 261-66
Johns Hopkins University, 10,
    70, 190
Joyce, Mary R., 67
Judaism, abortion and, 267-80

Kasun, Jacqueline R., 33-41
Keller, Helen, 66, 167
Kennedy Conference, 190
King, Martin Luther, 288
Koop, C. Everett, 45-73

LaChat, Michael, 161, 164
Lader, Lawrence, 188
Lancet, 194
Lejeune, Jerome, 195
Lenoski, E.F., 127
Lincoln, Abraham, 283-84
Lonning, Per, 250
Louisell, David W., 234
Lutheran Church-Missouri
  Synod, 67, 251, 258

Maguire, Daniel, 164
Maloof, George, 113, 118
Manney, James, 301-6
Marx, Paul, 160, 168
Masterson, John, 236
Matthews, John T., 83
McKernan, Martin, 234
medical ethics, 27-30
Melzack, Ronald, 146-47, 151
mental retardation, 5, 162, 170
Montagu, Ashley, 167
Morgentaler, Henry, 180, 188
Mormonism, 258
Mother Teresa, 179
Muggeridge, Malcolm, 177-84

Nathanson, Bernard, 114
National Association of
  Evangelicals, 251
National Right to Life
  Committee, 231-46, 299
Naziism, 4-6, 69, 72, 159-75,
  180-81
Nelson, J. Robert, 251
Neuhaus, Richard John, 283-94
*New England Journal of
  Medicine*, 6, 63, 187, 192
New York Medical Society, 68
New Zealand, 109, 170
Ney, Philip G., 123-38
Niederland, W.G., 125

Ninth Amendment, 15, 17, 24
Noonan, John T., Jr., 141-56
Norway, abortion in, 250
Novak, Michael, 199-201

O'Boyle, Patrick, 169
Oberstar, James, 235
Outler, Albert, 251

pain, 141-56
Paul VI, 265
Pearson, G.H.J., 125
Philo Judaens, 279
*Planned Parenthood of Missouri
  v. Danforth*, 249-50
Planned Parenthood, 6, 63, 196,
  201
Playboy, 83
Poland, abortion in, 60
population growth, 22, 27,
  33-41, 60, 64-65
pornography, 54
poverty, 22, 92, 290-91, 303
Powell, John, 3-11
Presbyterian Church in the
  United States, 251
Prism, 71
prostaglandins, 133, 221-22
Protestantism, 249-60
psychological effects of
  abortion, 90, 100, 123-38

Ramsey, Paul, 251
rape, 61, 110-13, 115-19, 270,
  276, 303
Rehnquist, William, 20
Rice, Charles E., 234, 236
right to die, 68
risks of abortion, 61, 97-105,
  274, 303
Rockefeller Commission, 72
Roe v. Wade, 15-26, 54-58,

234-46, 251-52, 256, 284, 286, 288, 302
Roman Catholic Church, 261-66
Roman Empire, infanticide in, 186, 189
Roosevelt, Franklin, 66
Rosen, Mortimer, 149
Rosenblum, Victor, 11, 192-93, 234
Rostand, Jean, 193-94

Sackett, Walter, 170
Sanborn, Agnes, 297-98
Scaife Foundation, 72
Schaeffer, Francis, 250-51
school prayer, 53-54
Schweitzer, Albert, 9, 48
Sender, Neville, 8
sex education, 131
sexual attitudes, 69, 87
Shaw, Anthony, 192
situation ethics, 165
Skinner, B.F., 188
Smith, Janet E., 77-95
Southern Baptist Convention, 252
Stanton, Joseph R., 185-98
Stout, Bill, 217-19
suicide, 61
Sunnen Foundation, 72
Supreme Court, 6, 15-26, 53-58, 77, 141, 152, 168, 186, 200, 234-46, 249, 267, 302
Sweden, abortion in, 86, 179
Sykes, Charles J., 159-75

Tempelman, Lord Justice, 192
therapeutic abortion, 63, 279-80, 304
Thielicke, Helmut, 250
Thirteenth Amendment, 244
Thompson, Francis, 290
Tietze, Christopher, 112, 124
Time, 71
Trinkaus, Walter J., 234

Uddo, Basile J., 109-22
unemployment, 38
United Kingdom, abortion in, 60, 86, 109, 177, 267, 273
United Methodist Church, 67, 251
United Nations, 54
United Presbyterian Church, 67, 251
Upjohn Corporation, 169

Vatican Council II, 263
Villanova University, 58
Von Galen, Clemens, 163

Waddill, William B., 199-201
Waltke, Bruce, 251
Warwich, Donald P., 64
Watson, James D., 71, 168, 188
Wertham, Frederic, 160-62
White, Byron R., 17
Will, George F., 203-207
Williams, George Huntston, 185, 189, 251
Williams, Glanville, 17, 55, 167
Williams, Robert H., 169
Willke, J.C., 235-36
Witherspoon, Joseph, 234, 236
Wogaman, J. Philip, 251
World Health Organization, 19, 58

Also from Servant Publications

What Is Secular Humanism?
*Why Humanism Became Secular
and How It Is Changing Our World*
By James Hitchcock

Helps you understand secular humanism and how it is influencing
our schools, mass media, courts, government, and even our
churches. Traces the history of this philosophical movement from
its medieval origins to its place of dominance in the modern world.
Illustrated. $6.95

The Christian Mind
How Should a Christian Think?
By Harry Blamires

A perceptive diagnosis of one of the key weaknesses besetting the
church today—the disappearance of a distinctively Christian worldview. Explains how to think as a Christian in a post-Christian
world. $4.50

Husbands, Wives, Parents, Children
Foundations for the Christian Family
By Ralph Martin

Helpful, well-balanced advice to help any couple strengthen their
marriage and family. $4.95

Available at your Christian bookstore or from

Servant Publications
Dept. 209
P.O. Box 8617
Ann Arbor, Michigan 48107

Please include payment plus 5% ($.75 minimum) for postage.
Send for our FREE catalog of Christian books, music, and cassettes.